THE NEWFOUNDLAND DIASPORA

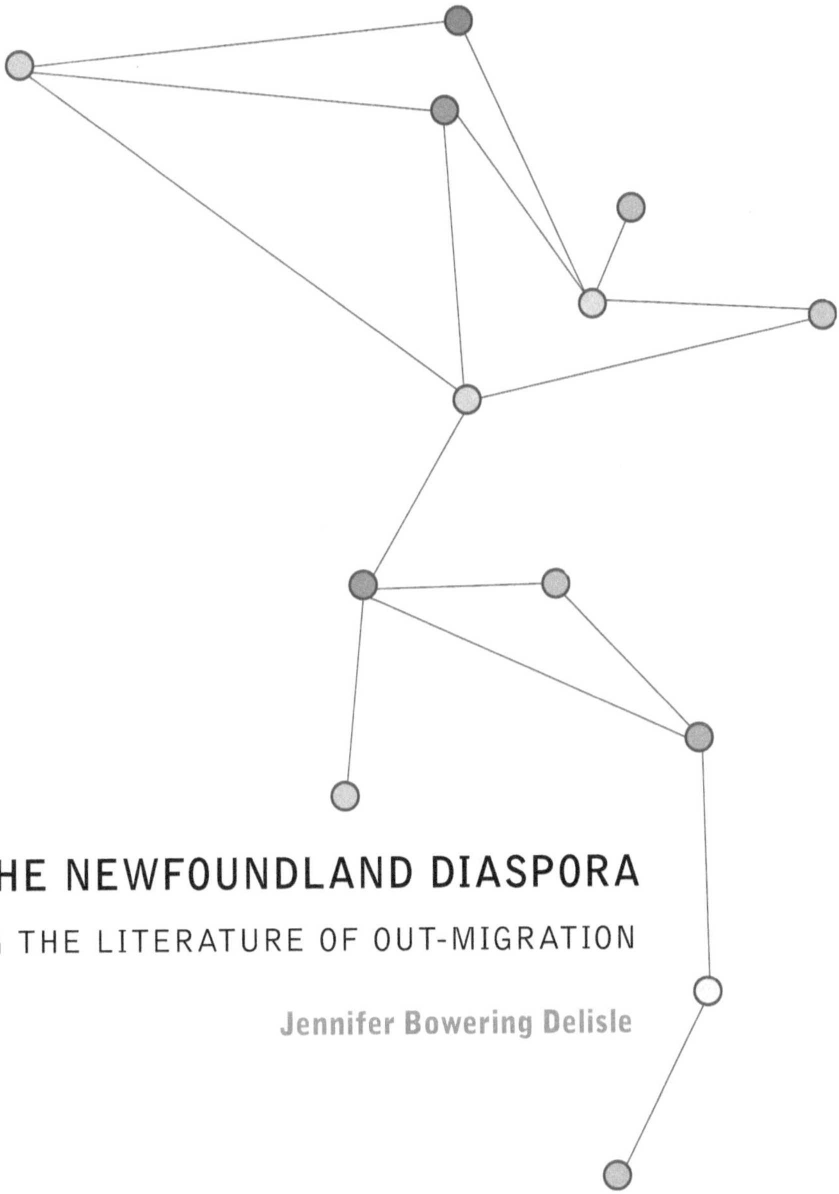

THE NEWFOUNDLAND DIASPORA

MAPPING THE LITERATURE OF OUT-MIGRATION

Jennifer Bowering Delisle

WILFRID LAURIER
UNIVERSITY PRESS

This book has been published with the help of a grant from the Canadian Federation for the Humanities and Social Sciences, through the Awards to Scholarly Publications Program, using funds provided by the Social Sciences and Humanities Research Council of Canada. Wilfrid Laurier University Press acknowledges the support of the Canada Council for the Arts for our publishing program. We acknowledge the financial support of the Government of Canada through the Canada Book Fund for our publishing activities.

Library and Archives Canada Cataloguing in Publication

Delisle, Jennifer, 1979–
    The Newfoundland diaspora : mapping the literature of out-migration / Jennifer Delisle.

Includes bibliographical references and index.
Issued also in electronic formats.
ISBN 978-1-55458-894-7

    1. Canadian literature (English)—Newfoundland and Labrador—History and criticism. 2. Emigration and immigration in literature. 3. Newfoundland, Island of (N.L.)—In literature. 4. Newfoundlanders—In literature. 5. Newfoundland and Labrador—Emigration and immigration—Psychological aspects. I. Title.

PS8131.N4D45 2013   810.9'9718   C2012-907184-6

Electronic monograph in multiple formats.
Issued also in print format.
ISBN 978-1-55458-895-4 (PDF).—ISBN 978-1-55458-896-1 (EPUB)

    1. Canadian literature (English)—Newfoundland and Labrador—History and criticism. 2. Emigration and immigration in literature. 3. Newfoundland, Island of (N.L.)—In literature. 4. Newfoundlanders—In literature. 5. Newfoundland and Labrador—Emigration and immigration—Psychological aspects. I. Title.

PS8131.N4D45 2013   810.9'9718   C2012-907185-4

© 2013 Wilfrid Laurier University Press
Waterloo, Ontario, Canada
www.wlupress.wlu.ca

Cover design by Martyn Schmoll. Cover photograph by Kenton Delisle. Text design by Daiva Villa, Chris Rowat Design.

The selections from E. J. Pratt—"Newfoundland," "Newfoundland Calling," and "Newfoundland Seamen"—are reprinted from *Complete Poems*, Volumes 1 and 2, ed. Sandra Djwa and R.G. Moyles (Toronto: University of Toronto Press, 1989), and appear here with permission of the publisher. The selections from Carl Leggo are reprinted with permission of the author.

Every reasonable effort has been made to acquire permission for copyright material used in this text, and to acknowledge all such indebtedness accurately. Any errors and omissions called to the publisher's attention will be corrected in future printings.

No part of this publication may be reproduced, stored in a retrieval system, or transmitted, in any form or by any means, without the prior written consent of the publisher or a licence from the Canadian Copyright Licensing Agency (Access Copyright). For an Access Copyright licence, visit http://www.accesscopyright.ca or call toll free to 1-800-893-5777.

CONTENTS

Acknowledgements vii
Introduction: Mapping the Literature of Out-Migration 1

Part One
Defining the Newfoundland Diaspora
1 Newfoundland and the Concept of Diaspora 9

Part Two
Affective Responses
2 Donna Morrissey and the Search for Prairie Gold 31
3 "The 'Going Home Again' Complaint": Carl Leggo and Nostalgia for Newfoundland 49

Part Three
Is the Newfoundlander "Authentic" in the Diaspora?
4 E.J. Pratt and the Gateway to Canada 65
5 "A Papier Mâché Rock": Wayne Johnston and Rejecting Regionalism 85

Part Four
Imagining the Newfoundland Nation
6 "This Is Their Country Now": David French, Confederation, and the Imagined Community 101
7 Writing the "Old Lost Land": Johnston Part Two 115

Part Five
Postmodern Ethnicity and Memoirs from Away
8 Helen Buss / Margaret Clarke and the Negotiation of Identity 145
9 The "Holdin' Ground": David Macfarlane and the Second Generation 167

Conclusion: Writing in Diaspora Space 181
Notes 189
Works Cited 195
Index 207

ACKNOWLEDGEMENTS

This research has been generously funded by a Social Sciences and Humanities Research Council (SSHRC) Canadian Graduate Scholarship, a Grant Notley Memorial Postdoctoral Fellowship, and a SSHRC Postdoctoral Fellowship.

Parts of this book were previously published in *Narratives of Citizenship: Indigenous and Diasporic Peoples Unsettle the Nation-State* (University of Alberta Press) and in *Canadian Literature* 196.

I am grateful to Laura Moss for her unwavering support, helpful suggestions, challenging questions, and sharp editorial eye. Thanks to Margery Fee, who has also been a crucial source of information, advice and encouragement. Thanks to Glenn Deer, Kevin McNeilly, Carl Leggo, Ronald Rompkey, Stephen Slemon, and Daniel Coleman.

Thanks to my friends and colleagues, with whom I have shared resources, helpful reading groups, and many stress-relieving beers.

Thanks to my family, whose stories of "home" began the thinking behind this project.

Thanks, finally, to Kent. This book would not have been possible without his patience, love, and support.

Introduction

MAPPING THE LITERATURE OF OUT-MIGRATION

> Hines, in his sermon/column, forever likened Newfoundlanders to the Jews, pointing out parallels between them. There was a "diaspora" of Newfoundlanders, he said, scattered like the Jews throughout the world. He saw himself as their minister, preaching to his flock from his columns, most of which began with epigraphs from the Book of Exodus.
> —Wayne Johnston, *The Colony of Unrequited Dreams*

> I dredge these silted beds
> but there is nothing left—
> the sea is torn, bone-seeded.
> even my lanky brother has gone
> west to the mountains.
>
> The winter beach is strewn
> blue with mussels sucked dry.
> I have abandoned my home.
> —Carol Hobbs, "Trawl"

In the 1970s my parents, newly married, left their home province of Newfoundland for Alberta. They expected to return in a few years. Two children and more than three decades later, they have not returned to Newfoundland to live. I grew up in Edmonton with my parents referring to Newfoundland as "home," eating Newfoundland meals, hearing traditional songs, and using Newfoundland expressions without realizing my friends did not understand me. Growing up I did not really consider myself an Albertan, even though I had never lived anywhere else. I constructed my identity out of my Newfoundland heritage. My grandparents were always five thousand kilometres away, but I had cousins to play with—many of my parents' siblings were also compelled to leave.

My family's is a common story, and an old one—Newfoundland's economic hardships have propelled a continuous stream of out-migration, not only since Confederation with Canada in 1949, but for well over a century. David Alexander explains that Newfoundland's primary economy, its fishery, simply could not sustain its labour force even as early as the late nineteenth century ("Economy" 29). For some, seasonal work in other places was the solution, but for many, seasonal migration led to permanent settlement elsewhere. As the nineteenth century ended, industrial Cape Breton drew thousands of Newfoundlanders, and the Canadian government actively recruited Newfoundlanders for the western provinces (Crawley 43). Before Confederation, the United States was an even bigger draw; in 1915 there were already 13,269 Newfoundlanders living in Massachusetts alone (Reeves 35). During World War II thousands of Newfoundland women married American servicemen and moved to the States. Following Confederation, Newfoundlanders tended to migrate to Canada rather than the US, most drawn to urban Ontario in search of work. According to Wayne Johnston, by 1963 an estimated two million expatriate Newfoundlanders and their descendants were living elsewhere in Canada or the US—four times the population of the province (*Baltimore's* 49). Out-migration was further boosted by the collapse of fish stocks, which culminated in a moratorium on the northern cod fishery in 1992. Between 1971 and 1998 the net loss to out-migration amounted to 100,000 people, about 20 percent of the province's population (Bella 1). As the final report of the Newfoundland Government's Royal Commission on Renewing and Strengthening Our Place in Canada (2003) reflects, this dramatic population loss "is a shocking indicator that something has gone seriously wrong in the economy of Newfoundland and Labrador" (35).

While many Canadian provinces, particularly other Atlantic provinces, have experienced out-migration for similar reasons,[1] Newfoundland's population loss stands out for its sheer numbers, at times reaching a net rate of more than 6 percent of Newfoundlanders aged five and older (Statistics Canada). Moreover, this statistic does not include the significant amount of seasonal migration that brings Newfoundland labourers back and forth several times a year. As of 2003, Newfoundland's expatriate community was estimated at a total of 220,000 (Royal Commission i)—a staggering number considering that the province's population in that year was just 512,500. This long period of population loss may finally be slowing; in 2008 and 2009 the province experienced a brief population increase for the first time in fifteen years (Statistics Canada). Yet census data since then again show an annual population loss to out-migration. The province's unemployment rate remains the highest in the country, at 13 percent as of June 2012 (Statistics Canada).

Out-migration has not been limited to former fishers or young blue-collar labourers. Professionals and artists have also left. Others have left in search of better education. Aging parents have followed their children to their new hometowns in Toronto or Fort McMurray in a "second wave" of out-migration (Royal Commission 39). While not every Newfoundlander's reasons for leaving are the same, together they have formed a culture of out-migration, in which leaving is often expected or considered inevitable, and in which returning is a powerful but often unfulfilled dream. Together, these migrants constitute a Newfoundland diaspora.

...

This book examines how this diaspora has impacted Newfoundland literature, both as the subject of much of the work and as a condition from which many writers write. In Newfoundland, critics have explicitly connected the development of a distinct literature to the massive change resulting from Confederation, the government resettlement program of the 1940s and '50s, and the collapse of the fishery (Gwyn; Rompkey, "Colonial"). This book argues that much of Newfoundland's current literary production is also a result of, or a response to, diaspora. The idea of a "Newfoundland diaspora" does not just refer to the post-cod-moratorium outflux, then, but to a larger social phenomenon that has shaped Newfoundland literature and culture. Malcolm Macleod's review of Helen M. Buss / Margaret Clarke's *Memoirs from Away* suggests the way in which the Newfoundland diaspora can be considered in terms of a broad literary history: "'Memoirs from away' is the title of this one book, but it is a fitting label for a whole category of writing about Newfoundland. While Newfoundlanders have been massively re-locating themselves in North America for 120 years, literary elements in the diaspora have often penned accounts of displacement, adjustment and nostalgia for a distant, past homeland" (98). This migrant literary tradition can be traced back to the early twentieth century and the poetry of E.J. Pratt and the stories and essays of the Montreal-based magazine *The Atlantic Guardian*. Contemporary narratives of out-migration also frequently locate themselves within a long historical diasporic trajectory, so that Wayne Johnston's memoir of family and displacement, *Baltimore's Mansion*, for example, looks back at the retreat of one of the colony's first settlers, Lord Baltimore, as the beginning of a social pattern. In this book, then, rather than moving chronologically through the texts, I take a comparative approach, examining how diaspora influences writers of diverse eras and genres, and how diasporic subjectivity intersects with the theoretical flashpoints of affect, authenticity, nationalism, and ethnicity.

It should be mentioned that I concentrate on the literature of the island of Newfoundland and Newfoundlanders, excluding Labrador. Newfoundland has traditionally considered Labrador to be its backyard fishing ground, and Labrador figures prominently in the literary imagination of Newfoundlanders. But in reality it constitutes a separate literary culture with unique issues and concerns, which merits its own critical study. To include Labrador in my study would be to draw a literary community along provincial political lines rather than cultural ones, which is a move that I want to oppose rather than support. It would also allow the political concerns of the Innu and Inuit peoples to be swallowed by a falsely homogenized provincial identity.

In Chapter 1, I draw on interdisciplinary theoretical work on diaspora to examine the implications and the value of applying this label to Newfoundland out-migration. The concept of diaspora is undoubtedly in vogue in both academic and popular discourse, raising concerns about its integrity as a term. Wariness of its increasing capaciousness and anxieties about its homogenizing or celebratory tendencies in an age of transnationalism both point to the problems of thinking about diaspora as a label to be pasted onto a particular group rather than as a concept that helps to articulate experience and identity. I adopt Canadian diaspora theorist Lily Cho's idea that diaspora should be understood not simply as an object of analysis but as a "condition of subjectivity" ("Turn" 11). Newfoundland out-migration is not automatically a diaspora; rather diaspora is a means of describing the particulars of out-migration as a collective experience. In this vein I outline several major connotations of diasporic subjectivity as they apply to the history and experience of Newfoundland out-migration.

Diaspora involves not just physical migrations from point A to point B, but the emotional experience of leaving a homeland behind, of finding oneself in a place that is foreign, and of finding oneself a foreigner. Affective responses to place and displacement are central to the construction of diasporic identities and the formation of diasporic communities. In Part II, "Affective Responses," I show how labour migrations can be characterized by profound feelings of pain and longing. In Chapter 2, I read Donna Morrissey's 2008 novel, *What They Wanted*, as a testimony to the psychological and cultural damage done by economic instability and the destruction of the island's resources. In Chapter 3, I theorize nostalgia as a literary practice in the poetry of Carl Leggo. While nostalgia has often been considered a pejorative term in literary criticism, I argue that it plays an important role in coping with the losses of displacement, and even in political critiques of present society or the new hostland. As an affective response to diaspora, nostalgia can be a driving force behind powerful and moving forms of creative production.

Nostalgia is often considered an "inauthentic" response to displacement. In Part III, "Is the Newfoundlander Authentic in the Diaspora?" I problematize this notion of authenticity as a means of policing identity, and of commodifying places. Literature about Newfoundland has in recent years enjoyed a newfound popularity in Canada and abroad; tourists now flock to Newfoundland's outport communities in search of the Newfoundland depicted in the film version of Annie Proulx's *The Shipping News* or Bernice Morgan's *Random Passage*. This desire for the exotic traces of Newfoundland culture raises serious questions about cultural authenticity, appropriation, and the line between the preservation of culture and the perpetuation of regional stereotypes. If literature shapes conceptions of Newfoundland identity, what is that identity? Who has the right to construct it? Do outsiders like Annie Proulx have the right? What about diasporic Newfoundlanders? I address these questions by considering the different standpoints from which claims to cultural authenticity are asserted and denied over time. I examine the reception of E.J. Pratt and Wayne Johnston, two diasporic writers writing more than half a century apart, who are both represented as delegates of an essentialized "regional" culture.

In Part IV, "Imagining the Newfoundland Nation," I continue my analysis of Johnston, examining how texts by Johnston and David French construct nationalism and Confederation in 1949 from the perspective of the diasporic Newfoundland community. The recent memory of a Newfoundland independent from Canada differentiates this diaspora from other interprovincial movements, in that it contributes to a sense of being a distinct society within the federation. Diaspora and Confederation are also often metaphorically intertwined, as both involve the loss of the Newfoundland nation and the threat of Canadian assimilation. Yet for these authors diaspora can also be a useful position from which to reimagine the Newfoundland nation. The Newfoundland diaspora thus involves multiple imaginaries — the "diasporic imaginaries" or communities abroad, the "imagined community" of the Newfoundland nation, and the literary reimagining of home in the face of change and loss.

Finally, in Part V, "Postmodern Ethnicity and Memoirs from Away," I consider alternatives to this nationalist identification, by examining displaced Newfoundlanders' claims to "ethnicity." Through analyses of memoirs by Helen M. Buss / Margaret Clarke and David Macfarlane, I ask where Newfoundland identity fits within the Canadian discourse of multiculturalism, which as both a public policy and a cultural ideal attempts to manage ethnic bodies (Kamboureli, *Scandalous* 89). Monika Fludernik argues that the popularity of the term "diaspora" is in part derived from "the communitarianism that has been sparked off by the multiculturalist movement," meaning that "the terms exile, immigrant, expelled, refugee, expatriate or minority no longer fit the experience" (xvi). The multiculturalist roots of diasporic identification, then, suggest that the concept of a Newfoundland diaspora cannot be based solely on an intense regional or neo-national affiliation, but rather demand that it be considered in terms of the multicultural delineations of both ethnicity and race. In Chapter 8, I draw on Ien Ang's concept of "postmodern ethnicity" as a potential means of negotiating the ethnic and racial facets of diaspora. In Chapter 9, I take these considerations into a discussion of the second generation of the Newfoundland diaspora, drawing on the theory of postmemory to elucidate the ongoing connections that the children of migrants feel to Newfoundland as a distant homeland.

My analysis of the Newfoundland literary diaspora, then, has implications for the broader institution of Canadian literature, which increasingly questions the place of regional, national, and ethnic affiliations within a literature drawn along the borders of the nation-state. Canadian literature is today as much as ever being shaped by global movements — from international networks of technology and capital, to the visceral images of shiploads of refugees off BC's coast. In turn, the study of Canadian literature is increasingly turning its attention to the forces of globalization, to the ways that, as Smaro Kamboureli puts it, the normative multicultural idiom has been "challenged by the immediacy of diasporic and transnational politics in our daily lives" ("Preface" xii). I argue that the literature of the Newfoundland diaspora both contributes to and responds to critical movements in Canadian literature and culture as it interacts with other Canadian diasporic and regional literatures. The Newfoundland diaspora plays a part in defining Canada even as it looks beyond the borders of Canada as a literary community.

PART ONE

DEFINING THE NEWFOUNDLAND DIASPORA

ONE

NEWFOUNDLAND AND THE CONCEPT OF DIASPORA

I am not the first to apply the term "diaspora" to Newfoundland out-migration. In their article on the use of the Internet in diaspora communities, sociologists Harry Hiller and Tara Franz define Newfoundland out-migration as a diaspora because of Newfoundland migrants' strong attachment to place, community affiliation, and "unique identity" (747). Other instances, including those in literary criticism, are casual, without exploration of the term's theoretical history and complexity. Shane O'Dea refers to "various diaspora groups (Jews, Irish, Newfoundlanders)" (379). Stan Dragland, reflecting on the Newfoundland literary scene, muses, "I know that a vibrant paper nation might look ironic to those in the Newfoundland diaspora who can't afford to live here" (206). Photographer Greg Locke hosts a website titled "Dispatches from Exit 0: Going Down the Road with Newfoundland's Diaspora." In his informal meditation *Leaving Newfoundland: A History of Out-Migration* (2007), Stephen Nolan calls the "tumultuous upheaval" of Newfoundlanders from their home a long-standing "diaspora" (2). I do not quarrel with these examples of the term. But their offhand usage does mark the need for a theoretical investigation of the implications of the term in the Newfoundland context, particularly in the field of literary studies.

The concept of diaspora, as noted earlier, has proliferated in recent years, in both academic and popular contexts, and so too have debates over the term's definition. While "diaspora" originated as a term for the dispersal of the Jews, as Avtar Brah writes, "to speak of late twentieth-century diasporas is to take such ancient diasporas as a point of departure rather than necessarily as 'models'" (181). Indeed, in *Powers of Diaspora: Two Essays on the Relevance of Jewish Culture* (2002), Jonathan and Daniel Boyarin argue that "the cultural strategies of Jewish diaspora—of regeneration through statelessness—speak well [...] to the dilemmas and the possibilities of the 'new diasporas' born in the midst and in the aftermath of the modern world-system" (vii–viii). The Boyarins affirm that "we should not define diaspora such that some are more 'diasporic' than others, and we must watch the intellectual trap of speaking as if the concept *produces* the various phenomena rather than merely helping us *think them together*" (28). But while diaspora has become a useful model to describe a multitude of movements in our current transnational moment, anxieties nevertheless remain over where the boundaries of diaspora should be drawn. Diaspora theorists like William Safran and Robin Cohen have formed lists of criteria for societies to qualify as diasporas. But James Clifford convincingly argues that "no society can be expected to qualify on all counts, throughout its history. And the discourse of diaspora will necessarily be modified as it is translated and adopted. [...] A polythetic field would seem most conducive to tracking (rather than policing) the contemporary range of diasporic forms" (306–07). Following Clifford, I am not interested in proving how or whether Newfoundland out-migration meets each criterion, as though "diaspora" is an exclusive club that can accept or deny membership (though maintaining some definitional integrity is important). Rather, as a "condition of subjectivity" (Cho, "Turn" 11), diaspora articulates the collective, affective experiences of Newfoundland out-migrants in relationship to homeland and hostland. Considering migrant cultures in diasporic terms provides a space in which to "think them together," and provides an enabling frame of reference through which to better understand experiences of displacement, as well as the literature that these experiences generate.

"Diaspora" is a useful term to describe Newfoundland out-migration in that it captures the magnitude of the phenomenon and its impact on Newfoundland literary culture. The term connotes what I identify as five main aspects of the migration experience: (1) painful displacement and a condition of loss; (2) a continued connection to homeland; (3) the formation of diaspora communities abroad; (4) the construction of homeland in neo-national rather than regional terms; and (5) a sense of difference and marginalization in the new home. These elements are not definitions of diaspora but rather connotations of diasporic subjectivity, which helpfully elucidate the experience of Newfoundland out-migration and its literature.

Painful Displacement

In her essay "Confederation," which won first place in the Newfoundland literary journal *TickleAce*'s essay contest marking the fiftieth anniversary of Confederation, Kay Anonsen uses second-person narrative to tell the story of a woman twice displaced from Newfoundland. The first time, she leaves as a child with her family in the 1960s. She returns as an adult, only to leave again after two decades in the province. We are not told the circumstances of the family's original migration from Newfoundland to Ontario, but the father's relationship to his birthplace implies a lack of choice: "your old Dad who lies far away from everything he understood told you many times that there was no one else worth knowing except a Newfoundlander" (51). His burial in Ontario, "far away from everything he understood," emphasizes both the rupture of identity caused by diaspora and its tragic permanence. Anonsen's description of having to give up one's Newfoundland driver's licence is equally powerful: "the woman took your information and your picture and your money and then she asked you for your Newfoundland driver's license and you asked why and you didn't want to give it to her, did you? It was the last proof of who you were, wasn't it?" (50). This simple scenario, and the protagonist's reaction to it, demonstrate how out-migration painfully represents both the loss of homeland and a threat to personal identity.

Diaspora theorists such as Paul Gilroy, Khachig Tölölyan, and Cho all argue that trauma and loss are central to the concept of diaspora. Anonsen's piece shows that out-migration is profoundly painful for many Newfoundlanders, but can a situation in which people choose to leave for economic reasons, rather than being forced to leave by violence, legitimately be called a diaspora? Gilroy argues that "diaspora" is "not just a word of movement, though purposive, desperate movement is integral to it. Under this sign, push factors are a dominant influence. The urgency they introduce makes diaspora more than a voguish synonym for peregrination or nomadism [...] life itself is at stake in the way the word connotes flight following the threat of violence rather than freely chosen experiences of displacement" (123). Gilroy suggests that diasporas are provoked by the violence of "slavery, pogroms, indenture, genocide, and other unnameable terrors" (123), rather than more benign labour or economic pressures. But while Gilroy's work has been profoundly important to the development of diaspora research, and while violence certainly figures prominently in theories of diaspora, most theorists do not confine the term exclusively to such displacements. In contrast, Robin Cohen, in *Global Diasporas: An Introduction*, analyzes what he calls "labour diasporas," which arise when groups not only leave a homeland in search of work, but also demonstrate a "strong retention of group ties," a strong connection to a homeland, and the inability to easily assimilate in the host society (57–58). Cohen's work goes to the opposite extreme to Gilroy's; his wide definition of diaspora even includes a form of "imperial diaspora," which is marked by "a sense of forming part of a grand imperial design—whereby the group concerned assumes the self-image of a 'chosen race' with a global mission" of colonial expansion (67). Cohen traces the word's etymological origins to Greek imperialism, and while he notes that these origins have "virtually been lost" in deference to the biblical usage, he uses this history to justify "imperial diaspora" as a category. Yet the predominance of the Jewish Diaspora in the term's development, and its more recent appropriation by post-colonial theory, has shifted it from its Greek imperial origins to a very different meaning, with hundreds of years of persecution, slavery, and indentured labour behind it. This history cannot be reversed as easily as Cohen would have it. Much of diaspora theory is concerned with resolving Gilroy and Cohen's extreme positions, with staking out a ground for diaspora somewhere in the middle that provides both the limits of meaningful definition and room for effective comparison and dialogue between displaced groups. Such work is not merely a question of quibbling about semantics, since both claims to diaspora and moves to exclude certain experiences from it involve profoundly emotional negotiations.

Staking out the ground for diaspora is therefore a project with both practical and ethical implications. In an issue of his influential journal *Diaspora*, Tölölyan identifies the term as having once been "saturated with the meanings of exile, loss, dislocation, powerlessness and plain pain" ("Rethinking" 9). While Tölölyan reluctantly concedes that "the definition has changed" (13), he effectively argues that the "amnesia" concerning the term's long-standing connotations of trauma and loss is problematic. In a Canadian context, Cho also expresses dismay that recent claims "divorce diaspora from histories of loss and dislocation" ("Turn" 12). These are concerns that I share. At the 2006 Canadian Metropolis conference for Research on Immigration and Integration in the Metropolis (RIIM) in Vancouver, sociologists Kenny Zhang and Yuen Pau Woo argued that the 2.7 million Canadian citizens living abroad could constitute a "Canadian diaspora." While Canadians abroad may retain a group identity and connection to home, according to Zhang and Yuen, this "Canadian diaspora" includes the thousands of Asian immigrants that have returned home after only a few years in Canada (n. pag.). By this definition, all that is required to be part of a diaspora is legal citizenship. While a "Canadian diaspora" may be possible, Zhang and Yuen do not attach the phenomenon they study to any shared sense of cultural identity or community abroad. Such a "loose" usage of the term, as Yuen himself describes it (n. pag.), renders "diaspora" meaningless—it collapses a multitude of movements and experiences into one term, emptying it of any sense of collective identity, traumatic displacement, or cultural significance. The application of the term "diaspora" to Newfoundland must therefore be carefully considered.

For Newfoundlanders the rupture from the homeland is obviously not violent like other diasporic engines such as slavery or war, but it is often experienced as a moment of painful loss propelled by forces beyond the migrant's control. The Royal Commission on Renewing and Strengthening Our Place in Canada states that "with job losses in many parts of the province being so severe, and without sufficient growth in employment opportunities elsewhere in the provincial economy, people have been forced to choose between unemployment and out-migration" (35). For people struggling to support themselves and their families, the choice between unemployment and out-migration is not much of a choice at all. As I began this research, this feeling of coercion was emphasized with CBC television coverage of the closure of another Newfoundland fish plant, and footage of a sobbing father shouting, "I'm the one that's got to go to my kid and explain to him why his father's got to leave and go to the mainland" (*The National*). This feeling of choicelessness, the splitting of families, and the loss of home have all contributed to a sense of anguish.

The sense that out-migration is unavoidable is not simply the outcome of economic insecurity, it has also become a more complex social phenomenon. On Newfoundland's Great Northern Peninsula in the early 1990s, sociologists Peter R. Sinclair and Lawrence F. Felt found that "migration in search of work plays an important role in legitimating young men's position in the local society" (22). One interviewee explained this phenomenon:

> It's kind of expected, especially for males, that they go somewhere else to find a job if they can't find nothing here. If you lose the job or find something better here at home, it's all right, because at least you went away. My parents encouraged most of us to move away at least for a year or so to look for work and maybe try to save something before we would be welcomed back. Even the UIC (Unemployment Insurance Commission) people seem to treat you better if they knows you've been away to look for work. I knows that some people who never have left had it thrown up in their face when they go to stamp workers to try and get on make work projects so they can qualify for UI. (13)

The feeling of lack of choice is not merely created by economic factors, but by the pressures of society. Not only is it expected that young people will *need* to move away, it is expected that they *should*. It has become a "*rite de passage*" in this region (Sinclair and Felt 13), an important part of being accepted in the community. In her more recent study of youth in a small Newfoundland community, Dona Lee Davis found this phenomenon still at work ten years after the cod moratorium. She discovered that all the young adults she interviewed had been "raised to 'get out'" (191), experiencing pressure from their parents, teachers, and peers to leave so that they would have more opportunities. The idea of "choice," then, is not black and white; Newfoundlanders who make the *decision* to leave may not feel as though they had a *choice*.

For those who do "choose" to leave, the loss of the homeland can still be extremely painful, as it often constitutes both a rupture from place and a rupture of identity. In Anonsen's "Confederation," the second time the protagonist moves away from Newfoundland, the move is economically motivated. It also seems to be a positive choice: "you're so happy to go to a place that has opportunity and good weather and the possibilities are endless" (49). But once the protagonist has left Newfoundland, the sense of loss is acute: "you walked out into the baking sunlight and realized how lonely you were, how lonely for Newfoundland, how lonely for Newfoundlanders" (50). This passage reveals the profound ambivalence of Newfoundland out-migration, the loss of identity and feeling of pain that accompany even situations where people "choose" to leave. Applying the term diaspora here necessitates a rethinking of labour and economic migrations in terms of these affective connections.

Connection to Homeland

In Anonsen's essay, the connection to Newfoundland remains strong, and it is manifested in the collection of material items that represent the place, foster memories, and mark identity. "You asked your sister to send you bumper stickers or license plate holders or anything that would signify you as a Newfoundlander," she writes. "You put up Newfoundland memorabilia all over the house and you gazed with love at that old ratty hooked mat of the island and you read avidly anything in the paper about Newfoundland and you'll never feel like an Ontarian or even a Canadian" (50). This connection to homeland is a salient feature of diasporic experience. As Clifford writes, "the language of diaspora is increasingly invoked by displaced peoples who feel (maintain, revive, invent) a connection with a prior home. This sense of connection must be strong enough to resist erasure through the normalizing processes of forgetting, assimilating, and distancing" (310). The speaker in "Confederation" manifests her connection with her homeland in material symbols of home, and her need to make this connection tangible illustrates her resistance to those forces of forgetting, assimilating, and distancing.

Newfoundland migrants may also maintain a connection to homeland through political activism. In his unpublished study of Newfoundland expatriate communities, Cory Thorne recounts how the large Newfoundland population in Cambridge, Ontario, founded Leave Our Fish Alone (LOFA) in 1987 in response to the federal government's decision to increase cod quotas for France, "despite mounting evidence suggesting that Newfoundland's fishery was in danger of collapse, and that this disaster was being perpetuated partially through illegal trawlers from France" (154). The group held rallies, organized protests, and started petitions, all within the community of Cambridge, Ontario. Safran suggests that a salient quality of diasporas is that their members "believe that they should, collectively, be committed to the maintenance or restoration of their original homeland and to its safety and prosperity" (84), a commitment clearly demonstrated by this political movement launched by migrants who no longer had any direct personal investment in the fishery.

Not all migrant Newfoundlanders would consider themselves part of a "diaspora"—some leave without a desire to ever return, and abandon their Newfoundland identity. But for many, the desire to return is strong—for some even strong enough to impel them to move back. In *Newfoundlanders: Home and Away*, Leslie Bella reports that between 1971 and 1998 over 350,000 Newfoundlanders left the province, but 250,000 returned. Of course this still left a net out-migration of 100,000, or 20 percent of the province's population (1). Bella found that for many migrants returning is not realistic, for the same reasons they left—unemployment and economic hardship. Sinclair and Felt's 1993 study of return migration to Newfoundland's Great Northern Peninsula found that while return migration is significant, it does not guarantee that former migrants will not have to leave again (21). But for Newfoundlanders in diaspora, the desire to return is not only driven by economics, or even by the draw of family and friends, but by a profound attachment to place, the pull of the idea of "home" (Sinclair, "Moving" 211). Bella discovered that "missing Newfoundland's ocean and the landscape was more emotionally significant for some than missing family or culture" (95). Jonathan and Daniel Boyarin argue that while the term "migrant" indicates a forward trajectory, presupposing the "ontological priority" of the new home, "diaspora" indicates a looking back at the original home (27). A "Newfoundland diaspora," then, connotes this continued attachment to homeland, often accompanied by a strong desire to return.

The Formation of Diaspora Communities
As Anonsen's protagonist turns in her Newfoundland driver's licence for an Ontario one, she meets another displaced Newfoundlander:

> He also held a Newfoundland driver's license in his hand which he showed you, like a credential [...]. You told him he was the first Newfoundlander you'd met since you got here and he said the man who owned the company he worked for was a Newfoundlander and everyone who worked there were all Newfoundlanders, every one. You made some kind of envious murmur and he said sure the first apartment building he moved into here was all Newfies, every single tenant in the whole building. (50)

Diasporas by definition involve the movement of groups, rather than the travels or exile of individuals. For Newfoundlanders, diasporic subjectivity leads to both the construction of practical collectivities and a more intangible group consciousness. Newfoundlanders in other provinces or countries tend to form "ethnic enclaves" or "little Newfoundlands" (Bella 21);[2] they may subscribe to *Downhome Magazine,* devoted to displaced Newfoundlanders; they often follow friends or family to the new destination in a pattern of "chain migration" (Bella iv); and they often form new connections with other migrants in clubs (Bella 44). They check websites like NewfoundlandersAbroad.com for businesses run by Newfoundlanders in their area. Hiller and Franz found that modern technology has meant that Newfoundland's diaspora community can exist across great distances and borders, through email or online chat rooms. Thorne contends that while for Newfoundland migrants "geographic commons have been destroyed," through the preservation of Newfoundland folklore and the construction of public spaces in the host communities "social commons have been consciously built" (81). These physical and virtual communities constitute what Vijay Mishra calls "diasporic imaginaries": "any ethnic enclave in a nation-state that defines itself, consciously, unconsciously or because of the political self-interest of a racialized nation-state, as a group that lives in displacement" (423). Such ties mean that individuals do not experience their personal migrations as unique, but rather as part of a collectivity with a common experience.

Another moment in Anonsen's piece suggests the ways in which these imaginaries can be formed not only out of mutual cultural identification, but also out of class solidarity:

> And when your sister moved to Toronto and worked in a factory filling aerosol cans, and came home for the weekend and you all sat around the kitchen table to hear her news and she told you how many Newfoundlanders worked in the factory, none of you could believe it. And then she said it was immigrants and Newfoundlanders, that's who was working in all the factories, and your Mom clucked her tongue and your Dad said sure what's the difference, we're immigrants too. (49)

"Diaspora" signals this (imagined or real) shared experience of displacement between Newfoundland migrants and other immigrants. It also suggests an ongoing sense of group identity marked by a particular form of labour migration, and articulates the link between these connections and Newfoundland as an imagined community. But the concept of a Newfoundland diaspora is not limited to the labour migrations of the working class and those directly impacted by the fishery collapse. Certainly class plays a large part in Newfoundlanders' ability to stay at home, a fact that is exacerbated by a significant urban-rural divide within the province. Yet as Anonsen's piece shows it is not just the shared working conditions of the factory that constitute a Newfoundland diaspora, but also the shared markers of home and identity symbolized by driver's licences and bumper stickers — material representations of diasporic subjectivity that transcend economic status. Class is just one of what Brah calls the multiple "modalities" through which diasporas are lived. "All diasporas," Brah argues, "are differentiated, heterogeneous, contested spaces, even as they are implicated in the construction of a common 'we'" (184). The concept of diaspora, then, "delineates a field of identifications where 'imagined communities' are forged within and out of a confluence of narratives from annals of collective memory and re-memory" (196). Experiences differentiated by class, gender, religion, and generation together form a heterogeneous culture of diaspora through which migrant Newfoundlanders can identify with each other, and with other diasporic peoples displaced from real and imagined homes. Literature is a key means through which diverse diasporic imaginaries are formed.

For the father in Anonsen's piece, the term "immigrant" not only signals social and economic marginalization, but also triggers a latent nationalism left over from pre-Confederation independence. The father goes on to "[boast] again of when Newfoundland was a dominion and even had its own stamps, its own money" (49). He cannot seem to separate his understanding of his own displacement from the political history of his island; both are key to the way that he constructs his identity. In this sense the "imaginary" aspect of Mishra's "diasporic imaginaries" evokes a connection with Benedict Anderson's "imagined communities" (*Imagined* xi), a theory that has become central to the idea of nation. Both concepts emphasize the role that the individual plays in imagining connections with unknown others, thus defining broader collective identities. This linkage suggests the implications that diasporas have for various nationalisms, including the construction of Newfoundland as an imagined nation.

Nationalism

The relationship between the nation and the concept of diaspora is vexed and often contradictory. On the one hand, many diaspora theorists consider diasporas to be extensions of nation-states or proto-national in structure, as they are defined by collective identities usually rooted in the country of origin. On the other hand, the growing interest in diaspora as a concept has also been linked to forces of globalization; in this sense diasporas are often seen as challenges to the nation-state as the dominating structure of personal and political identification. Diasporas represent, in other words, the mobility of groups in a supposedly post-national world. What these seemingly opposite perspectives show in fact is how salient the nation-state remains in conversations about diasporic subjectivity. In my view, the concept of diaspora is related to but distinct from the more fluid concepts of globalization, transnationalism, and cosmopolitanism. Diaspora continues to imply not a celebratory post-national mobility but a subjectivity rooted in narratives of displacement and collective identities that are frequently framed by (or excluded from) national affiliations. In this sense, my understanding of the Newfoundland diaspora is intertwined with a salient Newfoundland nationalism, a nationalism that is not undermined but actually reinforced by Newfoundland's place within the nation-state of Canada. I would like to spend the next few pages elaborating on this Newfoundland nationalism, which is at once a political movement and a cultural phenomenon, dependent upon a distinct history and often manifested in artistic production.

Newfoundland nationalism is often built upon a collective memory of hardship and oppression going back to the earliest settlements in the seventeenth and eighteenth centuries. Years of toil, of threats of starvation, of exploitation at the hands of a corrupt merchant system, and of the constant dangers of life at sea, all contributed to what Patrick O'Flaherty calls the myth of the "hardy Newfoundlander" (56), a pride in an identity forged out of decades of hard work and suffering. In 1832, Newfoundland was given a system of democratic representative government, and in 1855 it was granted responsible government. These political changes transformed Newfoundland into a self-governing colony which, in 1907, became known, like Canada, as a dominion of Britain. These legal changes were accompanied by the gradual development of Newfoundland as a distinct cultural entity. Ronald Rompkey outlines how, by the end of the nineteenth century, "there was a growing acknowledgement of the existence of Newfoundlanders as a *people* with identifiable peculiarities of pronunciation and idiom, of song, proverb and folk tale" ("Idea" 267; emphasis in original). Shane O'Dea links this group identity to a growing sense of nationalism: "over the course of the eighteenth and nineteenth centuries as more people came to be permanent inhabitants and, more importantly, descendants of permanent inhabitants, the sense of person-linked-to-place which is the essential for nationalism, grew into being" (380). Despite this strengthening national identity, Newfoundland's self-government did not last even a hundred years. In 1933, faced with bankruptcy, the Newfoundland legislature voted itself out of existence, suspending responsible government in favour of a committee appointed by the British government. Established as an emergency measure, this unelected "Commission of Government" lasted until 1948, when referenda were held to determine whether Newfoundland would resume responsible government or join Canadian Confederation. Fifty-two percent of Newfoundlanders voted to join Canada, which it did on 31 March 1949. Confederation is thus a very recent event in what we might call Newfoundland's "cultural memory," and it remains an emotional and controversial subject. The slim majority of votes that led to the loss of the Newfoundland nation has spawned accusations of British and Canadian interference and conspiracy. In his historical study *Confederation: Deciding Newfoundland's Future 1934–1949*, James K. Hiller writes that while there is no convincing evidence that the votes or results were tampered with or manipulated, "that such allegations were sometimes made shows how divisive the issue became" (63). In the decades since, Confederation has continued to raise questions, both about the historical circumstances that led to it and about the economic and social consequences it has had for Newfoundland.

Today, Newfoundland nationalism is driven not only by a unique history and the collective memory of Confederation, but also by an ongoing sense of alienation from the Canadian nation-state. The same economic hardships that have propelled out-migration have also exacerbated a feeling of resentment toward the federal government, which controls the fishery. In a 2003 provincial opinion poll, 84 percent of respondents felt that the federal government ignores Newfoundland and Labrador (Royal Commission 433). The common feeling that government mismanagement is to blame for the collapse of the fishery leads to the view that the diaspora is driven not simply by the forces of nature and economics, but also by a federal government that does not care about Newfoundland. Bella contends that "Canada's political leaders benefit if Newfoundlanders leave their home province for employment in Canada. Therefore, even though Newfoundland has been a nation in its own right [...] Newfoundlanders' ethnic identity is ignored in Canadian public policy, and along with it their right to stay home after the collapse of the fishery, a collapse engineered by that same Canadian government" (ix). This claim that "Newfoundland has been a nation in its own right" is contestable, given the island's complex colonial history.[3] Nevertheless, what Michael Crummey calls the "lost nation" remains a powerful defining myth in Newfoundland culture, and is exacerbated by rifts between the province and the state. Newfoundland history, then, is characterized by a deep tension between the idea of a Newfoundland nation and the realities of a province that feels neglected within the federation.

Bella's assertion that the Canadian government "engineered" the fishery collapse might also be hyperbolic, but many experts have examined how the policies and failures of the federal Department of Fisheries and Oceans (DFO) and other ministries have contributed to both the fishery collapse and ongoing social problems, including out-migration. Sinclair and others trace the fishery collapse back to the Confederation period, when "the provincial government's push towards an industrial fishery coincided with the objectives of Canada's federal government" (Sinclair, "Narrowing" 238). The result was the development of unsustainable fishing practices with which small inshore producers could not compete, the devaluation of traditional management practices, and consistent overestimation of remaining fish stocks (see also Matthews and Phyne; Neis and Williams; and Cadigan "Moral Economy"). Barbara Neis and Rob Kean point out that in the 1980s, in association with these overestimates, the DFO allocated between 10,000 and 20,000 tonnes of northern cod to European countries in return for access to European markets for Canadian goods, like grain, a move that seemed to favour the welfare of other Canadian producers over that of Newfoundland fishers (77). The federal government has also been critiqued for failing to protect the resource from illegal European fishing.

Many Newfoundlanders also feel that the federal government has failed them in the aftermath of the fishery collapse. Sharon Taylor, in her work on The Atlantic Groundfish Strategy, or TAGS, shows how this program to retrain fishers affected by the moratorium has failed its beneficiaries by treating the fishery as "the domain of individuals, separate from community and family life" (249). By helping fishers who qualified but ignoring the impact of the fisheries crisis on the next generation, the program left many young people with no other choice but to migrate to the mainland, in turn eroding the communities in which they grew up. Barbara Neis and Susan Williams add that "the federal government has treated the crisis with short-term programs, when in reality, fish stocks in some areas are recovering slowly and some may never recover, threatening the displacement of future generations" (354). There is a widespread belief, then, that not only did the Canadian government allow the fishery collapse to happen, it has also abandoned Newfoundlanders in the aftermath.

While it would be simplistic and inaccurate to place all the blame for the fishery collapse on the federal government, what is important to acknowledge is the strong belief in the minds of many Newfoundlanders that the Canadian government, because of a perceived lack of caring and understanding, allowed or caused the collapse to happen. This belief is reflected in the passionate reactions of the people most directly affected: the fishers and their families. In *Hard Rock and Water* (dir. Barbara Doran), Lisa Moore interviews cod-fisher-turned-crab-fisher Tom Best, who asserts that "the reality of our situation is that if our resources were dealt with properly and had been managed properly by the government of Canada we wouldn't be looking for handouts from anyone, we'd be just as powerful and just as rich *as a nation*" (my emphasis). Best's statement not only conveys deep feelings of injustice, but is also haunted by the loss of nationhood and autonomy. In this view the decisions that purportedly led to the fishery collapse, which in turn led to increased out-migration, are perceived as being out of Newfoundlanders' hands, and in the hands of federal lawmakers with other priorities. Cadigan notes that the depopulation caused by the fishery collapse "is likely welcomed by most of the officials responsible for the management of natural resources" ("Moral Economy" 14). Some even feel that the TAGS program is part of a covert resettlement plan, the ultimate goal being to get rid of small outport communities (Taylor 251). For many Newfoundlanders, then, out-migration is seen not just as an unfortunate consequence of economic hardship, but as a phenomenon encouraged by the federal government.

This rift between province and state has not been restricted to issues surrounding the fishery. At the end of 2004, Premier Danny Williams refused to fly the Canadian flag on government buildings, as a protest against the federal government's latest offer in negotiations over Newfoundland's oil revenues. Cadigan critiques such political strategies as "neo-nationalist Ottawa-bashing to distract the people of Newfoundland and Labrador from the failures of provincial policies and to co-opt their support" (*Newfoundland* 296). But regardless of the motivation, Williams's move appealed to a latent sense of alienation from the rest of Canada that has been sustained in the province for the last sixty years.

The conflict between Newfoundland and the rest of Canada is felt not only in political and economic terms, but also as a cultural difference and a threat of assimilation. Anonsen's protagonist looks pessimistically into the future, imagining a time when Newfoundland's unique communities have disappeared, leaving only major centres, and future generations of Newfoundlanders will finally consider themselves Canadian. "And then we'll have true Confederation because we'll be like everyone else" (51), she writes. "True Confederation," for this speaker, means the loss of a distinct identity. Alexander is more optimistic about Newfoundlanders' ability to maintain cultural difference in the federation. He argues that Canada simply "cannot be a national state" because of the strength of regional and provincial identities ("New Notions" 29). According to Alexander, "this provincial identity may be felt and expressed more strongly in Newfoundland than in any other province of English-speaking Canada" (31). Canada is a prime example of Tölölyan's claim that the existence of "infranational" diasporas challenges the cohesion imposed by the state and that nation-states therefore "may not always be the most effective or legitimate units of collective organization" ("Nation-State" 4). While diasporas are typically thought of as international movements, such "infranational" dynamics exhibit the interactions typical of diasporic contact.

The fact that Newfoundland is a province of Canada is, in this context, secondary to its distinct culture, and to an ongoing *Newfoundland* nationalism that replaces the dominance of the Canadian nation with the memory or possibility of an independent Newfoundland nation. In the Royal Commission's 2003 provincial opinion poll, 12 percent of Newfoundlanders polled felt that Newfoundland should separate from Canada (439). While the Commission considered this number small (143), to me it seems rather large. Historian Jerry Bannister agrees, adding that by framing the question of nationalism in such limited terms, "the commissioners failed to explore the many different ways in which nationalist sentiment is expressed beyond the political aim of separation" (187). Bannister suggests that literature and historiography are two other key forms of this "nationalist sentiment," which is a response to Newfoundland's ongoing economic struggles. This nationalism is not merely a post-cod-moratorium phenomenon. Cadigan documents the rise of nationalist rhetoric in provincial politics through the tenure of Premiers Frank Moores (1972–1979) and Brian Peckford (1979–1989). In his 1987 study on "emergent nationalism" in Newfoundland, sociologist Harry Hiller shows how a rise in cultural awareness coincided with economic concerns through the 1970s, creating a nationalism that is both politically and "ethnically" motivated (269). This "emergent nationalism" has resulted in nationalist and separatist political movements, the incorporation of cultural nationalism into secondary and post-secondary education, and the rise of a local publishing industry (269). Cadigan objects to the concept of a Newfoundland nation, arguing that "nationalism is an ideological construct partially based on the fabrication that peoples of diverse interests are really one and should mobilize in support of a particular interest group or party" (*Newfoundland* 296). Yet this "fabrication" of unity is precisely what makes the concept of the nation meaningful for many Newfoundlanders in search of cultural and even ethnic common ground in the face of perceived economic and political threats. Indeed one might ask when a nation is *not* a fabrication of unity. As Stuart Hall argues, "a nation is not only a political entity but something which produces meanings—*a system of cultural representation*. People are not only legal citizens of a nation; they participate in the *idea* of the nation as represented in its national culture" ("Question" 612, emphases in original). For many Newfoundlanders, the "idea" of the nation exists regardless of its current political status, and it is embodied in both political resistance to the Canadian state and a feeling of cultural difference.

This cultural nationalism has been linked directly to the development of Newfoundland literature. In a 1976 article in *Saturday Night*, Sandra Gwyn famously hailed the "Newfoundland Renaissance," a flourishing of theatre, literature, and visual art. This movement, Gwyn argued, was in part driven by nationalism: "Separation would be an economic absurdity. But anti-Confederacy, partly pure nostalgia, partly an expression of outrage at the colonialization [sic] of a proud and unique society, has become a vibrant force" (40). Since Gwyn, others have echoed this connection between nationalism and culture. Rompkey also highlights the role of Confederation, arguing that while Newfoundland previously displayed the national elements of a unique cultural tradition and history, "ironically it took Confederation itself to bring about what is sometimes regarded as their 'renaissance,' a flowering of cultural expression similar to those taking place in newly independent countries the world over ("Colonial" n. pag.). The loss of the nation is imagined here, ironically, as a moment of new independence and cultural expression. Newfoundland's national culture underwent its greatest development when Newfoundlanders felt the greatest need to differentiate themselves from the rest of Canada, both politically and culturally. O'Dea argues that cultural production and nationalism are inextricably linked in Newfoundland, where nationalism refers to a sense of national identity and "pride in place" (385). As I discuss in detail in Part IV, the nationalist drive behind Newfoundland creative production is often intensified by diaspora, because in diaspora the cultural identity and difference of migrant individuals come into direct tension with the assumptions of other Canadians.

The sheer number of pieces in *TickleAce*'s Confederation special issue that reflect on out-migration further demonstrate this connection between nationalism and diaspora. Trudy J. Morgan-Cole's "Confessions of an Ex-Patriot" is exemplary: "despite having been born sixteen years after Confederation," she writes, "I am a Newfoundlander; nothing brought that fact home to me as much as living in Canada did" (52). In other words, the individual's displacement in the "Rest of Canada," as it is known, is central to her understanding of Newfoundland's identity and difference. The fact that Anonsen's essay, which focuses almost entirely on the experience of out-migration, is called "Confederation" also powerfully conveys how a complex post-Confederation nationalism is often felt as a symptom of diasporic displacement. Suffering from an intense homesickness, the speaker admits that she "will never feel like an Ontarian or even a Canadian. But you are a Canadian, your friend says to you. And you smile and agree. How can you explain to her that the transfer was never completed, or isn't yet completed because after all fifty years isn't a very long time and neither Canadians nor Newfoundlanders have had a chance to get used to each other" (50). The speaker's friend, as a non-Newfoundlander, cannot understand this alienation. But for the speaker it is profound. It is based not on political opposition but on cultural difference; Canadians and Newfoundlanders simply are not "used to each other." This difference prevents her from feeling truly "Canadian." Commenting on her father's insistence that only Newfoundlanders are worth knowing, she writes: "you let him turn your heart into a Newfoundland heart, not a Canadian heart, and your soul into a Newfoundland soul, not a Canadian soul, and the context in which you understood the world became a Newfoundland context, not a Canadian context and there's nothing you can do about it now, not a damn thing" (51). Newfoundland identity is defined in opposition to Canadian identity, and this contradiction is exacerbated by displacement. "Interprovincial migration" does not come near to describing the nature and complexity of this phenomenon, whereas diaspora's complex relationship with nationalism gestures toward Newfoundland's vexed position within the Canadian state.

Difference and Marginalization

Closely tied to this feeling of political marginalization, then, is a feeling of cultural marginalization. Newfoundlanders not only feel alienated by the Canadian state, but frequently also feel marginalized by fellow Canadian citizens. The same 2003 poll of Newfoundlanders commissioned by the Royal Commission found that 88 percent felt that other Canadians have stereotypes about Newfoundlanders, including "stupid," "lazy/don't work/don't want to work," and "not educated" (Royal Commission 429). One does not have to look farther than one of the country's national newspapers to see where this feeling of marginalization or prejudice comes from. *The Globe and Mail*'s Margaret Wente has become notorious for her anti-Newfoundland editorials. Her comments on 6 January 2005, while the province was refusing to fly the maple leaf, are exemplary: "I like Newfoundlanders. I really do. But their sense of victimhood is unmatched. [...] Mr. Williams reminds me of a deadbeat brother-in-law who's hit you up for money a few times too often. He's been sleeping on your couch for years, and now he's got the nerve to complain that it's too lumpy" (A19). Wente goes on to complain about "all of the money we've sent you since you joined Confederation," in the form of equalization payments and make-work schemes—money that never seems to satisfy the "surly islanders." There is no acknowledgement of Newfoundland's contribution in terms of its natural resources; instead she chooses to stereotype Newfoundlanders as complaining, lazy, greedy deadbeats. Interestingly, diaspora plays a key role in an article ostensibly about provincial policies:

> We send more money so that people can stay in the scenic villages where they were born, even though the fish are gone and there's no more work and never will be, unless they can steal some telemarketing from Bangalore. [...] But who can blame people for wanting to stay put? Not me. No one will ever gobble down a plate of cod tongues and pen

an ode to Scarborough. Scarborough is not romantic. It is filled with ugly high-rise towers of immigrants scrambling to gain a foothold in a new land far from home. The difference is that, when they do it, we congratulate them and call it enterprise. No one will ever buy a scenic picture postcard of a strip mall. But Scarborough supports itself, and Newfoundland does not, and I wish Danny Williams would explain why it's a good idea to keep picking the pockets of Chinese dry cleaners and Korean variety-store owners who work 90 hours a week in order to keep subsidizing the people who live in Carbonear, no matter how quaint and picturesque they are. (A19)

In a fascinating move, Wente compares the industriousness of Chinese and Korean immigrants in Scarborough, Ontario, with Newfoundlanders who refuse to migrate, and therefore, it is implied, are too lazy to support themselves. The profits from Newfoundland oil that Williams is requesting be returned are imagined as being directly taken away from these hard-working, "good" immigrants. Canada (read Ontario) is imagined as a benevolent host to immigrants who, through hard work, can make something of themselves in their new home. But this land of opportunity is not available to all Canadians. Simultaneously, the sting of potentially leaving home is transformed into a selfish desire for "romantic" scenery. Wente's words exemplify what Herb Wyile calls the "glorification of mobility and flexibility within neoliberal thinking," which cultivates the mindset that "an attachment to place is disadvantageous, inconvenient, even retrograde. In such a mindset, people's deep attachment to an economically marginal region such as Atlantic Canada may come across as a stubborn refusal or even incapacity to get with the times and be realistic" (*Anne*, 244). In the context of massive out-migration, this "liberal individualist logic of post-industrial capitalism" (245) merely exacerbates Newfoundlanders' feelings of alienation.

Most of the Newfoundlanders that form this labour diaspora are white and enjoy relative privilege compared to the racialized immigrants that Wente evokes. Yet they are sometimes subjected to the "othering" that accompanies diaspora. Safran identifies one of the defining characteristics of members of a diaspora as the belief that "they are not—and perhaps cannot be—fully accepted by their host society and therefore feel partly alienated and insulated from it" (83). Newfoundlanders are often easily identifiable by their accents if not their appearance, while others go to great lengths to adopt a mainland accent in an attempt to assimilate (Bella 56). Anonsen describes the feeling of otherness that diasporic Newfoundlanders often experience: "And you never ever felt like a Canadian. You were from Newfoundland. Other kids you knew had moved to Ontario from Saskatchewan or British Columbia and no one noted it. But you were marked. You were different. You might as well have been from another country" (49). Newfoundlanders' difference, then, is not always chosen or intentionally performed. In their study of the controversial term "Newfie," which is often considered an ethnic slur, Ruth King and Sandra Clarke argue that "expatriate" Newfoundlanders "are a minority group and their ability to object to outsiders' constructions of their ethnic identity is influenced by this minority status, particularly if their socioeconomic situation is tenuous" (549). This otherness and minority status is central to Newfoundlanders' experience of diasporic subjectivity, despite the fact that they have moved within their country of citizenship.

King and Clarke's comment that Newfoundlanders' minority status is exacerbated by "tenuous" socio-economic situations points to the way in which Newfoundlanders' marginalization is tied to widespread class stereotypes that not only are emotionally hurtful but can present practical barriers to adaptation in the new home. If Newfoundlanders in Newfoundland feel stereotyped by other Canadians, this discrimination is acute in diaspora. In her interviews with Newfoundlanders in the diaspora, Bella found that migrants frequently encountered "Newfie jokes" and stereotypes that Newfoundlanders are drunken, stupid, unreliable, and always on EI. Some Newfoundlanders have been denied jobs or credit explicitly based on these stereotypes (48–49). As patterns of out-migration follow provincial economic disparities, class hierarchies frequently become mapped onto regional and cultural identities. As Anonsen reveals, even so-called "positive" stereotyping of Newfoundlanders can reinforce feelings of otherness in diaspora. Her description of this process hints at a slightly patronizing tone in the comments of well-meaning neighbours: "You were always the Newfoundland family on the block wherever you lived. That meant you were the nice, friendly people who loved to see you come, who were so much fun, so generous and likeable. And after the neighbours left to go back to their own houses, your Dad would say, goddamn fools, and your Mom would say, they're only trying to be nice" (48). Anonsen's slightly sarcastic tone here emphasizes the frustration and isolation that cultural stereotyping can cause. The term "diaspora" acknowledges this feeling of difference and these experiences of prejudice and marginalization.

Defining the Diaspora

The concept of diaspora takes our understanding of Newfoundland out-migration beyond the clichéd images of fishers forced to work the oil rigs of Alberta; it articulates how the experience of migration has become a common narrative in Newfoundland's cultural memory. Floya Anthias warns that the idea of diaspora may homogenize groups, eliding the different historical contexts in which migrations occur and the different circumstances that people face in various new homes (564). For Anthias, this internal heterogeneity renders the concept of diaspora inadequate as both a theoretical and a social category. But the concept of diaspora need not exclude the evaluation of internal gender, class, and even racial formations; rather, the common connotations of the term connect disparate experiences of out-migration in a shared diasporic subjectivity. Newfoundlanders, like any group, are not homogeneous. While the number of "visible minorities" is very small, it is made up of Mi'kmaq, new immigrants from around the world, and second, third, or fourth-generation "hyphenated" Newfoundlanders. Deep-seated conflict between Catholics and Protestants still occasionally rears its head. Tension between the "baymen" and the "townies" (the outports versus St. John's) is also prevalent, and is often connected to class conflict. But despite these internal differences, many Newfoundlanders do share a distinct sense of identity, and the term "diaspora" unites this heterogeneous group of migrants in a shared cultural narrative.

This narrative has become central to Newfoundland culture in general. In a 2011 article for *The Walrus,* acclaimed Newfoundland novelist Lisa Moore writes that "perhaps the most defining characteristic of life in Newfoundland has been the need to leave coupled with the desire to stay" (24). The irony of defining a place through the leaving of it is not lost on Newfoundland's writers, and they use their work to both tell the many stories of the Newfoundland diaspora and to connect these stories to a collective imagination and culture. In her work on diaspora and multiculturalism, Monika Fludernik argues that literature is central to the formation of diasporic imaginaries, "that web of images and dreams which creates a consciousness of ethnic belonging and collective identity in the hearts and minds of expatriates" (xxviii). As I argue throughout this study, literature is a space in which writers, and their readers, imagine Newfoundland—its culture, its landscape, its past, and the nation it might have been—and in the process both document the forces of diaspora and resist its losses.

PART TWO
AFFECTIVE RESPONSES

 TWO

DONNA MORRISSEY AND THE SEARCH FOR PRAIRIE GOLD

> Now over the years when things aren't the best,
> A lot of our fellers head out for the West.
> But everyone knows that they ain't gonna stay,
> They'll always come back with those up-along ways.
>
> No one suspected we'd ever have oil.
> The Newfies took off for Alberta awhile.
> They traded their rubbers and their warm worsted caps,
> For rodeo boots and big Calgary hats.
> — "Saltwater Cowboys," written by Bud Davidge

In 2006 Newfoundland photojournalist Greg Locke was commissioned by the *Financial Post Business* to do a photo series of Newfoundlanders on their way to jobs in Alberta's oil sands. In the accompanying story that he later published in the magazine *The Current,* provocatively titled "Mexicans with Sweaters," Locke reflects:

> Contrary to what many of my mainland colleagues thought (some of whom are influential business journalists), a plane full of Newfoundlanders heading to well paying jobs in Alberta was not going to be a "Party Plane" with happy people heading to a new, bright future. They couldn't understand that the majority of the people on Air Canada's new direct 7:00 AM flight to Fort McMurray were middle age men with grey hair. They were in a somber mood for having to leave their wives, children, grand children, and homes behind because there is no room in the new Newfoundland economy for them and their primitive resource

and trades based skills. It was not a party plane but one filled with people resigned to a new life they don't want. ("Fort McMurray" n. pag.)

This migration—sometimes seasonal, sometimes permanent—has become a bit of a cliché. So many Newfoundlanders have migrated to Alberta for work that Fort McMurray is often jokingly referred to as Newfoundland's third-largest city. But Locke's passage captures the very serious features of this labour migration: the stereotypes about Newfoundlanders being hard-drinking partiers grateful for the opportunities Alberta has benevolently bestowed upon them, the sense of class difference, and the uncomfortable ethnic or even racial comparisons referenced in the title "Mexicans with Sweaters." Most prominent here is the Newfoundlanders' affective response to their situation: the feelings of pain and loss, of resignation or choicelessness at leaving their home.

Donna Morrissey's 2008 novel, *What They Wanted*, dramatizes this labour migration to Alberta. Two young Newfoundlanders, Sylvia and her brother Chris, leave home for the oil patches of Grande Prairie, drawn by the promise of a thick and steady paycheque to send back home. For these siblings, the motivations for leaving and their feelings about it are complex. But like the subjects of Locke's photos, they are tied to a homeland that they are compelled to leave and to which they might never return. If, as I argued in Chapter 1, painful displacement and a condition of loss are important connotations of the term "diaspora," this novel demonstrates how this outflux is not simply a labour migration brought on by uneven regional development, but a diaspora with a powerful emotional impact for both those who leave and those who are left behind.

Morrissey constructs full characters whose complex and shifting motivations reveal, as the story develops, the dramatic personal and cultural impact that out-migration has on Newfoundland society. As the sequel to Morrissey's *Sylvanus Now*, which followed Chris and Sylvia's parents through their youth, *What They Wanted* stands as a new chapter in a longer social story of a faltering economy and fading morale. The novel is set in the 1980s, beginning when Sylvia returns home from her job in Alberta to visit her father in hospital. Through Sylvia's memories, we are told of her childhood in the outports of Cooney Arm and Hampden, of her strained relationship with her mother, and of her university romance with her brother's friend Ben. We are also introduced to a place where, as Herb Wyile argues in his book on Atlantic Canadian literature and globalization, people must grapple with "the erosion of traditional social structures in an environment of economic restructuring and the reconfiguration of space within global capital" (*Anne* 100). This is a place where the primary economy, the fishery, is collapsing, rapidly forcing outport Newfoundlanders to reassess the way they have always lived.

This swift social change leads to instability in the very definition of "home" throughout Morrissey's novel. Avtar Brah, in her well-known work *Cartographies of Diaspora*, points out that "on the one hand, 'home' is a mythic place of desire in the diasporic imagination. In this sense it is a place of no return, even if it is possible to visit the geographical territory that is seen as the place of 'origin.' On the other hand, home is also the lived experience of a locality" (192). For Sylvia, home is Cooney Arm, where she was born, and it is Hampden, the outport where she grew up and where her family still lives. It is her mother's house, the bosom of her family, and the bond with her mother that she is forever seeking. It is the place where she currently resides, the tent outside Grande Prairie, Alberta. And it is a state of being, a spiritual space of comfort and belonging. As Roberta Rubenstein puts it, home is "not merely a physical structure or geographical location but always an emotional space" (1). As the meaning signified by the word "home" shifts, Sylvia feels a perpetual sense of homelessness, a restless feeling of always being in-between these multiple home spaces. And as industrialization, environmental destruction, and cultural erosion take hold, the characters' claims to home are further compromised. As an emotional space, this shifting meaning of home reveals the psychological and cultural damage done by economic instability and the destruction of the island's resources. But Morrissey also suggests that home can be carried within by preserving one's ties to family, culture, and spirituality.

Initial Displacements
Morrissey's 2005 novel, *Sylvanus Now*, the precursor to *What They Wanted*, tells the story of a young man named Sylvanus as he tries to make a living off the inshore fishery in the 1950s and '60s. While his family has lived in the same tiny outport of Cooney Arm for generations, Sylvanus comes into adulthood at a time of great change. The traditional salt cod market is giving way to increasing global demand for frozen fish, and many fish processing plants are being built to replace the flakes on which cod has been salted and dried for centuries. Both Canadian and foreign fishing are expanding, making use of new technologies including massive small-mesh nets, floating freezers, and fish-finding technology. As these unsustainable practices become widespread, Sylvanus finds his own catch rapidly diminishing and begins to worry about his ability to support his family. This rapid industrialization is not only challenging traditional fishing practices, it is also threatening the sustainability of the fish stocks.

Simultaneously, the Newfoundland government is pressuring families in small outports to relocate to larger communities. Between 1935 and 1965, the Newfoundland Centralization Program gave families in small outports welfare assistance in return for relocating to larger centres where access to basic services could be provided more easily. Between 1965 and 1975, a joint program between the provincial and federal governments took over, which dictated that such families move to particular "growth centres."[1] Unfortunately in the new "growth centres" unemployment was already at about 20 percent, the best fishing grounds were reserved for long-term residents, and the new settlers were rarely able to find work outside of the fishing industry they had always known. The small assistance that they received did not come close to the value of the homes they were forced to abandon, and many could not afford homes in the new centres where costs were suddenly driven skyward. All totalled, about 250 communities — about a quarter of the outports — disappeared. Sylvanus's brothers take advantage of this program, but as he considers the prospect of leaving his home he is overwhelmed with nostalgia and loss.

Sylvanus initially refuses to abandon his old cod jig for the larger boats and the dangerous gill nets that consume everything in their path. But faced with a diminishing resource and government pressure to leave Cooney Arm he must make a difficult choice: adapt to the new ways or leave the only home he has ever known. Sylvanus chooses to use the new unsustainable nets in order to continue making a living off the sea. While his choice takes place in the late 1950s, as part of a novel published in 2005 his dilemma anticipates the difficult decisions that other fishers like him will have to make following the total collapse of the cod fishery in the early 1990s. The threat of coercive resettlement as part of the Newfoundland Centralization Program resonates with ongoing forces of urbanization and out-migration. The more recent mismanagement of the fishery and the failure of the government to provide adequate alternatives for employment are seen by many as an unacknowledged reprise of the resettlement agenda. The current economic and social pressure to leave outport communities does not just involve relocation to larger urban centres within the province, but relocation to other parts of Canada. Morrissey uses the historical novel to show that the pain of leaving one's home, whether on the level of the individual community or of the larger imagined community of the island, is devastating to both one's happiness and one's sense of personal identity.[2] *Sylvanus Now* ends on a note of hope, with the birth of Sylvanus and his wife Adelaide's first child, Sylvia, after three traumatic stillbirths. But this happy ending comes with lingering doubts about how long the family can continue to live in the isolated community that their neighbours have already abandoned.

The prologue to *What They Wanted* answers these doubts, as an adult Sylvia reflects on her childhood:

> I remember clear as yesterday those last days in Cooney Arm, the sea dying around us and taking Father's spirit with it. And my, but he had fought. Long after his brothers and the others left he'd stayed, netting cod, netting salmon, spearing flatfish, hauling crab-pots, trapping eels and rabbits, hunting seals and turrs and boo birds, and landing capelin and squid and all else the sea hove at him.
> Then the ocean gave no more. (1)

With three young children, Sylvanus and Adelaide, along with Sylvanus's mother, have to finally face reality and move to the larger community of Hampden where Sylvanus can find work in the logging industry. The family, then, experiences their first displacement early on.

For seven-year-old Sylvia, this original displacement is traumatic. Since birth she has been living in her grandmother's house, a few feet from her parents' door, because her mother was ill after giving birth. While this illness is never fully explained it seems to be postpartum depression brought on by the unshakeable fear that her daughter will die like her first three babies. Sylvia, then, is being uprooted from her grandmother's house, and from the only environment she has known—the meadow and beach, the graveyard where the bodies of her unknown siblings are buried. Sylvia has been accustomed to playing in the haunted abandoned houses, the "worlds hidden amongst the emptied bedrooms and drawers, whose voices remained locked into the wood as though awaiting the souls that once were to come back and reclaim them" (10). She senses the terrible loss in her father, and as her parents falter she trembles, "for in that moment I saw how that which contained me could be broken" (3). The violence of the chainsaw carving the house in half in order to float it through the channel to its new place in Hampden is terrifying to the young child and symbolizes the divisions within the household as well as the destruction of home.

For Sylvia, this rupture has a lifelong impact; she forever feels out of place, away from home, and this theme of homelessness lays the groundwork for her diasporic subjectivity. Sara Ahmed argues that "the question of home and being-at-home can only be addressed by considering the question of affect: being-at-home is a matter of *how one feels or how one might fail to feel*" (*Strange* 89; emphasis in original). While Sylvia has a house to live in with her family, it is not home because it does not *feel* like home. If home, by its very definition, is affective, then moving away is also, in Ahmed's words, "always affective": it also "affects how 'homely' one might feel and fail to feel" (*Strange* 89). Sylvia spends more years in Hampden than in her original home of Cooney Arm, but the traumatic move means that Hampden is from then on marked as not-home, as the place associated with feelings of rupture and loss. This affective response to home and its loss will become central to Sylvia's experience as part of a larger labour diaspora of Newfoundlanders in Alberta.

A few years later, Sylvia discovers the truth in the adage "you can't go home again" when on a return visit to Cooney Arm with her father she finds the village in a disturbing state of decay. She trails "along the beach, stepping over anchors left behind by the uncles and now bleeding red onto the rocks [...]. The ribbed skeleton of a boat, tossed inland by the sea, lay behind the abandoned house where I'd crouched with the spirits" (69). When Sylvia was a young child here she liked to explore the boarded-up houses, fascinated by ghosts. She plagued her grandmother "with questions about ghosts and how come they got lost, and do they never find their way home, and where's home anyway" (53). The old houses were always abandoned and haunted during Sylvia's lifetime, with walls that seemed to "sing." But in contrast to these memories of a place alive with both spirits and the living, upon her return there is a new sense that everything "felt like death" (69). Ahmed argues that home is constructed in memory, but that this imaginative construction is idealized and bound to the past. Therefore "it is impossible to return to a place that was lived as home, precisely because the home is not exterior but interior to embodied subjects" (*Strange* 91). If the feeling of being at home is constructed through idealized belonging and memory, then leaving home is not just leaving a physical place, but irreparably leaving the past behind.

As the opening to the novel this displacement not only provides the background for Sylvia's personal psychology, but also establishes the fragile connection between outport Newfoundlanders and their livelihoods. Forced by a dying fishery and government pressure to abandon their homes, these Newfoundlanders are, as Locke's article puts it, "resigned to a new life they don't want." With this resettlement the very nature of home is permanently altered, even lost. While the distance that the family must move is short, the painful move forced by economic circumstances and government mismanagement portends the more dramatic diaspora that will eventually come with the total collapse of the fishery.

The Maternal Home

Sylvia's vexed relationship to home is complicated by her strained relationship with her mother. Rubenstein argues that "memory traces of *home* are inevitably linked with those of *mother*" (24, emphases in original). But Sylvia feels as though she "had always been coming from a distance towards [her] mother" (49). Sylvia overhears a conversation between her mother and her mother's friend Suze that explains how Adelaide felt "cursed" after her first three babies died: "Ohh! All those nights I worried, waiting for little Sylvie to be taken. Always thought I was going to be punished again, that she'd be taken. Was always waiting for more punishment. Truly I never felt like a mother till Chris was born and took to my breast" (81). While this revelation makes it clear that Adelaide's emotional distance from her daughter was a result of an intense fear of loss, for Sylvia the words reopen old wounds. "Was there never a time when I'd been first in my mother's thoughts?" she wonders. "Even during those first days—first *moments*—of life, I was viewed as some kind of check mark, some pending sign, some outcropping from an ongoing struggle between her and God? Small wonder her breasts wouldn't milk—not out of fear for the poor suckling babe, but out of fear for herself" (82). With the birth of Chris, Adelaide's second surviving child, her fear of "punishment" was finally assuaged, and she was able to let herself give in to a deep maternal love. But the distance and fear that she felt toward Sylvia never subsided, and their relationship continues to be strained by jealousy, misunderstanding, and fears of loss. "Don't know if I've ever really felt at home," Sylvia explains to her brother. "In Gran's house I was always looking to Mother's, and then in Mother's I was always looking to Gran's. No matter whose table I was sitting at, or how sweet the jam, it always felt like I was just halfways home" (113). Her initial displacement from her mother's house, her early displacement from Cooney Arm, and her eventual displacement from Newfoundland altogether, all contribute to this lifelong sense of homelessness. Ahmed articulates this kind of perpetual homelessness for diasporic individuals when she writes that "the narrative of leaving home produces too many homes and hence no Home, too many places in which memories attach themselves through the carving out of inhabitable space, and hence no place that memory can allow the past to reach the present (in which the 'I' could declare itself as having come home). The movement between homes allows Home to become a fetish, to be separated from the particular worldly space of living *here*" (*Strange* 78). Sylvia becomes restless, forever in search of an idealized home separate from the "worldly space" she lives in. But as Rubenstein writes, "the original home is less an actual place than a site located in memory and fantasy, a psychic space invested with nostalgia for an idealized notion of wholeness. By the time it can be imagined, home is always already lost" (127). Sylvia is seeking a connection to her mother that will finally provide her with a feeling of belonging and of being at home. In this search, ironically, she physically becomes farther and farther distant from her mother.

As a child, in an effort to get her mother's attention, Sylvia frequently told her mother that she dreamed of travelling the world as Adelaide herself once aspired to do. But the brief moments of connection and approval that Sylvia's goals received soon died off, and ultimately we are never really sure if Sylvia actually wanted to travel or merely adopted her mother's lost dreams. Adelaide bought her daughter suitcases for her sixteenth birthday, a gesture intended as encouragement for her dreams of travel but interpreted as an attempt to get rid of her. In the end, "we'd never made peace with each other and had bickered and chaffed each other till the day I packed those three matching suitcases and eagerly left home for university in St. John's three months before enrolment started" (83). Sylvia's leaving, then, is intertwined with her particular relationship to her mother as an ideal home.

Sylvia now has a bachelor's degree in philosophy from Memorial University. But her friend Myrah happens upon a "grand opportunity" in the local newspaper—"a bar in Grande Prairie, Alberta, looking for Newfoundland waitresses, paying triple the wages offered around town and quadruple the tips. With my degree filling one pocket and student loans depleting the other," she tells us, "I was soon flying into the sunset with Myrah" (159). While Grande Prairie may not be as romantic as her earlier dreams of Rome, the five-thousand-kilometre journey nevertheless fulfills the ambition that she set for herself as a child and convinced herself she wanted. Now Sylvia dreams of going to graduate school someday and sends her brother Chris, a talented artist, brochures for an art school in Halifax. She cajoles him with the idea of sharing an apartment as they both attend school. Sylvia does not understand why her brother seems frightened to leave, asking, "What keeps you on this stupid, friggin wharf?" (44). Chris explains that he stays to help his father: "So's you can go. Somebody's got to be here. Somebody's got to help him [...]. Jeezes, Sylvie, he'd be dead by now if not for the bit of help I gives him" (45). When Sylvia suggests that he could send money home, Chris is curt: "That right? And how much they paying art students these days?" (46). Sylvia believes that her brother needs to be "nudged out of the nest" in order to "find his own way" (87). But this desire may be motivated by her own complex relationship to home and a need to justify her mother's remoteness: "it's not such a big deal, you know," I blundered, "leaving a dead-end logging town built around a post office" (22). But this "blundering" suggests that she protests too much, that her dismissal of her hometown is a defence mechanism against the guilt, loss, and homesickness that she feels.

Sylvia likes Grande Prairie and is caught up in the romance of adventure. She recalls how in letters to her brother she described "feelings of ease upon that endless land with the big blue sky reaching down around me like a bell jar, fat clouds floating overhead. [...] A day rolls on forever and you can track the sun from dawn till night, and with no dirty old water slopping at your window" (131). But while in her letters she dismisses her home and the ever-present sea, she regrets this attitude, and the fact that her mother found one of the letters. She admits that "I'd been joking. I loved the water slopping at the window. I'd written further down on the page how I missed the damn old water slopping at the window [...] even missed groaning with Mother about the slob ice filling the bay and seagulls shitting on the wharf" (131). Sylvia attempts to reject nostalgia in favour of her new home but ultimately cannot deny her homesickness.

When her father, Sylvanus, has a heart attack while out in his boat, Sylvia returns home for a few days. The affective relationship between mother, home, and migration is further explored in a tense argument between Sylvia and her mother at the hospital. Sylvia overhears her mother say that she refused to buy Chris the suitcases that he asked for last Christmas, a refusal that reinforces Sylvia's belief that the suitcases her mother bought her a few years before were "an invitation to leave home" (83). Sylvia argues that "*all* of one's offspring [should] be encouraged to go off and make lives of their own" (83). But her declarations here are inextricable from her defensive, sensitive relationship with her mother. She both wants freedom and to be needed and nurtured. Sylvia carries on: "'Suppose none of us ever left—how would we ever create new ways if we're held back in the old?' Mother balked. 'And what do you think happens to us who never leaves home, Sylvie—you think we grows stagnant like bog water?'" (84). Adelaide defends her attitude, saying that she encouraged Sylvia to leave because she wanted to, but that some, like Chris, don't have to leave home to learn "how to think and how to work" (85). But these steady and convincing words are undone by her emotion, as she goes on to accuse Sylvia of trying to "lure" Chris from home (85). Sylvia will later admit that she thinks her mother is right. But in this moment she cannot separate her opinions on leaving home from her own private emotions.

The role of the mother, then, is a delicate balance between providing a space of nurturing and belonging, and knowing when to let go, encouraging her children to expand their horizons. Throughout the novel mothers fail at this duty, either by failing to adequately nurture, as in Adelaide's case, or by failing to let go. Suze is described as having a perverted relationship with her son Ben, "handling" him too much, forcing him to nurse until the age of four (94). Ben's friend Trapp's mother is even more extreme, always calling out to rock him with a "crazy look in her eyes," a smothering that leads to serious damage to Trapp's social skills. These mothers highlight the ongoing emotional impact of home and childhood on one's sense of self. In 1980s Newfoundland finding this delicate balance between nurturing and smothering is made more difficult because of particular cultural and economic pressures. Sylvia reflects that everybody in the outports was always "wanting everybody home. Not for worries about the one leaving, but for them left behind, as though a house couldn't properly shore itself without all hands abide" (121).

Sylvia's grandmother recognizes the difficulty of a mother's task within the context of a failing industry and a remote and intimate community. When Sylvia asks her why everyone gets so upset whenever anyone leaves, her grandmother responds "From the way we used to live, I suppose. All by ourselves, getting what we wants from the other. When somebody leaves then, we feels crippled" (128). Confronted with a fishery decline, the outports are torn between wanting to preserve their communities and wanting their children to have opportunities in life. Sylvia believes that Chris needs to go to university, asking her mother, "you think he's gonna be fishing and logging his whole life? You think he's fit for no more than that?" Adelaide argues that it should be up to Chris to choose and is offended by Sylvia's dismissal of the outport way of life: "no fool is your father or your grandfathers. And they fished and logged all their lives" (123). Leaving, then, to Adelaide, means more than just leaving home, it also means abandoning the traditional way of life that defined their ancestors. But she does not know how to negotiate between her own emotions, dreams, and beliefs, or how to interact with her two very different children.

Despite this tension, when Sylvia is about to leave home to return to Grande Prairie she is overwhelmed by homesickness upon hearing the sounds of early morning: "water lapping against the pilings, the timbre of wavelets upon rocks, the far-off drumming of sounders—surely they must've been my first sounds, for I was suddenly soused with loneliness, a longing for that lullaby of long ago" (129). Amid these womb-like sounds she must resist a sudden impulse to rush back inside to her family instead of getting in the car to the airport. Sylvia is ambivalent, then, towards home, at once happy to be free of it and nostalgic for it. Home, here, is defined by longing—not the place where she is currently standing, but a place associated with a lost past, an idealized feeling of belonging. Svetlana Boym writes that "to feel at home is to know that things are in their places and so are you; it is a state of mind that doesn't depend on an actual location. The object of longing, then, is not really a place called home but this sense of intimacy with the world" (251). As Sylvia is overwhelmed with longing for sounds she associates with "long ago," she is longing not for place but for a feeling of belonging in her family and her life.

While Sylvia is characterized through her tense relationship with her mother, Chris is often characterized in relationship to his father. Sylvanus is defined by the sea and a fisher's way of life. As he lies in his hospital bed, his sleeping face launches Sylvia into remembrance of her father as a younger man: "laying my palm against his cheek, I felt its roughness, almost tasting the salt from the days he straddled his boat in the stiff morning gales, hand-jigging codfish in the ways of old, face bared to the wind, legs anchored to the sea" (25). In contrast, his face now is pale and his eyes are squinty and "so looking like death it was as if they knew what death was." Indeed, she adds, "in a sense he did know what death was — or a form of death. From the moment he picked up his chainsaw and started his first summer in the woods he cursed over the sweltering heat away from the sea, and the flies" (25). Sylvanus is so defined by his way of life as an inshore fisher that his displacement from Cooney Arm and his new job in the logging industry are seen as akin to death. Sylvia remembers how even after a full day's working in the woods he would immediately go out in his boat without even eating or resting, "to breathe" (25). Sylvanus is "scattered about [...] his soul wandering the emptied fishing grounds of Cooney Arm, his heart fighting for resurgence in some hospital room in the city" (37). Chris is physically similar to his father — "his eyes the same glistening brown as Father's, his hair the same thickness and coarseness." He even smells like his father when Sylvia hugs him (12). But Chris is not a natural fisher like his father. He admits, "I'm not cut from his stock; I'm not good at any fuckin' thing [...] drawing *birds* when I was suppose to be launching the boat alongside of him" (45). Chris feels responsible for his father's heart attack, since he was supposed to go out with his father that morning. While Sylvanus recovers in the hospital, Chris tries to help out with the seal hunt. But he fails to secure his father's new boat, which drifts away in the night. Knowing that Sylvanus cannot afford to replace the boat, and knowing that its loss will be a severe blow to his already ailing father, Chris decides to leave after all — not to go to art school, but to go to Alberta with Sylvia to get a high-paying job in the oil patch, to buy a new boat and send money home. He makes contact with Ben, an old friend already working on a rig near Grande Prairie, and secures a position as a "greaser," a dirty and dangerous position in one of the rough and noisy camps. While Sylvia wanted Chris to expand his world beyond the "dead-end logging town" (22), she is upset that he would choose to leave while his father is still in hospital, to go to Alberta instead of to university.

Adelaide is devastated, and blames Sylvia for encouraging Chris to leave home. But Sylvia hopes that somehow her mother understands that both her children "needed a larger world to draw upon than a rocky cove, no matter the sweetness of its shores." She reflects:

> Had [her mother] not pined for that something other once? And perhaps life had planed away that unrest inside of her, but surely she remembered her want for some one thing that was just out of sight down the road, the key to some heavenly room perhaps, if she could just walk far enough to reach it. For what is life if not that vitality of spirit, if not the tension between what is and what could be if one were to walk a little farther down that road? And in that, perhaps, mother had failed

herself, or had given over to a different want. Surely she would come to see that, and be glad of Chris's having left. (133)

Sylvia's image of a "heavenly room" recurs throughout the book, as a space of comfort and contentment, a spiritual home. Tellingly, the word "room" suggests the physical space of home. But Sylvia does not yet know where to find this "heavenly room," assuming that it exists in some distant locale. Sylvia seeks a feeling of belonging and of being at home without recognizing that this "heavenly room" may be a state of mind rather than a physical location.

"Room" also suggests the rooms of the abandoned houses in Cooney Arm, whose walls seem to "sing" with the spirits of their lost owners. Sylvia feels an affinity with these homeless ghosts, and through this haunting these rooms become objects of longing, symbols of loss. When Chris asks her what the ghosts want — a question that grants the novel its title — she replies that she does not know (261). Yet when Chris tells her "they're your ghosts, you made them up, you should know what they want" (261), we sense that she wants the same thing: a "heavenly" room, a space of belonging and memory and of connection between generations, the lost homes from which they have been severed by economic pressures as well as personal conflicts and desires. Displaced from home at an early age, Sylvia seeks her "heavenly room" in distant locales, trying to convince herself that she does not need to be at home to find peace.

Leaving, then, for both Sylvia and Chris, involves a delicate negotiation with the needs and desires of their parents and their community, and despite Sylvia's university education, their choices are still limited by economic pressures. Neither really seems to know precisely what they want for themselves, and amid this confusion and emotion they find themselves caught up in a growing Newfoundland diaspora.

The Diaspora

The Alberta oil patch is full of other Newfoundlanders. Ben's friend from home, Trapp, is also working the same rig. The town itself "quadrupled in size overnight, and you'll be hard pressed to find an old person strolling the sidewalks — or even a local. Throngs of young people is mostly what you see — all from back east" (174). The imbalance of wealth between east and west is ironically referenced in a conversation Sylvia has with her boss in the bar as he gathers up a pile of change. "'Hear that — prairie gold,' he drawled, rattling the coin into his till." "Yeah, count it wisely," Sylvia responds. "Back home we could walk on water once, the fish was so thick" (177). This change in Newfoundland's fortunes is mentioned cavalierly here, but it points to the vast impact that the downturn in the fishery is having on Newfoundland's labour market and social structure. While Sylvia and Chris's reasons for being in Alberta are personal and specific, the siblings are part of a much larger community of labour migrants pushed away from their homes by a failing economy overly dependent on a single industry.

Chris, unlike Sylvia, is disdainful of Grande Prairie and its living conditions. A housing shortage means that Sylvia lives in a tent city with other migrant workers. But she tells him that people are "sleeping in cars, everywhere. We're lucky. And beside, it's just for the summer; why waste money on high rent? Cripes, a thousand bucks for a porch is what they're charging" (153–54). Sylvia refers to the tent as "home," illustrating a profound rupture between home as location or residence and home as place of origin. The tent is a distorted home, temporary by design, and precariously pitched by the side of the river.

But they do not stay in the tent for long. When Sylvia finds out that Ben has gotten Chris a job on a rig, rather than the safer construction job in town that she had envisioned, she is furious. She observes the rig workers in her bar with "their scarred hands and fingers missing, their bruised and scratched skin, their wearied, overworked eyes." She ponders the statistics: "Thirty-nine dead in the past three years, eleven dead in the past ten months... some crushed under tons of steel, others hit by whiffs of poison gas, food wolfed down in between one-minute pipe changes, lotsa money and lotsa cost of flesh and blood, inexperience, insufficient training, fatigue, twelve-hour shifts, fourteen days on, seven days off, work fast, make money, get out" (182; ellipsis in original). When it becomes clear that Chris will not change his mind, however, Sylvia quits her own job and follows her brother to the camp to work as a cook.

It is immediately evident that Chris is out of place here as a dreamy artist who goes into periodic "trances" that may be epileptic seizures. As the novel develops, so too does an intense foreboding. Before the trio even reach their rig, they witness the explosion of a nitrogen tanker at a service rig, simply because "somebody pulled the wrong lever" (204). While no one is hurt, in the confusion and the thick white nitrogen fog Chris's new boss Push lures Trapp into the open septic hole. This cruel joke is Sylvia and Chris's first introduction to Push and the tense conflicts that divide the crew. The rig itself is a stinking, screaming "jungle of machinery," whose noise is constant and inescapable and traps the men in their own thoughts so that every small conflict gets "more festering time than it deserves. Turns the mind to rot after a while" (206–07). The details of the rig operation are complex, mysterious, and dangerous—Ben explains that "one bad-assed pocket of gas can send them pipes shooting through the air like spaghetti" (217). Catching the warning signs of such life-threatening problems involves guesswork and gambling on the part of rough men who work while drunk and do not trust each other.

This mood of foreboding only intensifies as the novel progresses. Conflict between Trapp and another member of the crew flares up in the cookhouse and the two draw knives on each other. While the situation is quickly controlled, the tension and volatile atmosphere linger on, and Sylvia becomes more desperate to get out. She tells her brother that her father would be ashamed of them for working in that place: "He wouldn't have you here for ten trucks, for ten boats. You insult him if you think that" (253). But despite these wounding words Chris and Ben refuse to leave. Not long after, Sylvia wakes up in the middle of the night when the rig sounds unusually loud, and she catches words of a conversation outside—"Mud. Pressure. Arsehole Push" (276). The next morning the night crew comes in covered in mud from a "spillover." Over breakfast Sylvia hears the crew arguing about the cause of the mud backing up the pipe. They argue over whether or not to wake Push, but upon the insistence of the engineer they decide the problem is minor, and the day crew, including Chris, go to work. Throughout these scenes there is a gripping sense of impending disaster, with all the inevitability of a Greek tragedy.

Sylvia, feeling worried and sick, decides to call home and is delighted to hear a new lightness in her family. Her father's boat has been found, washed up on a nearby island. Chris is released from his obligation to replace it. But this news is tempered by her father's strained words: "They're leaving in droves—all the young people, leaving in droves, tell [Chris] the fishery's all but dead—not just the inshore anymore, Dolly, it's the offshore too now, she's all but gone [...] get him in school, Dolly, nothing here for the young" (287). Even her mother admits now that she was wrong, that her father is right about them going to school. While some of the family's money problems are solved by the found boat, the long term implications of her father's news are much bleaker. As Newfoundland's resource-based economy is failing, there is little for Chris and Sylvia to return to.

The climax finally comes when Sylvia goes out to the rig floor to deliver lunch to the men. She pauses for a moment to watch them work and spots Chris watching "the chain wrap itself around the pipes, and a roughneck moving in with jawlike tongs to torque them up. Chris shivered. I could see that he shivered. There, I thought with sudden clarity, he's awakening to the beast. He's seeing it as I do. He's seeing the grease secreting through its pores. He's nauseated by the bad blood flowing through the crew as they feed like parasites upon each other" (289). As Sylvia heads back to the camp she hears a roaring sound, and turns to see pipe "spitting out through the side of the derrick and shooting like a black spear three hundred feet into the grey sky then breaking off in lengths" (289). Chris, stopped in another of his daydreams, does not run in time like the others and is killed when a length of chain wraps around his chest, puncturing his organs. As Sylvia runs toward the rig she already knows her brother is dead—"a part of me had known it all along. It had been born with me, it had shown me through his dreams, for they were never of the ordinary, but of Christ. Of moons without planets. Without time—as his art, his dreams too, were without time" (291). Sylvia wonders if Chris always knew somehow that he would die, and that that was why he was afraid to leave home: "had it been built inside of him, somewhere, this knowing of his fate?" (313). Chris's death, then, seems inevitable, destined. As an almost Christ-like figure his death is more than the untimely loss of one young man, but a death that embodies the destruction of Newfoundland's way of life. His loss to the destructive and inhuman working conditions of the Alberta oil patch dramatizes the broader economic losses that leave, in Sylvanus's words, "nothing here for the young" (287). He leaves his home in order to make enough money to replace his father's boat and support his family, assuming the traditional masculine role of breadwinner. But for Chris, so much like his father, his severance from home is unnatural, even deadly.

The Heavenly Room and Cultural Mourning
The day before his death, Chris recalls a recurring dream in which he is his father, sitting in his boat. In the dream he feels "totally content. More than content. Like this was everything—sitting in the boat" (278). This dream takes on added importance after his death, when Sylvia discovers the last sketch that Chris drew:

> It was a night sketch of our father sitting in his boat. He was sitting with his back to me, his face held towards the huge expanse of darkened sky. But his hair was light in colour, and longish, curled around his collar—it was him, Chris. It was both Chris and Dad. It was his dream. The both of them sitting as one in the boat, the water rippling beneath them as they held up a paddle looking expectantly towards that other, more ancient sea, darkling amidst its stars. (312)

Upon seeing this last sketch Sylvia thinks "I needn't have feared Chris standing gutted on a wharf like Father with his rotting boat and stage after the fish had gone. The thing Chris created lived in my hands, his breath upon my face. He had found that heavenly room, he'd never been without it" (314). For Chris, then, the "heavenly room," the spiritual home that Sylvia is always seeking, is a state of being, a contentment and connection to a higher power found through his art. Sylvia finds the archetypal images of Chris's dreams and drawings demonstrate that "we are but shadows, our thoughts shifting like clouds, never returning to what they once were, always searching for elsewhere. And yet some things are more solid than rock. [...] we are never born and we never die, like the waters in a flooded riverbank, simply finding different channels along which to flow" (314). While Chris's death represents significant cultural losses, then, it also marks a moment of transition, a hope for the future that does not lose sight of the past from which we have come.

Chris's death also enables Sylvia to move toward the home she has always searched for. First, it is the catalyst to Sylvia and Adelaide's reconciliation. Overcome with grief at Chris's death, Adelaide finally opens up to her daughter, revealing that "I always believed if another was taken from my breast, it would've been you. And so I let Gran keep you, and I was afraid to love you. And I poured my love into Chris, but no matter how tightly I held him, I never felt full. I was the mother who cleaved her baby in half; I sacrificed one half for the other, and prowled every living day since, pining for them both" (304–05). In this moment of grief Sylvia finally finds the connection with her mother that she has been craving, as Adelaide flies to Alberta to retrieve not her son's body but her living daughter. Now Sylvia finally yearns to return home, recognizing that the "huge want" she had always felt in her heart cannot be filled with romantic love, as she had previously thought. Instead, she realizes "that it was never a need for someone that I felt but simply a desire to return home, to that room Chris always felt in his heart, the one that fed him contentment, no matter which wharf or rock he sat upon" (316). Sylvia's restlessness is finally quieted, as she recognizes that the "heavenly room" is home, and that home is a state of being. Yet this hard-won knowledge is also tinged with loss, as her brother's death has changed the shape of home forever.

Sylvia does move back to her parents' house, but outport Newfoundland is still changing around it. Sylvanus has a new job erecting a salmon fence and policing the river for poachers, and it is the only thing that allows him to stay in Newfoundland. He tells his daughter that his brother, Sylvia's Uncle Manny, has been laid off from the fish plant and is leaving for Toronto: "'No fish in the offshore waters, now,' he said sullenly. 'All gone the way of the inshore—as we all said it would happen. Gawd-damned arse-up government. Soon there'll be nothing living in the water. Barren. Imagine that, the ocean barren'" (319). As she takes in this news Sylvia sees fear in her father's eyes:

> Fear for his brother Manny, who had lived his life on the sea and was moving to a factory job in the city; Manny, who had lived his life amongst three dozen people, now moving to a city of three million. Jeezes, and Father shivered in his boots, dipping his hands into the river as though assuring himself it was there and not some illusion he might wake up from and then have to pack his bags like his brother and turn his back to his only salvation. (319)

With this devastating loss and fear Morrissey depicts what Rubenstein calls a "cultural mourning": "the literary representation of mourning that results from cultural dislocation and loss of ways of life from which an individual feels historically severed or exiled" (38). This labour diaspora involves the affective responses of loss and alienation, and an ongoing longing for "connection to a collective cultural history and home" (38). It creates a sense of mourning not only among individual migrants and their families but in Newfoundland society as a collective. Like the fishery downturn in *Sylvanus Now*, this image of "the ocean barren" anticipates the imminent cod moratorium of 1992. The sense of inevitable doom that characterizes the action leading up to Chris's death is now matched by the inevitable doom of the final collapse of the fishery. The "cultural mourning" elicited in these scenes, then, is not grounded in a specific historical moment, but is rather part of a larger, ongoing mourning for a way of life that is lost.

Sylvia connects this sense of mourning to her childhood ghosts, seeking home: "No wonder the houses of Cooney Arm are haunted, I thought. Fishermen like my father, his brothers, may have moved on, but, as with the linoleum on the floor, the hinges and locks on the doors they left behind so too are their spirits still back there, hooked into the generations that lived on the land and in those houses before them" (319–20). These fishermen are not only displaced from their homes but separated from their own spirits. In this novel, then, the ghosts are not the dead but rather the living who cannot let go of the past and their traditional way of life. They remain "hooked" into their homes and earlier generations. Sylvia and Chris are also "hooked into the generations" that preceded them, as their emotions, desires, identities, and fates are bound up with that of their parents. But as Sylvia observes her father's fear she also figures out "what they wanted, those ghosts in the walls of Cooney Arm. They wanted to be freed from those walls, freed from the confusion and blindness of times since passed, and brought forward into the mindfulness of the living" (320). This goal is not simply to be free of the past, to move on with a changing Newfoundland, but to bring that past forward into the present, to maintain a connection with generations of tradition while finding a way to live in the here and now. This is the difficult negotiation that Sylvanus and Adelaide must make at the end of *Sylvanus Now*—and now it is their daughter's turn to find that balance. She recognizes "two rivers of feeling" within her: "one flowing towards time and tomorrow, the other flowing backwards, seeking its source. It feels like those times I used to stand by the footbridge in Cooney Arm, looking towards Mother's house and looking back to Gran's, always feeling halfways home" (323). But "halfways home," now, is the location of life itself, somewhere between the past of one's ancestors and the future of her own making. Sylvia must finally learn to "chart [her] own map" through life (325), coloured by, yet independent of, romantic love, grief, and childhood longings.

What They Wanted illustrates the complex motivations that lie behind this labour diaspora, and how leaving home involves the affective responses of loss, longing, and cultural mourning. Like Locke's more recent Fort McMurray migrants, Sylvia and Chris, Ben, Trapp, and Uncle Manny, all demonstrate the gravity of the Newfoundland diaspora for both personal and cultural well-being. For Morrissey's characters, out-migration is always imagined as a temporary solution. Yet Morrissey's novel connects the stories of these individuals with a much broader social movement in Newfoundland, a mass exodus arising from the total collapse of the island's primary industry. For these characters, then, the pain caused by their severance from home is made more acute by the much broader, and permanent, destruction of the home they have known.

 THREE

"THE 'GOING HOME AGAIN' COMPLAINT": CARL LEGGO AND NOSTALGIA FOR NEWFOUNDLAND

> The summer madness is now at its riotous peak. It's a deep-down yearning for the homeland in summer afflicting most of us Newfoundlanders exiled on the continent, especially in cities removed from the salt water. We call it the "going home again" complaint.
> This longing to go back and perch for a spell on the sea-rocks of nostalgic memory—to listen to the waves and smell the cool ocean—attacks us a year or so after we leave the island, as soon as the novelty of the new place wears off, and stays in most cases until we die.
> —Ron Pollett, "Summer Madness"

Nostalgia has long been an important aspect of Newfoundland diasporic literature. In the 1940s, Arthur Scammell and Ron Pollett became the two main voices of the *Atlantic Guardian*, a magazine for expatriate Newfoundlanders published in Montreal. Their work features nostalgic idealizations of the outports of the past: fond boyhood memories of catching trout or collecting "hosstingers" (dragonflies), and tales of heroic deeds and honest hard work. Pollett in particular often emphasized his diasporic location in the process of recalling the place of his youth. He begins his article "There's No Place Like an Outport," for example, by admitting: "It's pretty well known that while I write of the restful Newfoundland countryside where I was cradled and schooled, I live and bide in the rip-roaring city of New York. […] But what makes me happy, now that I'm getting up to the age when a man sits around in his socks and ruminates over his past—what makes me happy is to be able to look backward on a childhood and youth spent in an outport" (*Ocean* 97). Nostalgia provides happiness in both age and displacement, allowing him to dwell on memories of tobogganing, picking mussels, or looking out the kitchen window at the sunset on the water. Pat Byrne calls Scammell and Pollett the "romantic realists," because "even though they elected to present a rather idealized picture of the traditional outport culture in their writings, they had experienced the realities of that culture firsthand and were products of it" (68). Byrne's label indicates an almost oxymoronic quality of one form of nostalgia: a simultaneous drawing from deeply personal and heartfelt memories, and the rendering of those memories in romantic or idealistic, and therefore suspect, terms.

Critics have been wary of these romantic depictions of Newfoundland that Byrne argues became "unintentional parodies" after Confederation (74). The nostalgic memory of the out-migrant, James Overton warns, can often create a distorted image of Newfoundland: "The literature of exile [...] contains an 'out of time' vision of Newfoundland. One obvious clue to this is that it represents a vision of Newfoundland frozen at the time of the migrant's departure" (129). Patrick O'Flaherty is also wary of the romantic realists' diasporic writing. He warns that Scammell's work represents "the old outport seen from a distance of time and space, through the distorting prism of middle age, with the pain filtered out. It is the product of expatriate sentimentality" (154). By these accounts, nostalgia is dangerous because it creates an "idealized mental construct" (Byrne 74) rather than an "authentic" representation of Newfoundland to bring into Confederation and modern times. But as I will explore further in the next chapter, "authenticity" is itself a problematic concept, homogenizing experiences of home, privileging realism over other aesthetic forms and techniques, and reinforcing cultural stereotypes. Moreover, the idealization of a lost homeland reveals an emotional truth, if not an accurate geographical and social depiction; such fondness demonstrates the exile's feelings of loss and longing. If we reject "authenticity" as a means of evaluation, we must ask ourselves, what role does nostalgia have to play in diasporic literature? As an affective response to loss, can it ever be more than sentimental idealism?

This question becomes more urgent when we consider that diasporic or immigrant writing in general is often dismissed as being "merely" nostalgic, as fixated on the past to the exclusion of social and political integration in the new home. Critiquing the different responses to Indian-Canadian writing both in Canada and India, Arun Mukherjee notes that immigrant writing is often perceived as nostalgic for the original homeland, and is therefore seen as being "caught between two worlds" and "unable to 'become' fully

Canadian." She writes: "Immigrant writing, it seems, is always about longing for homes lost, about the pain of transportation, about adjustment and not about the 'ongoing dialectic' of a society. [...] There is something very smug about this kind of response. I see it as a denial of the possibility that an 'immigrant's book' may also have some relevance to readers in India. It seems that 'the immigrant's experience' is relevant to no one except 'the immigrant'" (35–36). Sneja Gunew similarly points to "the repeated and often dismissive response that ethnic minority writing 'simply' deals with nostalgia, and that its mode is elegiac [...] The logic appears to be that this writing deals with a landscape of the mind, of memory, which being apparently of minimal relevance to the here and now is therefore something to be outgrown" (Framing 111–12). The dismissal of nostalgia in these contexts becomes a dismissal of diasporic writing in general—the literature is seen as being fixated on the past, a perspective that is somehow considered regressive. Instead of dismissing it as "something to be outgrown," I want to revalue nostalgia as a deeply personal response to the losses of diaspora.

Nostalgia is not an inherently pejorative term. Derived from the Greek nostos, meaning "return home," and algia, meaning "pain" or "longing," it simply denotes a feeling of longing for a home distanced by time or space. Despite its bad reputation, nostalgia is a driving force behind many literary texts, particularly diasporic texts, and therefore a theoretical analysis of nostalgia and its functions is crucial. Some critics have begun this work, including Roberta Rubenstein, Svetlana Boym, Andrea Ritivoi, and John Su. Their timely analyses consider both the dangers of nostalgia and its potential usefulness. But throughout these studies nostalgia remains an elusive term. Su rightly notes that in the popular imagination "'memory' signifies intimate personal experience, which often counters institutional histories," while "'nostalgia' signifies inauthentic or commodified experiences inculcated by capitalist or nationalist interests" (2). But Su also shows that nostalgia in literature is in fact much more complex. Nostalgia, for Su, refers to both an individual's reflection on personal memories and a larger political desire for pre-colonial communities that no living person can remember, or that never existed. It is at once an act, a feeling or state of being, a "tone," an aesthetic style, and a political strategy. It is sometimes specifically a synonym for longing for a lost homeland, at other times for commodified tourist kitsch. Of course nostalgia *is* all these things; it no longer only signifies the specific disease state named by a medical student in 1678, but is a term with multiple applications and nuances. This slipperiness is in many ways what makes nostalgia such an interesting and necessary topic for literary analysis. But it also means that the different manifestations of nostalgia in literature must be carefully differentiated, in order to explore how nostalgia is constructed in specific diasporic contexts, and the role it plays in recovery from personal and collective losses.

Rather than the touristic desire for the simulacra of the past, this chapter focuses on what I call "experiential nostalgia," a term that references the affective response to memories of individual lived experience. While experiential nostalgia is felt on a personal level, this quality does not exclude elements of broader cultural symbolism; it may in fact be mediated by familiar codes, even stereotypes or clichés. The distance between the nostalgic subject and the memory object, however, is short, since the memory object is reconstructed from personal experience rather than the historical images of popular culture. Experiential nostalgia abounds in the diasporic poetry of Corner Brook native Carl Leggo, who now lives in British Columbia; it acts as a crucial means of coping with the pain of displacement and of maintaining identity. This productive nostalgia, in turn, provides his readers with a vivid picture of the affective experience of diaspora.

Carl Leggo and Experiential Nostalgia

Carl Leggo's three books of poetry, *Growing Up Perpendicular on the Side of a Hill* (1994), *View from My Mother's House* (1999), and *Come-By-Chance* (2006), are undeniably nostalgic, and in this sense are emblematic of the connection to homeland that is a main feature of diasporic subjectivity. In the first two books, the poems are connected in a larger narrative; all the poems are grounded in Lynch's Lane, Corner Brook, where the speaker grew up, and concentrate on recounting significant childhood memories. In all three collections, the first or second poem establishes that the speaker has left Newfoundland; thus the nostalgia of these poems is created by both temporal and spatial distance. There is a tone of loss, then, that haunts these poems, as in the lines from "Scratch in My Throat" in *Come-By-Chance*:

> I live with the past
>
> trailing like a train of U-Hauls stuffed
> with stories I no longer need. It is always hard
> to clean the closet, especially in winter
> when the stories, like old sweaters,
>
> might still be missed (lines 12–17)

There is a tone of guilt or sheepishness here, as Leggo's speaker admits to his own nostalgia for the past but confesses that he cannot seem to let the past go. Leggo's poems are a prime example of experiential nostalgia because the source of the nostalgia is the speaker's own memories and experiences. Leggo, in fact, considers his poetry "life writing," a genre that he considers to be performative but also identity-forming, dependent upon "blood, life, and memory" ("Writing Lives" n. pag.). While the poems may involve distortions, fictionalizations, or common cultural symbols like boyhood chums and wise father figures, they are formed out of the speaker's personal relationship to his own past and to the homeland that he has left behind.

In her cultural analysis of nostalgia, Svetlana Boym introduces a helpful typology of nostalgia that can further classify the experiential form. "Restorative" nostalgia, as she defines it, stresses the *nostos* part of the word, the return home, and therefore "attempts a transhistorical reconstruction of the lost home" (xviii). "Reflective" nostalgia, on the other hand, stresses the *algia*, the loss, and therefore thrives in "the longing itself" (xviii). Leggo's poems exhibit both restorative and reflective nostalgia, at different times. In many of the poems, the experience, person, or moment being remembered is itself emphasized. Leggo populates his books with interesting or significant characters from his speaker's childhood neighbourhood. Several of his poems are slices or vignettes of memorable moments and events, collected together like snapshots in an album. This snapshot quality is referenced by the title of the poem "Light Snaps" in *View from My Mother's House*, in which neighbours get married, have babies, die, and even win the lottery. Together, the poems become a memoir of childhood, with the repeated refrain of "Cec, Frazer, Macky, my brother and me," engaged in various forms of boyhood mischief, unifying the poems and their speaker across the books. These poems are light and often funny, featuring one- or two-liners like "when Nan heard the Pope had died, / she said, his wife must feel some bad" ("Light Snaps" 51–52). They evoke a mood of happiness and safety as they reconstruct the remembered moment.

A few of the poems, however, such as "Scratch in My Throat" above, are "reflective." "Tangled," the last poem in *Growing Up Perpendicular on the Side of a Hill*, is subtitled "Lines from Edmonton to my father in Newfoundland." It immediately immerses us into algia, into loss, with the first lines "far away / in a city you will never know" (1–2). The poem describes a memory of the speaker in a dory with his father, as his father tries to untangle the speaker's fishing line. The memory blends in without pause to a reassertion of distance:

and I wouldn't look at you
because I knew you were mad
and I had to look
and you weren't mad

>   you were smiling
>   and where I live now
>   there is no ocean
>   unless you stand on your head
>   and pretend the sky is ocean
>   but it's not. (26–35)

The lack of punctuation and the repetition of "and" at the beginning of most of these lines connects the memory of the event with the loss created by distance, the fact that "where I live now" is far away from both the ocean and the father. Toward the end of the poem the untangled fishing line becomes a metaphor for home and identity:

>   you knew
>   an untangled line could be thrown
>   into the ocean's black silence
>   and
>   anchor you to the bottom. (43–47)

But the speaker cannot establish a connection between himself and his new place of residence because

>   the line I throw out
>   never hooks into the sky
>   but always falls back
>   and tangles at my feet. (36–39)

The tangles, both in the memory of the dory and in the figurative image of throwing a line into the sky, represent the speaker's restlessness. But he knows that it is the connections with both family and place, the untangled line thrown into the ocean, that have the power to "anchor" him, to mitigate the loss of diaspora. The "line" also has a dual meaning: not only the fishing line, but also the line of poetry. It is the nostalgic verse, then, that has the potential to reconnect him with his homeland. The "restorative" poems, the ones that dwell in recovered moments of the past, are thus all tinged with the losses that are animated by other more reflective, meditative moments.

Are these poems overly sentimental and therefore inauthentic? Are they representative of a regressive preoccupation with the past and the homeland? Rather than contributing to an unhealthy fixation on the past, the nostalgia in Leggo's poems is in fact central to the speaker's recovery from the pain of displacement. In her book on nostalgia and immigrant identity, Andreea

Ritivoi notes that nostalgia, by revisiting the positive aspects of the past, is a self-reinforcing tool (30). In post-traumatic moments, such as diaspora, nostalgia helps one to locate a self that existed outside of that trauma, an identity that is not defined by the moment of loss or alienation, but also by positive memories. As it affirms personal identity, nostalgia also affirms survival of a traumatic event. Drawing on the work of philosopher David Lewis, Ritivoi uses the example of surgery to explain this process: "I confirm my survival by observing the continuity and mental connectedness between who I was prior to the event and the person resulting from the operation" (128). An important means of observing that connectedness is nostalgia for the time before the event; memory confirms the continuation between the old self and the new self. While Ritivoi's examples involve more traumatic scenarios, the concept can be helpfully applied to situations in which a profound change has occurred in the speaker's life, which may not have involved trauma but which nevertheless has caused a crisis of identity. In *Yearning for Yesterday* (1979), sociologist Fred Davis notes that nostalgia often accompanies the milestones typical of the life cycle; the passage from adolescence to adulthood, marriage, the rearing of children, retirement. In moments when identity is threatened by a feeling of discontinuity, Davis argues, nostalgia provides a feeling of continuity, of connection with our earlier selves (49). Leggo's poems are exemplary of this function of nostalgia, since they focus on detailing memories and experiences of a Newfoundland childhood, on connecting the adult self in displacement with the boy growing up in Corner Brook. In "Eight Windows," the second poem in *View from My Mother's House,* the speaker establishes in the first stanza his childhood desire to leave his home and explore the world:

> growing up I saw
> from eight lean windows
> in my mother's house
> pitched in the gravel
> of steep Lynch's Lane,
> my whole known world,
> culled in the compass
> of the Humber Arm
> and Long Range Mountains,
> like a fortress,
> and always I wanted
> to see far beyond
> the horizon. (1–13)

The desire to leave is fulfilled in the final stanza, in which we are told that the speaker now lives in Richmond, BC, where "the only hills / [are] stockpiled sand dredged / from the Fraser" (187–189). While growing up he longed for a different view from that which he saw through his mother's eight windows, now he finds himself

> in a world flat pressed
> under gray soft skies,
> seeking the same view
> through eight lean windows
> of my mother's house,
> years ago bulldozed. (193–98)

Now that he has seen the other coast, he looks for the same view of his childhood neighbourhood and the landscape of home, a view that will connect this older, displaced self with the self who years ago "walked off Lynch's Lane" (177). The nostalgic journey that the speaker takes through the rest of the book, through childhood memories of people and events, seems to achieve this goal. "Coastlines," the final poem of *View from My Mother's House*, recalls "Eight Windows." In this poem, Leggo describes daily walks on the Pacific Coast, where the speaker sees

> my image
> upside down in the smooth
> Fraser River, all the world
> topsy turvy, but
> still in balance. (18–22)

His own image is reversed, corrupted in his new home, or rather *by* his new home, represented by the Fraser River. In the final part of the poem, the speaker expresses his desire to be like the eagle, gull, or heron, which "sees the world / from other locations" (55–56), but instead he is

> calling out the view, far
> from my mother's house,
> seeing still all the world
> through eight windows. (61–64)

The image of the speaker "seeking" the view of eight windows at the beginning of the book is now transformed into "seeing" that view. While the speaker has moved to the coast on the opposite side of the country, he still sees the world from the same perspective of his birthplace and therefore confirms that he is the same person. This perspective, manifested in nostalgic remembrance of that birthplace, maintains or restores personal continuity even though the world around him is "topsy turvy." The past, as a shaping force of identity, is not left behind, but rather transforms his experience of the new home. The two opposing homes, the two opposite coasts, are held in "balance."

Nostalgia is not only a means of affirming survival of displacement, it can also be a means of coping with the ongoing pain that that displacement causes. As Boym writes, nostalgia is the desire "to revisit time like space, refusing to surrender to the irreversibility of time that plagues the human condition" (xv). The act of nostalgic remembrance temporarily replaces the feeling of loss or alienation with happiness and familiarity. In her article "Nonlinear Dynamics and the Diasporic Imagination," Minoli Salgado theorizes that "a form of temporal reversal is a key feature of the diasporic imagination in its quest for wholeness and connection with the past. While the lived reality of the writer undeniably affirms the violent temporal rupture that migration enforces [...] this very dislocation creates the conditions for the imaginative desire to negate time, reverse it and enact an endless return to the past" (188). Nostalgia conflates time, so that the past is experienced as though it is the present, replacing, albeit temporarily, feelings of alienation with feelings of comfort, and overcoming loss through the power of memory. Leggo displays this effect in his poem "Lynch's Lane," in which the street where the speaker grew up is so intimately connected with his identity that "Lynch's Lane is etched in my body" (4). In this poem, the speaker's nostalgia has a definite "rose-coloured" quality, as he tells us that

> none ever tasted as good
> as the first orange popsicle
> of summer. (7–9)

But the memory of this taste leads to a flood of other associated sensory experiences:

> sweat stinging sunburn
> water and tar on the lane
> to keep dust down
> Skipper mowing the grass
> with whistles of the scythe. (10–14)

The memories listed in this poem evoke all the senses, and are written in the present tense. The speaker, then, is not just recalling events and experiences set firmly in the past, but is walking down Lynch's—and memory—Lane as though he is experiencing these tastes, smells, sounds, sights, and touches in the present. In *The Senses Still*, C. Nadia Seremetakis expands on the Greek etymology of nostalgia to explain the connection between it and the senses, and argues that memory and the senses are intertwined in such a way that memory is "a sense organ in-it-self" (9). The memory of a taste becomes a re-experiencing of that taste; the opposite of *nostos*, she notes, is *a-nostos*, lack of taste. As Ritivoi explains, "If I can only relate to my past in a mediated way, through symbolic representation, at times I might also feel separated from it, so intensely aware of the constructed nature of my representations that the representations no longer feel authentic. But when the past seizes me, and it seems as though I am perceiving, rather than remembering it, I can nurture the illusion of a perfect connection to it" (35). In this moment Leggo's speaker has been "seized" by the past, and has managed to collapse time, to travel to and re-experience the past through the memory of the senses, and therefore momentarily overcome the pain of diaspora.

There are several moments, however, when the speaker in "Lynch's Lane" re-establishes the distance between the moment of remembering and the past remembered: where his restorative nostalgia becomes reflective. The seasons are conflated so the summer popsicles of the second stanza are replaced by "icicles knocked from the eaves" in the fourth; we know the descriptions are in the past because memories of different seasons are remembered simultaneously. The speaker is also split. He is able to see himself as a child:

with Cec, Frazer, Macky,
my brother, and me playing war
cricket kick the can at day's end. (22–24)

The passage of time has created a disjuncture between the voice speaking now and the "me" playing kick the can. Thus even as the speaker re-experiences these moments through nostalgia, he, and we as readers, are not allowed to fully forget that the moments have been lost through the passage of time and space. We are confronted, then, with what Roberta Rubenstein calls the "presence of absence," an absence "that continues to occupy a palpable emotional space" (5) in the form of nostalgic loss.

In this sense nostalgia is not just a mode of recall but an emotion in itself, inseparable from feelings of both fondness and loss. Sara Ahmed argues in *The Cultural Politics of Emotion* (2004) that "emotions are not 'in' either the individual or the social, but produce the very surfaces and boundaries that allow the individual and the social to be delineated as if they are objects" (10). In other words, emotions, as the way we "respond to objects and others" (10), are what create the very surfaces of the self as a being in the world. If we consider nostalgia as a kind of emotion, then, it represents the clash between the individual body and the new environment, the not-home. The emotion is not fully contained within the nostalgic subject but rather marks the interactions between that subject and other people or places in his or her surroundings. Even in its most "restorative" moments, then, nostalgia is a marker of loss as it shapes the division between the diasporic subject and the memory of place.

But this loss does not make the journey futile. Rubenstein argues that nostalgia confronts the past in order to "fix" it, in both senses of the word: to "*secure* it more firmly in the imagination and also to *correct*—as in *revise* or *repair*—it" (6, emphases in original). In other words, through nostalgia authors may "reconstruct and thus restore or repair the emotional architecture" of home (6). For Leggo's speaker, idealistic memories of childhood and homeland are fixed, perfect moments in time that mediate "the gap between longing and belonging" (6). As Ritivoi argues, "constant 'mental visits' to an inaccessible home or one forever relegated to the past become a way of adjusting to change and coping with difference" (31). Thus the final stanza of Leggo's poem brings us back to a slightly revised version of the initial image of the place "etched" in his body:

> like black lines pricked in skin
> with a needle for focusing
> India ink in a point
> Lynch's Lane is tattooed in my body. (45–48)

The memories are not just located in the brain, but are part of the body, re-experienced by the ears, eyes, nose, mouth, and skin. They also mark the body, and therefore become an important part of his identity. The image of the tattoo, in its permanence, reveals the fact that the speaker carries these memories with him now, mitigating somewhat that disjuncture between the self of the past and the self of the present. As a mark on the surface of the body, it becomes a link or seam between the "inside" of the self and the "outside," what Ahmed calls the "stickiness" of emotions as objects meet in the world (*Cultural* 91).

Experiential nostalgia, then, does not just maintain or preserve the connection between the speaker and his past self, it is also a crucial part of the construction of diasporic identity. Davis convincingly argues that if nostalgia is a means of relating our past to our present and future, it is "deeply implicated in the sense of who we are, what we are about, and (though possibly with much less inner clarity) whither we go" (31). It helps us to "salvage a self from the chaos of raw, unmediated experience" (33). The memories, and the place remembered, become a crucial part of who the speaker imagines himself to be. As Monika Fludernik asks, "how, except by clinging to what one knows, can one manage to face the new and survive the challenge [of diaspora]? Given this dilemma, the memory of the past and its re-invention as an imaginary homeland are of the utmost psychological significance. Identity operates through narrative, and narrative needs to start in the past and pace its way to a future that embraces and resolves the discrepancies between past and present" (xxviii–xxix). In other words, the diasporic speaker constructs a narrative of his past that places his present situation within the larger story of his life, thereby constructing an identity that accommodates both past and present. Fludernik's reference to Salman Rushdie's phrase "imaginary homeland" is crucial here. The speaker's past, his home, is "imagined" in that it is reconstructed by memory, or nostalgia, rather than empirically described. But this imagined quality makes it no less significant psychologically. It is essential to that narrative of identity, to the extent that it becomes "tattooed on the body."

Leggo's poetry reveals that experiential nostalgia can be central to coping with the experience of diaspora. But the psychological functions nostalgia can serve in diasporic literature do not mean that diasporic works should be dismissed as "merely" nostalgic. Experiential nostalgia does not necessarily signify sentimentality and cliché, nor does it necessarily entail inauthentic, idealistic, or disingenuous engagements with the homeland. Rather, as the admittedly sparse reviews of his work assert, Leggo's voice is both "personal and approachable" (Sullivan B4), and demonstrates sensitivity and "great care" (deBeyer 114). As a source of intense and personal emotion for the diasporic speaker, experiential nostalgia can create highly sensual and passionate images, it can reveal the complex construction of the speaker's personal identity, and it can emphasize both the importance and the imagined nature of place in our own ideas of home.

The Nostalgic Reader

As these personal emotions are translated into literature, they can become an important part of constructing a broader diasporic community, or what Vijay Mishra calls the "diasporic imaginary." The act of reading itself becomes a nostalgic return to the homeland. In *Marketing Place: Cultural Politics, Regionalism and Reading* (1993), displaced Newfoundlander Ursula Kelly describes how reading Newfoundland literature in diaspora effects a nostalgic conflation of the present with the past:

> The dead of winter. Again. Someplace, anyplace, not my place. Toronto, maybe. Or Halifax. At every turn, loss. [...] Then, in the sneaking, unsuspecting way that need sometimes seems to collide with com-

modity, I happen on a book of poetry, sitting unwrapped but unread, a
ghost of Christmas-just-passed. It is *The Time of Icicles* by Mary Dalton.
I read. I devour. Now fits—of pain, rage, laughter, tears. My readings,
labour. At book's end, I close my eyes. In my mind's eye, then, I see
myself. I am laughing, crying, dancing. And I am home. (2)

While she is "home" only in her "mind's eye," she is nevertheless there; reading literature has transported her to her home, has collapsed the distance of both space and time that has made her feel lost in Toronto or Halifax.

The *Atlantic Guardian*, to return to where we began, is a good example of the community-forming role of nostalgic literature in the diaspora. Despite his hesitations about the authenticity of Pollett's nostalgic memories, O'Flaherty concedes that "In Pollett's life we see a pattern that repeated itself in the biographies of thousands of his fellow countrymen, who uprooted themselves from familiar rural settings to pursue, at great cost, economic opportunity in urban North America. Part of Pollett's value as a writer is that he speaks for a mute multitude of emigrant Newfoundlanders" (155). This "multitude," then, becomes a "diasporic imaginary," a community of Newfoundlanders connected by their displacement, and their memories of home. Byrne agrees, placing Pollett's nostalgia in the context not only of displacement, but also of the massive change that Newfoundland was undergoing at the time:

> There is little doubt, and letters to *Atlantic Guardian* confirm this, that part of the explanation for Pollett's popularity was that in his attempt to rediscover and reconstruct the world of his own childhood from afar, he stirred in his readers nostalgic recollections of an outport way of life which, because of the changes that occurred between 1945 and 1955 in the aftermath of the war and with the advent of Confederation, many who had never left the Island felt was becoming equally as remote for them as it was for Pollett. (70)

Byrne goes on to explain the psychological importance of this nostalgia for the readers: "the depiction of the traditional Newfoundland way of life contained in the writings of the romantic realists was obviously general and idealized, but coming as it did at a time of social and cultural transition, it provided people, for a time, with a benchmark, or a 'holdin' ground,' to use [Ted] Russell's term, against which to measure and evaluate the changes" (73). Experiential nostalgia thus leads to what Rubenstein calls "cultural mourning," "an individual's response to the loss of something with collective or communal associations" (5). As other Newfoundlanders, both at home and in diaspora, read about the personal experiences of others whom they have never met, they generalize those stories and images to their own histories. They identify with both the memories described and the feeling of loss associated with them. They too take comfort from "reliving" the writer's Newfoundland.

This transfer of nostalgia through literature, then, is one form of what Teresa Brennan calls the transmission of affect, as it involves the passage of nostalgia from the individual to a larger group. This transmission, however, is dependent upon a sense of genuine feeling on the part of the original speaker, and on the recognition of personal lived experience. Recognition of the *experience* behind experiential nostalgia prevents any easy distortion of shared memories into tourist kitsch or trite cliché, and acknowledges the strong affective responses that diasporas evoke. As we read through Leggo's speaker's nostalgic attempts to live with his displacement, we too are touched by the deep emotions induced by his experiences, whether we recognize ourselves in them or simply sympathize with the raw feelings of loss and longing. The idealization of Newfoundland in these works, then, is not a distortion of place, but an accurate picture of the emotional geography of diaspora.

PART THREE

IS THE NEWFOUNDLANDER "AUTHENTIC" IN THE DIASPORA?

 FOUR

E.J. PRATT AND THE GATEWAY TO CANADA

When E.J. Pratt left Newfoundland in 1907 at the age of twenty-five he was not unusual; Patricia Thornton estimates that in the first decade of the twentieth century net migration amounted to a loss of 16,700 people from Newfoundland, or 8 percent of the population (25). But Pratt was perhaps the first significant literary figure in the Newfoundland diaspora. Of course, at this time, he was not leaving one province of Canada for another, but literally emigrating to another country. Much has been written on Pratt's poetry, including detailed textual analyses by Frank Davey and Sandra Djwa, biographical work by David Pitt and Susan Gingell, and scholarship by Northrop Frye, John Sutherland, Desmond Pacey, and others that locates Pratt's poetry within a developing Canadian national literature. Little has been written on Pratt, however, in the last twenty-five years. A large proportion of the scholarship, then, particularly that coming out of the thematic criticism movement of the 1970s, reflects a particular period in the development of Canadian literary criticism as a field working to assert the texture and the value of a national literature. Analysis originating in Newfoundland in this period, such as Patrick O'Flaherty's important 1979 literary history of Newfoundland, similarly reflects a rise in cultural nationalism in a province struggling to define itself in relationship to the rest of Canada. Much of this Pratt scholarship, then, discusses the ways his poetry does or does not reflect his childhood in Newfoundland as a provisional Canadian space.

Debates over Pratt's "authenticity" as a Newfoundlander largely took place in the context of the post-Confederation nationalism of the Newfoundland Renaissance, revealing more about the tenor of the 1970s than about the time in which Pratt himself was writing. My concern here is not so much with a reading of Pratt's poetry or with rehearsing the analyses that have proliferated over the last century, but with an examination of the ways in which he has been appropriated by and excluded from particular cultural identities as a diasporic and national figure. My reading of Pratt and his critics in terms of the idea of cultural "authenticity" reveals many of the problems associated with diasporic identity and literature, not only in Pratt's time, but through the Confederation period to today. The rhetoric of "authenticity" demands that diasporic figures become delegates for their home culture, and values their work in terms of the accuracy of their representations. The concept of "authenticity" also traps critics like O'Flaherty into perpetuating cultural stereotypes and fetishizing the idea of a "real" Newfoundland, which hides the process of its own construction. As I will show in Chapter 5, the conservative regionalism that characterizes much of Pratt's criticism has not been outgrown, but continues to reverberate in discussions of contemporary Newfoundland diasporic authors.

Patrick O'Flaherty's "Emigrant Muse"

E.J. Pratt moved to Toronto in 1907 to pursue a career as a Methodist minister. He completed his M.A., B.D., and Ph.D. and was ordained, but instead of entering the ministry he was hired to teach in the Department of English at the University of Toronto. His first book of verse, *Rachel*, was printed privately in 1917, and throughout the next four decades he became well known as a poet with the publication of such works as *The Witches' Brew* (1925), *The Titanic* (1935), *Brébeuf and His Brethren* (1940), and *Towards the Last Spike* (1952). Though Pratt was not born in Canada, he spent his entire literary career, and indeed most of his adult life, in Toronto, and is often considered a transitional figure in the history of Canadian literature, bridging the gap between the late-Victorian romanticism of the Canadian Confederation poets and the new Canadian modernism espoused by the Montreal poets of the 1920s and '30s. His work reflects many of the contradictions and changes of his time; as Djwa explains, it shows the confluence in the 1920s of a developing Canadian nationalism, new cosmologies, and scientific movements ("1920s" 55). He both influenced and was influenced by the literary communities that developed around the conservative Canadian Author's Association established in 1921 and the younger poets represented in the influential 1936 anthology *New Provinces*, in which he was included.[1] By the end of his career Pratt had become known for his epic long poems, whose heroic themes and "elaborately rhetorical and prosodic features" mark him, Smaro Kamboureli argues, as "aesthetically and ideologically a solitary figure" (*Edge* 29). As a poet that "could be appreciated by a basically conventional audience" (Djwa, "1920s" 60–61), Pratt straddled a multiplicity of influences and critical categories.

Pratt's career coincided with a burgeoning Canadian nationalism, and Jonathan Kertzer suggests that he engaged in a deliberate project of building a Canadian national literature, particularly with works like *Towards the Last Spike*: "Through a battle of muscles, ideas, words, and images, Canada is moulded across the land and in the minds of citizens, who become authentic Canadians through this epic ordeal, and who find a national voice in Pratt's poetry" (12). Looking back on Pratt's career in 1968, Northrop Frye, long a champion of his work and its prominence in the Canadian literary tradition, declared that "Pratt has been, in Canada, a kind of unofficial poet laureate" (*Bush Garden* 188). But Pratt's status as the "first 'Canadian' voice in poetry" was recognized as early as the 1920s (Djwa, "Introduction" xiv–xv), even before his work took on national themes like the construction of the Canadian Pacific Railway. Djwa reflects that "Pratt's vision of nature and his original poetic voice were important qualities in a decade [the 1920s] characterized by a persistent call for an authentic Canadian poetry. Despite his Newfoundland birth (the province did not join Confederation until 1949), Pratt soon became recognized as Canada's national poet" ("Introduction" xv). One of the most important voices to declare Pratt's status as a Canadian national poet was A.J.M. Smith, in his *Book of Canadian Poetry*, first published in 1943 and revised in 1948 and 1957. Smith's anthology lauds Pratt for his attention to contemporary ideas and events and his universal scope, but also for his patriotic themes, finding in his work a cosmopolitanism that is "rooted" in Canadian life without being restricted by a colonial mentality (36). It was not only a retrospective process of canon-making, then, that secured Pratt's position as, in John Sutherland's words (in 1956), "the leading poet of Canada" (2), but rather the appreciation of his contemporaries in a time of nationalist desire for "authentic" Canadian literature.

Despite this place at the centre of Canadian nationalism, Pratt writes that his Newfoundland childhood had an important influence on his poetry, for "a man cannot get far away from his heritage" (*His Life* 14). Specifically, he identifies eccentric characters of the outports (14); the drama of storms and marine disasters and the heroism such disasters inspire; and nature (4–5) as strong memories or influences from his early life. These local images and themes are easy to spot in his early collection *Newfoundland Verse* (1923): the "old salt" in "Overheard in a Cove"; the sealing disaster described in "The Ice-Floes"; the personification of the sea in "Sea Variations" or "The Secret of the Sea." Susan Gingell claims that "habits of mind developed in his early years and images impressed on him at that time remained central factors in his verse-making throughout his poetic career" (104). In *E.J. Pratt: The Evolutionary Vision* (1974), Djwa finds not only thematic connections between Pratt's poetry and his heritage, but formal ones as well. She argues that the long poem *The Witches' Brew* (1925) is influenced by traditional Newfoundland folk ballads, particularly Johnny Burke's humorous tongue-twisting song "The

Kelligrew's Soiree." She convincingly concludes that the rhythm of his poetry reflects "the patterns of Newfoundland speech—a highly accented patterning which Pratt himself retained all of his life" (49). Djwa's reading effectively locates Pratt's work in relationship to a long vernacular narrative tradition on the island. In her introduction to *E.J. Pratt: Selected Poems* (2000), Djwa further explains that in the nineteenth-century Newfoundland in which Pratt grew up, "the poet is most often a storyteller and [...] the poem, like the folk song, has a public function in affirming community, celebrating heroes, and lamenting death" (ix). Djwa connects the public function of the Newfoundland ballad tradition to Pratt's lifelong belief that "poetry should express the speech and emotions of ordinary men and women" (ix). Clearly Pratt's Newfoundland upbringing, as both a source of vivid images and as a cultural heritage, did have a lot of influence on the content and the form of his work.

In a 1968 address in St. John's, Northrop Frye identifies the Avalon peninsula, the part of Newfoundland in which St. John's is located, as Pratt's "fundamental environment" as a poet: "like all poetic environments, his was a mixture of memory and literary convention, and many of you might not recognize it as the place that you actually live in. But it would certainly never have existed without this *actual place*" (*Bush Garden* 191; my emphasis). Here, before an audience connected to Newfoundland through the immediacy of residence, Frye's words raise questions about the relationship between the intangible influences of cultural heritage and the lived experience of place. Similarly, Gingell notes that "Pratt would go for the essence of Newfoundland experience rather than for individualized experience," which leads her to conclude that Pratt is not necessarily a "regional" poet because "he does not stress the particular" (97). But how does one define the "essence of Newfoundland experience," or even the "actual place"? And when do the failures of memory or the embellishments of literature lead to stereotyping, exoticization, and cultural appropriation?

In his memoir of Newfoundland, *The Danger Tree* (1991), David Macfarlane paints a less flattering picture of the poet, who had a loose acquaintance with Macfarlane's family:

> Once ensconced in Toronto, he rarely returned to Newfoundland. Eventually he became a professor of English, an enthusiastic golfer, and, in Canada, a famous poet. Staring from the window of his warm, comfortable house on Davenport Road in Toronto, while the wall clock ticked behind him and his wife prepared roast chicken for a Sunday gathering of his academic and literary friends, he composed verse about a wind-racked, rock-bound island he remembered, just as, while read-

ing Masefield and Kipling and Robert Bridges, he composed elegies to the fallen dead of a war he neither fought in nor saw. (58)

Macfarlane's disdain for Pratt is in part derived from his "old-fashioned, uninventive, and ornate" verse (59), but also from a sense of betrayal; Macfarlane recounts the story of how Pratt raised the money to leave Newfoundland by selling concoctions he called Universal Lung Healer in communities around the island (58). Pratt's con of trusting outporters terrified of tuberculosis is sharply juxtaposed with the above image of Pratt's eventual comfort in Toronto. While Macfarlane is critiquing Pratt's behaviour here as much as his poetic skill, Macfarlane continues to emphasize the distance that seems to betray Pratt's disingenuous connection to his countrymen. In *Acta Victoriana* Pratt published and introduced the last letter sent home by Hedley Goodyear, Macfarlane's great uncle, before Hedley was killed in World War I. Macfarlane describes the exaggerations, mistruths, and overly sentimental phrases in Pratt's introduction: "Pratt, writing from the distance of his Toronto study, seemed to be idealizing the Goodyears, if not inventing them" (278). As I discuss in Chapter 9, Macfarlane in his own work is not averse to fictionalizing events in his family's past, including a war "he never saw." But while Macfarlane himself writes about Newfoundland from the distance of Toronto, he cannot bring himself to excuse Pratt for claiming phoney intimacies and making a personal family tragedy "windy and meaningless" (277).

In contrast to Gingell, Djwa, and Frye, at least two Newfoundland critics reject Pratt as a "Newfoundland poet." In his foreword to the anthology of Newfoundland literature *Baffles of Wind and Tide* (1974), Clyde Rose writes that "presumably by choice, [Pratt] moved to Toronto and seldom returned to Newfoundland. His scholarly works [on Newfoundland] though accurate in detail lack the authentic sounds" (xii). For Rose, a feeling of "remoteness" and a resulting lack of authenticity make Pratt not a Newfoundland poet but "a Toronto poet who uses Newfoundland and its people as a canvas for his work" (xii). This assessment, which emphasizes Pratt's location in Toronto, leads me to ask to what extent his exclusion from Rose's collection of Newfoundland writers is a result of his dislocation, rather than the qualities of his work. In other words, can a Newfoundland writer in diaspora *ever* be an "authentic" Newfoundlander?[2] This question gestures toward the general question that diaspora theorist R. Radhakrishnan asks: "Is the Ethnic 'Authentic' in the Diaspora?"[3] Rather than attempt to answer the impossible question of whether Pratt is an "authentic" Newfoundlander, I contend that the anxieties surrounding this question point to the pitfalls of writing literature in diaspora, particularly in the aftermath of Newfoundland Confederation.

O'Flaherty, in his literary history *The Rock Observed* (1979), also takes serious issue with Pratt's treatment of Newfoundland, arguing that "Pratt succeeded in discarding, to the extent that it could be discarded, his ancestral claim on the Newfoundland experience" (126). He directly rejects Djwa's claim that Pratt's formal innovations can be connected to the Newfoundland folk ballad, stating that her "arguments are unconvincing" (125) without explaining why — an unfair dismissal of what I take to be an astute reading of *The Witches' Brew*. More than three decades on, O'Flaherty's book remains the only literary history of Newfoundland and has been profoundly influential in the field of Newfoundland literary criticism. His arguments are very much derived from the political and cultural context of the 1970s, problematically fetishizing the image of what he calls the "real" Newfoundland. Yet his work remains significant and widely read, framing, for example, Lawrence Mathews' introduction to *Essays on Canadian Writing*'s 2004 special issue on Newfoundland literature. His privileging of cultural authenticity continues to reverberate through Newfoundland literature and its criticism; I therefore examine O'Flaherty's analysis of Pratt's work at some length. O'Flaherty titles his Pratt chapter "Emigrant Muse," and while he does not unpack this phrase it immediately establishes two main aspects of his assessment of Pratt's work, the romantic quality of the poetry and Pratt's physical and emotional distance from his subject as someone who left his home.

One aspect of O'Flaherty's uneasiness with Pratt's Newfoundland work is inaccuracy of detail. Citing examples in Pratt's first published poem on Newfoundland, *Rachel* (1917), and his collection *Newfoundland Verse* (1923), O'Flaherty notes that Pratt is occasionally "careless" with facts. He mentions the non-existent "Gulf of Labrador," for example, and has a character describe the habits of a skunk, though there are no skunks in Newfoundland (O'Flaherty 120). While these details are not ultimately important in their respective contexts, they do, for those familiar with Newfoundland, jar. They eliminate any sense of intimacy with the setting and do not seem to serve any significant purpose. Rather, they merely add to what O'Flaherty sees as the overall inaccuracy of the representation of Newfoundland and Newfoundlanders. In *Rachel,* Pratt constructs "a Newfoundland glamorized, a fictitious 'Elizabethan' Newfoundland, lumbered with the stock imagery and themes of Victorian sea romances, and honoured, more in flattery than in truth, with a large share in the traditions of the English sea dogs" (121). O'Flaherty's criticisms of Pratt here are just — not because they reveal an inauthentic identity, but because they show evidence of sentimental images and flat, unoriginal characters. What O'Flaherty fails to consider in his critique, however, is the literary context within which Pratt was writing. Djwa explains that romantic poetry survived longer in Canada because of a unique reaction to the Great

War, reflecting a sense that the nation was "coming of age" and that the land itself provided a source of optimism and hope in contrast to the battlefields of Europe ("1920s" 56–57). While Pratt's work has often been noted for its representation of the harshness of the Newfoundland environment, this harshness is also often the site of the heroic. The romantic, Victorian quality to which O'Flaherty objects in Pratt's early work is more an indication of Pratt's literary and social influences than of an intentional misrepresentation of his homeland. But as O'Flaherty adds that "in fact, there is hardly any observation even of the land and sea that summons up the *real* Newfoundland" (121; my emphasis), we must ask what, exactly, *is* the "real" Newfoundland that O'Flaherty imagines?

O'Flaherty argues that "the essential vision of Newfoundland life contained in [Pratt's poems] is spare and bleak. […] Pratt's Newfoundland poems form a sombre chronicle of human defeat, displaying a gloomy but intense interest in the impassive forces of nature which unite to dwarf and destroy men" (123). This observation is easily supported; Pratt's often-quoted poem "Newfoundland" is written in broad, sweeping language that seems to encompass the island:

> Here the tides flow,
> And here they ebb;
> Not with that dull, unsinewed tread of waters
> Held under bonds to move
> Around unpeopled shores—
> Moon-driven through a timeless circuit
> Of invasion and retreat;
> But with a lusty stroke of life
> Pounding at stubborn gates,
> That they might run
> Within the sluices of men's hearts,
> Leap under throb of pulse and nerve,
> And teach the sea's strong voice
> To learn the harmonies of new floods. (1–14)

The title "Newfoundland" is juxtaposed with the "here" of the first line, implying that this "here" is not a particular outport or beach, but the entire island. The images do not name specific locations or describe the details of a particular moment in time; rather they are generalized, reflecting the "timeless circuit" of the sea. For O'Flaherty, this scope makes the content of the representation troubling. The romantic conflation of people with the environment, evident in images like the tides that run "within the sluices of men's hearts" (11), is celebratory, but it is also, as O'Flaherty contends, tragic: the winds "breathe with the lungs of men" (42), but

> Their hands are full to the overflow,
> In their right is the bread of life,
> In their left are the waters of death. (47–49)

The melodrama of these lines, emphasized by their placement at the end of the stanza, constructs a Newfoundland defined by hardship and a population that is present only in the "breath" of the winds. Indeed the "tide and wind and crag" (75) are active, personified, while humans are a ghostly presence represented by a "broken rudder" (30) and kelp "red as the heart's blood" (31). Yet O'Flaherty does not read the Newfoundland poems in the context of his larger body of work; the observation that his poems chronicle human defeat and the destructive forces of nature could be applied to much of his poetry, including those poems concerned with other Canadian locales. Instead O'Flaherty concludes that "when one considers the entire body of Pratt's Newfoundland poems—not a large portion of his *oeuvre*—what stands out are these images of horror and grief and the persistent theme of tragedy. The overwhelming impression given is that Newfoundland was a good place to escape from" (123). O'Flaherty thus directly connects Pratt's "bleak" representation of Newfoundland to his emigration from it: "Pratt's Newfoundland is seen in retrospect, simplified into images of cruelty and fear, reduced to the hard and fixed outlines to which memory often reduces the distant past. It is a Newfoundland jettisoned, and half remembered" (125). O'Flaherty thereby rejects Pratt's representation of Newfoundland as false and ethically suspect due to his willing emigration.

"The Heart of the Country"

O'Flaherty is not only concerned with what Pratt says, but also with what he leaves out. He adds that "Pratt did not attempt, much less achieve, a comprehensive statement about his homeland" (124). This statement begs the question, is "a comprehensive statement" about Newfoundland necessary to be a Newfoundland poet? While O'Flaherty qualifies (in what seems like a moment of self-contradiction) that "this is not to belittle what he did write," and that Pratt was nevertheless "Newfoundland's finest poet," he goes on to tell us that "it is still surprising to see what is left out of his poems on Newfoundland":

> Really his poetry showed no interest in Newfoundland history. He evidently had no interest in exploring the distinctive traditions and habits of speech of his people. There was nothing in his poems that showed

a genuine curiosity about the outport way of life, no fingering of out-harbour contrivances, no examination of the mechanics of fishing and sealing, no investigation of how the people adjusted to the demands of their harsh environment, no detailed studies of individual fishermen. The "drama of the sled and dory" is alluded to but not examined. (124)

By registering his "surprise," O'Flaherty is revealing his own prescription for what constitutes Newfoundland literature. Because Pratt maintained a Newfoundland "dialect" in speech, but wrote in educated English, O'Flaherty contends that Pratt's "literary language represents his almost complete dissociation from the culture into which he was born" (126). Again, O'Flaherty fails to consider the fact that the Canadian poetry of the 1920s rarely employed vernacular language or dealt with specific moments of everyday working-class life. While O'Flaherty's objection may be due to the contrast between Pratt's romantic Newfoundland lyrics and his later work, through which he became known for meticulously researching and cataloguing the technical details of ship parts, naval lingo, or the duties of workmen building the railway, I see this contrast as the result of his development as a poet over several decades, rather than a deliberate "dissociation" from his culture.

But O'Flaherty's comments here are representative of a prevailing attitude in post-Confederation Newfoundland literature and literary criticism, that the outport constitutes the "essence" of Newfoundland culture or, as Adrian Fowler puts it, "the prime source of Newfoundland's cultural identity" ("Myth" 71). The outport came to be privileged, by tourist and anthropological discourse, as the centre of Newfoundland identity—as, in O'Flaherty's words, "the real Newfoundland" (121). Overton relates how the idea of "The 'Real' Newfoundland" actually became a campaign for Newfoundland Tourism in the 1980s to capitalize on this desire for exotic authenticity: "'The "Real" Newfoundland' is the outports and 'the people,' 'the fishermen knitting their nets, caulking their boats, or building a wiggly garden rod fence'" (106). Arguing that this idea of a distinct Newfoundland culture rooted in rural life was largely generated from outside, Paul Chafe recounts how "Newfoundland satirist Ray Guy coined the phrase 'Newfcult' to describe this phenomenon in which Newfoundland became regarded as unique and unspoiled—a bastion of folksy humanity on the edge of the technocratic, metropolitan world" ("Hey Buddy" 72). "Newfcult" was internalized by Newfoundland's cultural producers; in his contribution to *Essays on Canadian Writing*'s special issue on the Literature of Newfoundland, Fowler outlines the development of the outport as a "major theme" in the literature, arguing that by the 1970s "the outport community was acknowledged to be the heart and soul of Newfoundland" ("Myth" 71). The pervasiveness of the outport as theme or setting was not limited to those writers who grew up there. In an earlier essay, published in 1985, Fowler wrote that even "the townie writer" (meaning one from St. John's) has "felt the need to come to terms with outport life" ("Literature" 128). The appropriation of the outport by the "townie" writer has been perceived as a way of tapping into the core of Newfoundland.

The idea that the outport contained the essence of Newfoundland culture was spawned in part by the threats to outport life posed by the unstable fishing industry and widespread poverty. Confederation and the following twenty-three-year reign of Joey Smallwood brought many more threats, perhaps the most significant of which was the Newfoundland Resettlement Program and its precursor, the Newfoundland Centralization program. Between 1935 and 1975, hundreds of families in small outports were moved to larger "growth centres," where they would supposedly have better access to services. A quarter of Newfoundland's communities were abandoned. The 1970s brought more changes, including the discovery of off-shore oil and the beginning of a battle with the federal government over ownership of the resource, and the province's attempt to renegotiate the terms of the 1969 sale of power from Churchill Falls to Hydro-Québec, all of which caused Newfoundlanders to question their province's place within Confederation. In this period of political dissatisfaction, provincial arts policy under Premier Frank Moores began to promote Newfoundlanders' identity as "a people with a unique way of life" (Rompkey, "Idea" 272). In a 1976 article in *Saturday Night*, Newfoundland-born journalist Sandra Gwyn famously hailed the Newfoundland Renaissance. The subtitle of her article read "destruction of the outports has unexpectedly spawned Newfcult, the miraculous and exciting revival of art and theatre on Canada's poor, bald rock" (38).[4] The comment is perhaps a little melodramatic, but it reveals the direct link that was made between the threat to the outport and creative—including literary—production. Gwyn writes, "What the planners overlooked was that these settlements—clusters of flat-roofed, white clapboard houses and churches on the brink of the Atlantic [...] and the people who left them for mobile homes and prefab bungalows, contained the essence of the Newfoundland mystique. [...] A way of life, *the* Newfoundland way of life, had been foreclosed. [...] This overpowering sense of loss and betrayal has permeated the consciousness of every artist working there, and suffuses every art form" (40; emphasis in original). Paradoxically, as she argues that "the old order that produced all of us is being smashed, homogenized, and trivialized out of existence," she is also arguing that this destruction is the very "source of inspiration" for cultural production (40). The destruction of culture perpetuates the production of culture.[5]

In 1979, then, O'Flaherty was reading Pratt at a time of both a growing Newfoundland cultural nationalism and profound social change, when the outport was regarded as the threatened "essence" of Newfoundland culture. His reading of Pratt's work, though the poems were written several decades earlier, was influenced by this cultural climate. By ignoring the common details of outport life, O'Flaherty argues, Pratt failed to imbue his writing with this authentic "essence." Ironically, then, while O'Flaherty criticizes Pratt for his use of romantic, "inauthentic" stock images, he simultaneously seeks other stock images of the "outport way of life" (124). This privileging of the threatened outport as the heart of Newfoundland culture could be regarded as a form of strategic essentialism, as an overemphasis of the cultural value of the outport in order to resist its dissolution and to unite Newfoundlanders as a distinct group. But strategic essentialism requires an acknowledgement of the constructedness of "essential" attributes, a self-reflexivity that is missing from O'Flaherty's critique. This idea, then, that there is an authentic "essence" of Newfoundland is highly problematic. It homogenizes Newfoundland culture, excluding experiences of life in the city in the process. If the outport as motif represents a "dying culture" and the loss of the old ways, then a Newfoundland identity defined by outport culture is deeply troubling, for this identity is seen as being under imminent threat, or even already dead. This idea also traps the island in a sentimental ideal, where technological or economic progress or change is seen not as supplemental to culture, but counter to it. In other words there is no happy medium between economic viability and cultural viability, and no space for exploring the concerns of contemporary rural communities.

While the idea that the outport represents the "real" Newfoundland has placed demands on writers within the province, O'Flaherty's critique suggests that diasporic writers in particular need to assert their identity by adhering to certain literary conventions or expectations. As a transplanted Newfoundlander who became well known as a poet in Canada, Pratt is a target of what Sneja Gunew identifies as the perception that the minority or diasporic writer's "function [is] a representative one (in the sense of delegation or speaking for)" (*Haunted* 76). Pratt is therefore charged with the responsibility of "correctly" representing his culture. At times, he embraced this role. He writes that as the son of an itinerant clergyman, "I had a good opportunity of getting acquainted with the heart of the country, which is essentially the outport life" (*His Life* 5). But according to O'Flaherty, the fact that Pratt's family moved every few years meant that he did not form strong attachments to the communities he lived in (117); he was always an outsider to the community, and his reflections on this "heart" of the country are therefore generalized and romanticized. Pratt's biographer, David G. Pitt, writes that he sometimes "conjured up a picture of himself when a boy as a 'typical' outport youth, a character whom he clearly admired: rough, tough, full of oaths and colourful braggadocio, 'heroic,' mischievous, a truant in more ways than one" (*Truant* 19). But even Pitt writes that

> it must be said straightaway that the self-portrait is largely if not wholly a fictive one. The circumstances of E.J. Pratt's early life made it impossible for him ever really to have lived the life of an *authentic* outport Newfoundlander, or to have known such a life as an actual participant rather than mainly as an observer, albeit a very percipient and sensitive one. The fact is, I think, of considerable importance in understanding and appreciating Pratt's perspective and perception of the outport world. It is a fact that largely accounts for the absence from his Newfoundland poems of any *real* identification with either the place or the people. (*Truant* 19–20; my emphases)

Pratt's family not only had to move frequently but also held a distinct and somewhat distant place in the communities in which they lived. Pitt writes that "the very fact of his birth into a Methodist minister's family meant that E.J. Pratt could never have been a full-blooded member of the local tribe. Only had he been born of the native stock, raised in one small village, and sent to sea, semi-literate at best, at the age of fifteen or earlier, could he have qualified for such membership" (*Truant* 20). Pitt's analysis reinforces the idea that Newfoundland "authenticity" requires an intimate connection with the outport. But Pratt's departure at the age of twenty-five cemented his position as a cultural outsider. For O'Flaherty, by failing to pay appropriate attention to everyday outport life in his poetry, not only did Pratt misrepresent his homeland, he misrepresented it *to* a foreign audience. This point raises crucial questions: If Pratt had written the same works, in the same way, but stayed in Newfoundland, would he be more of a legitimate Newfoundland poet in O'Flaherty's eyes, a poet capable of writing observations "of the land and sea that [summon] up the real Newfoundland" (O'Flaherty 121)? Would his authority to speak as a Newfoundlander have been questioned if he had written these works at home?

Sea to Sea

For O'Flaherty, it is troubling that "when Pratt became famous he grew fond of parading his Newfoundland background before the many audiences he addressed. It somehow became an ornament to be displayed rather than a limitation to be overcome" (126). Pratt's "boasting about Newfoundland" seems both exploitative and "patently contrived when one realizes how easily he broke his ties with the colony once he got the chance to leave for Ontario" (122). O'Flaherty thus claims that from 1907 until Pratt's death in 1964 "Toronto would remain his actual and intellectual home" (120). It seems then that for O'Flaherty, the problem with Pratt's depictions of Newfoundland is not only that they were contrived, simplistic representations of the place, but that they were representations born outside of Newfoundland, in what O'Flaherty perceives to be a disingenuous connection to the island. It is his "emigrant" status, then, that makes his depictions of Newfoundland suspect, relegating them to the category of appropriation.

O'Flaherty suggests that the problem with Pratt is that he substituted a new Canadian identity for his Newfoundland identity, at a time before Confederation associated the two: "Pratt in his maturity was obviously making an attempt to move beyond what two Canadian critics have called 'the lesser inspirations of Newfoundland' in order to become, 'apparently quite deliberately,' Canada's national poet.[6] This meant throwing off parochial concerns to take on bigger themes: the Canadian Pacific Railway rather than Newfoundland's narrow gauge line, Brébeuf rather than Coughlan or Jens Haven, the Iroquois rather than the Beothucks" (125). O'Flaherty interprets Pratt's adoption of Canadian themes in his work as a rebuff against Newfoundland. He argues that "Pratt succeeded in discarding, to the extent that it could be discarded, his ancestral claim on the Newfoundland experience" (126). The fact that he is "Canada's national poet," for O'Flaherty, precludes a Newfoundland identity. Before Confederation, Canadian and Newfoundland identities, it seems, are mutually exclusive.

O'Flaherty's reaction may be due to the way in which Pratt's Newfoundland heritage has been appropriated by critics into a Canadian national narrative. In his introduction to the 1958 *Collected Poems of E.J. Pratt*, Frye writes:

> His work began with Newfoundland, and his latest major narrative ends in British Columbia. On his seventy-fifth birthday the CBC recorded tributes to him from all over Canada, some of the most eloquent being from the province of the ice-floes and from the province of the last spike. It was a sign that the work he had helped to do had been, not of course done, but well begun. In defiance of every geographical and economic law, Canada has made itself not simply a nation but an environment. It is only now emerging from its beginning as a shambling, awkward, absurd country, groping and thrusting its way through incredible distances into the west and north, plundered by profiteers, interrupted by European wars, divided by language, and bedevilled by climate, yet slowly and inexorably bringing a culture to life. And as long as that culture can remember its origin, there will be a central place in its memory for the poet in whom it found its tongue. (xxvii–xxviii)

This nation "groping and thrusting" its way into existence begins with Newfoundland on the east coast and ends with British Columbia on the west, with no mention of the fact that Pratt's Newfoundland, exemplified in his 1923 *Newfoundland Verse*, long preceded Confederation in 1949. Pratt's Newfoundland, then, is anachronistically inscribed into the national story. Similarly, the thematic criticism of the 1960s and '70s easily found in Pratt's Newfoundland poems Frye's "garrison mentality" ("The societies in Pratt's poems are always tense and tight groups engaged in war, rescue, martyrdom, or crisis" [*Bush Garden* 226]), as well as the "survival" instinct that Margaret Atwood so famously identified as the heart of the Canadian literary impulse (33). "Seldom has a man been more faithful to his heritage," Peter Buitenhuis writes (48), citing the recurring theme of the sea in Pratt's poetry as his main evidence. He adds that "in the still-primitive conditions of the Canadian Far West and the Eastern seaboard, where Pratt grew up, the wilderness of plain, sea, and rock gave a meaningful setting to the clash of forces taking place within society. Pratt's work is filled with images of primitive nature and evolutionary history" (50). The significant body of criticism that emerged in this era worked simultaneously to identify Pratt as quintessentially "of" Newfoundland and to rewrite Newfoundland into a pre-Confederation Canadian literary tradition. Robert Collins, in his 1988 *E.J. Pratt*, writes that Pratt was a "Canadian poet—not in the limiting but in the truest sense: that is, he both spoke for the society and, in doing so, created a national tradition that helped define the country to itself in ways that accorded remarkably with the need of the Canadian people in the first half of the twentieth century" (vii). While this may well be true when one considers the full body of Pratt's work, Collins clarifies that

> paradoxically, the regional intensity that marked his youth contributed, as much as anything else, to make E.J. Pratt a national poet. [...] Rogue child though it was, Newfoundland is an indispensable part of what became a nation. The beginnings of Canada come out of that eastern sea, the Atlantic. [...] The sea-girt outpost of Canada, Newfoundland was truly the gateway through which Europe passed to become Canada, so long an outpost in the Atlantic that only in the mid-twentieth century did it become part of the confederation through which a political identity was given it. [...] It seems almost destiny, then, that the nearest thing that Canada has brought forth as an epic poet is a man whose childhood and youth were shaped by the fundamental thoughts and rich imaginative rhetoric of the outports of Newfoundland. (2)

For Frye, Buitenhuis, Collins, and others, the Newfoundland and Canadian identities, even before Confederation, are not contradictory or mutually exclusive, but rather fit together teleologically, in a sea-to-sea vision of Canadian unity. Thus Newfoundland is retroactively appropriated into the Canadian imagination, and Pratt's "Newfoundlandness" is defined in relationship to his "Canadianness."

In some contexts Pratt himself perpetuated this teleological vision of Canadian Confederation, particularly later in his career when the colony was embroiled in a passionate debate over the issue. In a letter to Joey Smallwood just prior to the referendum, Pratt wrote of his "personal wish that Newfoundland should 'come in.' [...] I find that such a wish is shared by the great majority of Newfoundlanders living in Canada" (qtd. in Pitt, *Master* 392). This enthusiasm is also expressed in "Newfoundland Calling," written in anticipation of the union. In this poem, Pratt links the place names of Newfoundland with that of Canada, declaring "The names will know their cousins when they see / Them, greet them with the same sonorous hail" (31–32). There are no people here, nor even places; rather the names themselves are personified and stand in for Newfoundlanders and Canadians, as well as their histories and cultures. He conflates the Newfoundland hardship that he so often lauds with that of other Canadian regions, so that together they form one history:

> They have survived through strains of genes and blood
> Storms, fishing admirals and dust-bowls; rolled
> On decks and log-jams; watched pitheads; withstood
> The prairies' drought, blizzard and rust, and told
> The explorers' yarns through a long Arctic night
> Till dawn broke with a soft Pacific light. (49–54)

Pratt thus performs the melding of Newfoundland and Canadian histories and identities, appropriately fixing his early work within a unified corpus as Canada's "national poet" (Collins 2; O'Flaherty 129).

But Newfoundland and Canada were (and in many ways still are) culturally and politically distinct, and in other contexts Pratt himself was quick to point out the differences. In his essay "Memories of Newfoundland" (1937), Pratt wrote that "so distinctive is the Newfoundland type that it is only with the greatest difficulty that one may translate it in foreign terms or communicate it even to Canadians" (*His Life* 6). Despite the gesture of "*even* to Canadians," Pratt goes on to assert the profound cultural differences between his birthplace and his adopted country in terms of cultural authenticity. The passage merits quoting at length:

When a half-dozen of us Newfoundlanders gather together in Toronto to smoke and yarn, the foreign born, if he happen to be invited to the company, finds himself only on the fringe of the charmed circle.

The conversation, once it has lapsed into dialect, is a closed book to him. He may know that haggis is a Scotch dish, or a particular hybrid of stew is Irish, but has he ever eaten brewis? No. His palate for dried cod is limited to a few tasteless fillets which the proprietor of a meat-and-fish store in the city claimed to have been cut from genuine cod. Has he ever eaten whorts? No, only blueberries—a fundamental error. Or bake-apples, or capillaire, or partridge berries? Never heard of them. Had he ever been stimulated by the smell of kelp after a northeaster had lashed the shores—a tonic like strychnine to the blood? Or by the smell of caplin three days after the tonnage had been deposited on the cabbage beds? No. Then he was forever excommunicate, a stranger to the true faith. How did he pronounce the name of the country? With the accent on the second syllable. That was enough—the final heresy. (6–7)

Here Pratt establishes his cultural identity, largely through the experience of particular tastes and smells. These experiences constitute an insider knowledge that amounts to something of a secret code determining authenticity. As Radhakrishnan points out, "ethnicity is often forced to take on the discourse of authenticity just to protect and maintain its space and history [...] It becomes difficult to determine if the drive toward authenticity comes from within the group as a spontaneous self-affirming act, or if authenticity is nothing but a paranoid reaction to the 'naturalness' of dominant groups" (210–11). Of course we can never know Pratt's intentions behind this narrative, if this was a "self-affirming act," or if he felt threatened by assimilation into the dominant Canadian culture, or if he was merely exoticizing or even making fun of his own identity as a celebrity poet. The religious rhetoric of "excommunicate," "true faith," and "heresy" emphasize the sacredness of this authenticity, as well as its mysterious exclusivity. His Newfoundland identity becomes akin to his religion or ethnicity. But the hyperbole of the religious metaphor also gives the entire passage a somewhat playful tone; the fact that Pratt was an ordained Methodist minister makes the passage seem almost tongue-in-cheek. In the end it is difficult to determine how serious this assertion of Newfoundland difference is meant to be.

Pratt does not declare his identity here by directly recounting his memories, but by framing the recollections within an imagined encounter between insiders and outsiders. This rhetorical strategy reveals the relationship between Pratt's cultural identity and his diasporic location; his identity is defined in contrast to that of his new neighbours. The essay was written for Joey Smallwood's mammoth compilation *The Book of Newfoundland*, and a primarily Newfoundland audience. The references to insider terminology and experiences thus serve to create a camaraderie between the diasporic subjects in the piece and their compatriots back home. The suggestion is that even as he is hailed as a great Canadian poet, he resists total appropriation into Canadian culture. Pratt's claims to Newfoundland identity are thus inseparable from his position as a diasporic figure; he needs to assert his cultural authenticity only because of his location in Toronto. In their introduction to *Theorizing Diaspora*, Jana Evans Braziel and Anita Mannur note that diasporic persons are often considered inauthentic "imitations of the real citizens in the home state" (8). Based on O'Flaherty's and Rose's criticisms, Pratt fits into this category. Yet Braziel and Mannur add that recent theorizations of diaspora have "offered ways out of the trappings of this hierarchical construct of nation and diaspora," by considering diaspora as "an alternative paradigm for national (or multinational, transnational, and even postnational) identification" (8). This new paradigm subverts what Gayatri Gopinath identifies as the old hierarchical construct of diaspora as the inauthentic "bastard child of the nation—disavowed, inauthentic, illegitimate, and impoverished imitation of the originary culture" (qtd. in Braziel and Mannur 8). In this newer model, the diaspora is not an inauthentic imitation of the nation, but rather a means of subverting the importance placed on nationhood in the construction of identity. For Pratt, there is no contradiction between supporting Confederation and the dissolution of the Newfoundland nation, and asserting his Newfoundland cultural identity in opposition to the dominant Canadian culture. His diasporic identity affirms that Newfoundland identity exists outside of political boundaries.

Pratt's self-positioning is thus shifting and strategic, and largely dependent upon his particular audience; he is also the first to capitalize on his Newfoundland identity, producing exotic, stereotypical images of his countrymen with ease. As a well-known poet and a Newfoundland expatriate, around the time of Confederation Pratt was asked repeatedly by Canadian magazines, newspapers, clubs, and societies for poems or addresses about the new province. His essay "Newfoundland Types" was written for this occasion; in it he outlines the "Newfoundland types" that he says "make up the bulk of the population on the fishing coasts" (*His Life* 9). With this phrasing he suggests that Newfoundlanders can be classified into stereotypical stock figures: the sailor with centuries-old "Devon blood," the preacher with a rough "native eloquence," the saucy, quick-witted child, or the community healer always fetched in a crisis (12–17). Interest in regional identities was commonplace at this time; as Lisa Chalykoff notes, critics such as Edward McCourt contributed to the view that regions are "imbued with a distinct native 'spirit' that exerts itself uniformly upon all subjects who exist within its borders" (164). Yet interest in the "Newfoundland type" specifically betrays a desire for the backward and the exotic. As Pratt wrote, "The appeal of this subject never seems to wear out. I have been asked to prepare next winter some broadcasts over the CBC for Ontario high schools and the director suggested that as far as possible I introduce a number of poems dealing with eccentric persons slightly off balance, not in their minds exactly, but in their tastes, hobbies, and preoccupations. Part of a writer's job is to collect and describe such characters" (*His Life* 15). While Pratt does not say so explicitly, the context of his comments suggests that the "eccentric persons" the director was asking for are the quaint and interesting "types" found in Pratt's Newfoundland work. Part of his appeal as a writer, it seems, is for this exotic or amusing representation of Newfoundland stereotypes. His poem "Newfoundland Seamen," published in several national newspapers on the day Newfoundland joined Confederation, and read by Prime Minister St-Laurent in his "welcoming broadcast" on "Confederation Day," is exemplary:

> This is their culture, this—their master passion
> Of giving shelter and of sharing bread,
> Of answering rocket signals in the fashion
> Of losing life to save it. (1–4)

While the poem is idealistic and reverent toward "Newfoundland seamen," its role as an introduction to Canadians of their new countrymen serves to essentialize the culture and people into an image of primitive struggle, hardly changed from when

> centuries before Argentia's smoking funnels,
> That small ancestral band of Devon men
> Red-boned their knuckles on the *Squirrel* gunwales. (14–16)

It is thus crucial to note that his assertions of a sort of Newfoundland "ethnicity" were often a response to Canadian requests for it. One might conclude that he recognized its marketability at this time. It is easy to see, then, how Pratt's shifting and potentially even disingenuous claims to "authentic" Newfoundland identity exacerbated the anxieties that grew in the post-Confederation decades and the nationalistic 1970s about Newfoundland's place in Canada, anxieties derived from both stereotyping and the threat of assimilation. What these debates also reveal, however, is the perceived effect of diasporic location on cultural identity, and the stakes for Newfoundland writers who leave the island. Cast as delegates for their homeland from both inside and out, they are charged with the impossible and restrictive task of accurately representing their culture to a foreign audience.

The idea of diasporic authenticity is always understood in relationship to external cultures, in this case, those of mainland Canada. O'Flaherty is by no means an anti-confederate; he believes that "opting as they did, in 1948, for a chance at a decent and secure mode of life, the people may have chosen, not assimilation, but a kind of freedom" (187). But while he believes that Canada can accommodate Newfoundland culture, he is wary of what he sees as a deliberate rejection of that culture in favour of membership in the dominant majority of central Canada. Insofar as Pratt perpetuates reductive stereotypes of Newfoundland, these are legitimate concerns. But ultimately, authenticity is a limiting concept because it oversimplifies the formation of identity. It asks diasporic subjects to choose either assimilation or the limitations of realism and cultural expectation. And it cannot easily accommodate the post-Confederation Newfoundland that Pratt dreamed of and saw come to fruition in 1949, a place in which one can, ostensibly, be both "authentically" a Newfoundlander *and* a Canadian.

Readings of Pratt's work that consider Newfoundland communities in terms of environmentally determined garrisons identify his depictions of local space as evidence of a Canadian nationalism; in Frye's assessment in the preface to *The Bush Garden*, "the question of Canadian identity, so far as it affects the creative imagination, is not a 'Canadian' question at all, but a regional question. [...] Identity is local and regional, rooted in the imagination and in works of culture" (i–ii). But while Pratt embraced an unabashed Canadian nationalism, the anachronistic readings of his work that retroactively appropriate Newfoundland into Canadian space oversimplify his national and diasporic identity, rewriting the Confederation moment as a natural "consummation devoutly to be wished" (D.W. Prowse, qtd. in Johnston, *Colony* 429) and perpetuating a marginal, homogeneous vision of Newfoundland culture. Pratt's location at a moment of Canadian literary nationalism and as a prominent figure when Newfoundland joined Canadian Confederation makes him a figure onto whom a series of anxieties about regional and national identity are projected. Critics who read his work for authentic expressions of a homogeneous regional identity oversimplify both the historical moment and the national and cultural identities struggling for articulation in a time of great change.

 FIVE

"A PAPIER MÂCHÉ ROCK": WAYNE JOHNSTON AND REJECTING REGIONALISM

While I have argued that the debate over Pratt's authenticity can be attributed to the cultural climate of the 1970s in Newfoundland and the rest of Canada, a similar debate has emerged much more recently around the work of Wayne Johnston. Johnston was born and raised in the small community of Goulds, just outside St. John's. He moved to Toronto in his early thirties. Though he has lived in Toronto since 1989, he continues to write primarily Newfoundland-centred books. He has become one of Newfoundland's best-known writers, with novels such as *The Divine Ryans* (1990), *The Navigator of New York* (2002), and *A World Elsewhere* (2011). Johnston's 1998 novel, *The Colony of Unrequited Dreams*, is his most popular work, and was shortlisted for the Giller Prize and was a runner-up on CBC's *Canada Reads*. The novel has been strongly criticized, however, for its fictionalization of Joey Smallwood, the province's first premier and the man who brought Newfoundland into Confederation. For those who remember Smallwood the man, Rex Murphy writes, Johnston's rendering amounts to a "pastework substitute" (49). In his review article in *Newfoundland Studies*, historian Stuart Pierson concurs, but extends the paste-and-paper imagery to Johnston's depiction of the island itself, which he lambastes for being full of factual inaccuracies: "his settings, as in the theatre, where a papier mâché rock can stand for any island in the world, do not carry with them, by themselves, any numinous significance" ("Johnston's" 283).

Such concerns are rooted in the same old anxieties about the "real" Newfoundland that characterized the Pratt debates of the 1970s, anxieties about the survival of Newfoundland culture and about representing regional and national identities, particularly in diasporic contexts. Pierson opens his article with an anecdote about James Joyce and the fact that the famous writer of the Irish diaspora wrote to his aunt in Dublin to confirm details about the city as he completed *Ulysses*. Pierson then goes on for two pages simply listing the geographical and historical errors in *Colony*: a house on Blackhead Road cannot look out on the harbour from the front and on the Atlantic from the back, Harbour Drive did not yet exist in the 1920s, the girls' and boys' schools Bishop Spencer and Bishop Feild did not back on to each other, et cetera ("Johnston's" 283–84). While Pierson does not say so directly, the comparison with Joyce suggests that to him the problem with Johnston's work is not simply sloppiness but failure to maintain an appropriate regard for the authenticity of place *in diaspora*. In her article for *Essays on Canadian Writing*'s special issue on Newfoundland literature, Danielle Fuller feels compelled to ask the question: Is Johnston a "Newfoundland writer"? "Johnston, born and raised in Newfoundland," she writes, "has lived in Toronto since 1989 and rejected the 'regional writer' label explicitly in an interview with *TickleAce* editor Bruce Porter. [...] For the purposes of this essay, Johnston [is a writer] with an intimate knowledge of Newfoundland who [has] written extensively about it" ("Strange" 47). While I read Fuller's question as a cautious attempt to avoid classifying Johnston in the essentialist terms of a native informant, the way in which she frames her query as a question of diasporic identity is telling. Unlike Pierson, Fuller recognizes that geographical inaccuracies serve particular aesthetic functions in this work of fiction, yet Johnston's dislocation still puts his identity as a Newfoundland writer into question. For Fuller, a "Newfoundland writer" is a "regional writer," and while in her book *Writing the Everyday: Women's Textual Communities in Atlantic Canada* (2004) she carefully differentiates between various definitions and forms of literary regionalism, here the term is left unexamined, raising questions about the connections between markers of identity and regionalism as a concept and practice. In the interview with Porter to which Fuller refers, Johnston does not reject a Newfoundland identity per se, but rather rejects the concept of considering literature in "regional" terms as too "self-contained" ("Time" 27). In this chapter, I show how Johnston's work exceeds the limitations of traditional regionalism as he plays with issues of representation of place, literary authority, and diaspora. Johnston makes intentional geographical and historical errors in his novel to challenge the very notion of authenticity and the restrictive cultural stereotypes imposed by conservative regionalist readings.

Johnston's Imaginary Homeland, or a Tree That Doesn't Look Like a Tree
The first words in *The Colony of Unrequited Dreams* in the voice of Joey Smallwood are "I am a Newfoundlander" (8)—his identity, indeed his life, are centred upon his relationship to his homeland, and Newfoundland is central to every aspect of the novel: its plot, its characters, and its theme. The novel

follows not only perhaps the most iconic figure in Newfoundland's history from birth to death but also Newfoundland itself through periods of great change, from the colonially influenced, class-based society of the turn of the twentieth century through the tragic sealing disaster of 1914, the collapse of responsible government, the influx of Americans and Canadians during World War II, and Confederation with Canada. The very title, "the colony of unrequited dreams," at once encompasses the island's colonial history and the legacy of what "might have been" (560).

Despite the centrality of Newfoundland to the novel, Pierson's comparison of Johnston with Joyce sets up his critique as a concern over diasporic authenticity. It asks us to read the novel's geographical inaccuracies as evidence of imposture. Newfoundland novelist Bernice Morgan, in her review of *Colony* for *TickleAce*, also admits that she was driven "to distraction" by the errors, particularly in descriptions of "the St. John's I have lived in all my life": "he keeps referring to 'the apron,' tells us coves are little streets between Water Street and the Harbour Drive," not to mention "crosses in Protestant homes, a bridge moved in from Kilbride, Newfoundlanders strolling into Fort Pepperell in wartime" (103). But Morgan also recognizes in Johnston's work a strong "sense of place and love of place" (103). She wonders, ultimately, "if a writer as confident and canny as Johnston could have set me up" (105). While Morgan's short review does not explain the literary function of such a "set up," her generous reading leaves room for a consideration of the aesthetic purpose of Johnston's fictionalized island.

I argue that what Johnston is doing here is creating Newfoundland as, in Salman Rushdie's terms, an "imaginary homeland." Reflecting on the process of writing his own novel *Midnight's Children* from his new home in England, Rushdie writes: "our physical alienation from India almost inevitably means that we will not be capable of reclaiming precisely the thing that was lost; that we will, in short, create fictions, not actual cities or villages, but invisible ones, imaginary homelands, Indias of the mind" (10). As with the criticisms of Johnston's novel, Rushdie found that people wanted *Midnight's Children* "to be the history, even the guidebook, which it was never meant to be" (25). Yet in attempting to remember the details of 1950s and '60s Bombay, Rushdie discovered that "it was precisely the partial nature of these memories, their fragmentation, that made them so evocative for me. The shards of memory acquired greater status, greater resonance, because they were *remains*" (12; emphasis in original). The very impossibility of "total recall," and the errors that will inevitably arise from the attempt, leads to a productive, creative reimagining of a space already mediated by its very centrality in the novel. For Johnston, like Rushdie, this "imaginary" quality is not a problem to be overcome, but is useful in the process of writing fiction.

In *Colony* many errors serve symbolic purposes. The location of Bishop Feild school on the corner of King's Road and Colonial Street—two streets which, as Pierson points out, do not cross—identifies the school as a juncture between imperial England and the colony and carries with it the tension between patronizing English teachers and Smallwood, one of the "savages descended from the 'dregs of England'" that they have been assigned to "civilize" (*Colony* 34). The idea that the harbour and the Atlantic are visible from opposite ends of Smallwood's childhood home similarly poises him between the "old world" and the "new." This location also places Smallwood's home in a particularly precarious position, vulnerable to harsh Atlantic winds from all directions, reflecting both the family's poverty and dysfunction and Smallwood's own psychic fragility. Rushdie explains that in his own writing the fragmentation and errata caused by his displacement "made trivial things seem like symbols, and the mundane acquired numinous qualities" (12). Some of Johnston's geographical inaccuracies do not seem to serve much of a narrative purpose, and it is unfortunate that they take some readers out of the story. But clearly other such inaccuracies play important symbolic, even "numinous," roles. Johnston sums up his approach to fiction with a simple analogy, declaring that his novel "is impressionistic writing in exactly the way that some painting is impressionistic painting. No one objects when an impressionistic painting of a tree doesn't look like a tree" ("Afterlife" 113).

Almost all of the errors that Pierson and Morgan cite above, moreover, are either Smallwood's or Fielding's, as they reflect on places and events of the past. For example, when Smallwood is on the south coast we learn that the people there do not have electricity, yet later Smallwood recalls: "take away their radios and they lived not much differently than people in such places had a hundred, even two hundred years ago" (388). What Pierson fails to recognize in pointing out this discrepancy is the fallibility and tone of condescension that this moment lends to the character. Memory is not perfect, and in a novel that is in large part about change, in a fictional biography that follows a character from childhood to death, these moments of imperfection give the voice depth. Smallwood is an unreliable narrator who is remembering, and as Rushdie puts it "one of the simplest truths about any set of memories is that many of them will be false" (24). Ironically, such falsehoods also have the potential to convey a character's powerful affective relationships to his or her geography. Chafe effectively explains another of Johnston's "errors," which occurs at the beginning of the book, in one of Fielding's journal entries dated not long after Confederation: "It must be noted that Fielding's depiction of a St. John's bathed in amber 'in the evening, in the morning' by sun shining through unfurled sails is impossible. Anyone possessed with a rudimentary knowledge of St. John's would know that the setting sun could never pass through the sails of schooners docked in the harbour and cast a glow across the streets. Fielding is creating a 'home in memory'" ("Scuttlework" 343). Chafe's subtle reading connects Fielding's feeling of homelessness in a place where "the past is literally another country now" (*Colony* 3) with the inaccurate idealizations of nostalgia. In other words, Johnston's "error" here is really a fault of Fielding's memory and exemplifies the disconnection that she feels from both her past and the nation that is no more. Fielding concludes her memory: "This was our city when we were still in school. This is what it looked and smelled and sounded like. But how it was before what happened between us, how it *felt* before we met, we can no more recall than we can how we felt when we were born" (8; emphasis in original). Here Fielding tries to do the impossible by disconnecting her memory of what the city looked like from how it "felt." In a moment of dramatic irony, she does not realize that in her physical description of the city her memory has already failed her. Thus the errors enabled by Johnston's own displacement become central to conveying Fielding's sense of disconnection. They become part of the "imaginary homeland" created by what Rushdie calls the "double filter" (24) between the writer and his or her subject. The distance created by both the passage of time and distance means that the Newfoundland constructed exists only in the imagination, thereby emphasizing the loss brought about by that distance. The opening passage of the novel, then, ends with a tone of loss that will shade the rest of the book.

Thus, for Johnston, dislocation is crucial to the creative process; he says he left Newfoundland "because I couldn't write about the island while I was there. [...] Life was too immediate. I was too inundated by the place and its details. I'd write about something and see it when I walked across the street the next day" (Holt n. pag.).[1] Radhakrishnan notes that this sentiment is not uncommon among diasporic subjects; he persuasively writes that "it is counterproductive to maintain that one can only understand a place when one is in it. It is quite customary for citizens who have emigrated to experience distance as a form of critical enlightenment or a healthy 'estrangement' from their birthland" (210). Rather than leading to inauthenticity, diaspora can lead to an objective, "nuanced historical appreciation of the home country" (210). Johnston's dislocation, then, enables him to make necessary errors, to achieve the distance needed for creative freedom. Rushdie writes that the diaspora can be a "fertile territory" for the writer to occupy: "If literature is in part the business of finding new angles at which to enter reality, then once again our distance, our long geographical perspective, may provide us with such angles" (15). In an interview with Herb Wyile, Johnston explains his displacement in similar terms: "When I'd been away for long enough, going on ten years—the spatial and temporal remove from Newfoundland, especially the spatial remove, finally allowed me to see things from a new perspective" (120). Johnston implies here that this remove enabled more than just symbolic alterations to geography; it enabled a more objective perspective on the island's culture and history.

Johnston also explains that *Colony* in particular required this distance because of its subject matter, since Newfoundland would have been a "censorious atmosphere" in which to write a book about so iconic a figure as Joey Smallwood, who at the time Johnston started writing the novel had been dead only three years ("Afterlife" 107). He adds that it "also removed an inhibition that I think a lot of Newfoundland writers feel about writing about Newfoundland in a certain way. When you're there, there are certain things that are *verboten*, things you don't mention. You don't portray a downtrodden Newfoundland or an embittered Newfoundlander or things like that, no matter how many of them there might be around. Thus that spatial remove is really important" (120). Johnston suggests, then, that Newfoundlanders are particularly protective of the way in which the place and its historical figures are depicted, since to portray "downtrodden" Newfoundlanders would be contributing to already common and damaging stereotypes. His diasporic position frees him to provide a different, if controversial, perspective on his homeland.

Resisting Regionalism

Despite the value evident in Johnston's "new perspective," there continues to be a strong anxiety in Newfoundland about "accurately" representing the island, an anxiety that has not changed much from the post-Confederation efforts to preserve an "authentic" culture in the face of a threatening assimilation. The sense that the outport and its fishing culture is the true essence of Newfoundland continues, exacerbated by the fact that this culture has been seriously threatened by the cod moratorium and the resultant slow death of fishing communities. There remains an internal pressure to preserve what is imagined as Newfoundland's "real" culture, which leaves some Newfoundlanders wondering where they fit in. As renowned Newfoundland writer Lisa Moore admits, "sometimes I feel like a fake Newfoundlander. I have no connection to the fishery. I'm a townie. I've never been in a dory. My family have never fished. I don't even like salt cod" (Doran). This statement, from a born-and-bred Newfoundlander and one of its strongest literary voices, is a testament to the pressure exerted by this notion of the "real" Newfoundland, even for resident writers.

Johnston uses his imaginary homeland to play with such pressures and stereotypes, subverting the very concepts of authenticity and cultural representation. Sheilagh Fielding, Smallwood's fictional life-long love interest and the novel's other narrative voice, reflects on this idea of authentic Newfoundland identity in her journal as she sails away from Newfoundland on her way to New York. A band on the boat is playing Newfoundland music, traditional songs about fishers and sealers, but as a doctor's daughter Fielding admits, "I know little more about the lives of such people than I know about the lives of Eskimos" (150). She passes the time making up titles of "white-collar folksongs" that mimic the structure of real Newfoundland tunes: "'Journalist's Jig,' 'Lawyer's Lament,' 'Concerning an Architect Named Joe,' 'The Chartered Accountant from Harbour Le Cou,'" et cetera. She muses:

> I remember my uncle Patrick singing, upon request at Christmas time, "The Ryans and the Pittmans," sitting in his chair with his head thrown back, his face flushed from drinking, his eyes closed as though he could smell the salt spray, as though he were revelling in voyages past, despite the fact that, so terrified was he of the water, he could not be coaxed into going once around the pond in his row-boat at the cottage.
> "The Ryans and the Pittmans" is sung to the tune of "Farewell and Adieu to You, Spanish Ladies," and everyone joins in the chorus: "We'll rant and we'll roar like true Newfoundlanders, / We'll rant and we'll roar on deck and below." (150–51)

Fielding's satirical song titles point to the way in which Newfoundland culture is traditionally defined by the rural working class and counter such homogeneous perceptions of the place. Her memory of her uncle simultaneously exposes the ease with which Newfoundlanders perform and perpetuate stereotypes of cultural identity. The lyric "we'll rant and we'll roar like *true* Newfoundlanders"—sung to the tune of an appropriately transnational folk song—finally becomes ironic, as we are left questioning who the "true Newfoundlanders" are, and who is excluded from this vision.

While Fielding writes these words in 1920, they are easily applied to contemporary representations of the island. As Fuller, Overton, Chafe, and Wyile have all recognized, this idea that outport life and fishing culture form the essence of a unique society is often appropriated by tourist discourse; Newfoundland is still regarded by many outsiders—and is often marketed to outsiders—as a marginal, exotic space. Such exotic visions of Newfoundland are still perpetuated by Newfoundland and Labrador Tourism, which capitalizes on impressions of the province as a "mysterious land" of "unmoving authenticity" (NewfoundlandandLabrador.com). The home page of Newfoundland and Labrador Tourism declares, "Come to Newfoundland and Labrador, a place that stays the same, but changes you forever." In this vision, Newfoundland is a primitive, anachronistic space, embodied by majestic landscape and "friendly people," where "authenticity" is somehow rendered a tangible commodity. Despite the novel's predominantly urban setting, many reviewers and critics have read *Colony* with a similar picture in mind. In his defence of the novel for CBC's *Canada Reads*, Justin Trudeau describes the book as "a story of barren rock upon which nothing was expected to grow [...] least of all a people as tragically beautiful and noble as Newfoundlanders" (qtd. in Chafe, "Hey Buddy" 69). In his review for the *New York Times*, Luc Sante writes that "Newfoundland is more than just a maritime province of Canada. Like few places these days, it seems remote, even exotic in a chilly way, and it's likely you haven't been there. It therefore can assert itself as a setting to the point of claiming a character role: a vast, desolate mystery hovering just over our northeast flank" (BR6). This perspective is also evident in scholarly articles. For example, in a 2007 article in *Studies in Canadian Literature*, Owen D. Percy reads Johnston's Newfoundland as a "peripheral, dangerous, and foreign [space] on the hazy edges of mainstream Canada" (214). He adds that Newfoundland is a region "with little or no place in the master narratives and History of the nation" (214). For Trudeau, Percy, and Sante, Newfoundland is an exotic hinterland.

In this construction of Newfoundland as an exotic, marginal, rural, working-class space, both Newfoundland and its literature are "regional," in the word's traditional association with "provincialism, with a rural context, or with local-colour writing" (Wyile, Riegel, Overbye, and Perkins xi). As perhaps the Newfoundland writer best known outside of the province, Johnston, and his Newfoundland, are considered representative of a peripheral space. Alexander MacLeod astutely notes that "for the vast majority of *Colony*'s reviewers, especially those outside of Newfoundland, Johnston's novel is not so much a playful re-telling of a history they have probably never heard in its original form, as much as it is an almost naturalistic representation of a harsh physical environment they have probably never visited" (70). Yet MacLeod reinforces these naturalistic interpretations, ultimately arguing that Johnston's novel represents a "deterministic reading of geography" (77). Drawing on theories of Canadian regionalism, he contends that Johnston's narrative is fused to what Lisa Chalykoff calls a "'first solitude' interpretation of regionalist environmental determinism," whereby social space is interpreted as "impenetrably 'natural' or objectively 'real'" (MacLeod 74). Yet Johnston's distortion of Newfoundland's geography belies MacLeod's reading; Johnston's Newfoundland is emphatically *not* "real." Rather, *Colony* subverts first-solitude regionalism by destroying the idea that space can be "authentically" represented and by replacing geographically determined representations of Newfoundland with a self-consciously constructed imaginary homeland.

The critical reception of Johnston's work emphasizes the urgency of this subversive project, as he continues to be read for his exotic subject matter rather than his literary prowess. Indeed Wyile suggests that much of the current popularity of Atlantic Canadian literature stems from a touristic desire for a quaint backwater culture at the country's margins (*Anne* 23–24). In this sense, the regional occupies the same rhetorical space as the minority, as Others excluded from the mainstream and defined by homogeneous stereotypes. Gunew contends that "minority writers" are

> invariably confined to the issue of their "identity" even in a poststructuralist world of decentred subjectivity. They function as what Gayatri Spivak (1988) has termed the "native informant", with an unproblematically coherent subjectivity projected upon them. They are constructed as "insider" sources for "information-retrieval" rather than being deemed capable of postmodernist writing. In short, their ability to produce "textuality" or to play textual games is rarely countenanced. As well they are legitimated in large part by their "eye-witness" accounts of certain minority histories which also confine them to realist genres. (*Haunted* 72–73)

Johnston resists such minoritizing visions of Newfoundland as a marginal but knowable space with playful postmodernism. Even as critics attempt to appropriate his novel as representative of an exotic Canadian regionalism, Johnston plays with and upsets these labels, calling into question the very categories of region, nation, and colony. Indeed the plot of the novel largely centres on Smallwood's desire to "measure up to such a place" (552) and the irreconcilable contradictions between the idea of the Newfoundland nation, its lingering colonial status, and its impending Confederation with Canada.

One of the ways he achieves this subversion of regional labels is by refusing to fulfill the expectations of a regionalist reading. Janice Fiamengo points out that "regions are thought to be natural entities, distinguished by a dominant geographical feature and an associated industry or way of life: we think, for example, of the Atlantic region's geographic and economic links with the sea" (244). Johnston's emphasis on the land rather than the sea subverts this definition of the Atlantic, or more specifically, the Newfoundland region, replacing a geographic determinism with an awe-inspiring but ultimately unknown interior space. Noting that "virtually the whole population lived on the coast, as if ready to abandon ship at a moment's notice," Smallwood laments that "of the land, the great tract of possibility that lay behind them, beyond their own backyards, over the farthest hill that they could see from the windows of their houses, most Newfoundlanders knew next to nothing" (139–40). Smallwood's fascination with the land shifts the attention from the coast, literally the periphery of the continent, to an interior reimagined as the centre. As Smallwood stares at his island from a boat off the southern shore, he muses that "it was hard to believe Newfoundland was an island and not the edge of some continent, for it extended as far as the eye could see to east and west, the headlands showing no signs of attenuation; a massive assertion of land, sea's end, the outer limit of all the water in the world, a great, looming, sky-obliterating chunk of rock" (347). In this image the sea does not mark the edge, the margins of the land, but rather the reverse; the margins of the sea mark the beginning of a large and powerful mainland. Elsewhere, travelling by train through the interior, Smallwood imagines Newfoundland not as an island, but as "a landlocked country in the middle of an otherwise empty continent, a country hemmed in and cored by wilderness, and it is through this core that we are passing now, the unfoundland that will make us great some day" (141). Here, Newfoundland is once again imagined as the heartland, centre of an undiscovered hinterland ripe for exploration and exploitation.

Johnston's Newfoundland is, certainly, bound up with images of geography, but rather than an environmentally determined regionalism and an imposed marginality, Johnston uses his diasporic position to create an imaginary homeland that challenges the marginalizing regionalism through which Newfoundland literature is often read. He adopts what Fuller calls a "'doubled' mode of representation," shifting between a narrative voice directed at "insiders," and an "anthropological style of narration" that describes the city of St. John's, as well as cultural practices such as drying cod ("Strange" 42). According to Fuller, this doubled narration both appeals to the consumption of place promoted by tourism and subverts the idea that such a mediated experience could lead to "authentic" encounters. While for Fuller this self-awareness operates separately from questions about Johnston's own Newfoundland identity, I suggest that this subversion of authenticity self-consciously pre-empts conservative objections to his own authority as a diasporic Newfoundlander. Johnston forces us into a St. John's and a Newfoundland of his own making, a place that plays with whatever preconceived perceptions we may bring to the novel and that therefore stands as the perfect backdrop for a Joey Smallwood who is equally fictionalized. Even as readers like Sante and Trudeau make claims about the harshness of Johnston's Newfoundland landscape and its peripheral position in Canada's hinterland, Johnston highlights the constructed and shifting nature of place as a locus of identity. The first-solitude regionalism of geographic determinism does not leave any room for Johnston's displacement and the important impact that out-migration has had not only on Johnston's own work but also on the culture of Newfoundland in general.

Diaspora means that Johnston's Newfoundland is, in Rushdie's terms, a Newfoundland "of the mind" (10). But this is not the same "of the mind" as what Chalykoff calls "second-solitude regionalism," either, which sees regions as mental, metaphorical constructs separate from real geographies. Rather, Johnston's imaginary homeland is a mental construction based on the materiality of place and a deep personal connection to home. Chalykoff acknowledges that "the very meaningfulness of the term 'region' derives from its capacity to represent some kind of collectivity or identity," but adds that "literary regionalists must interrupt the tradition of utilizing the *assumption* of regional social cohesion as an uninterrogated premise for theorizing regional space and begin to utilize it as an open-ended and self-conscious hypothesis for future theorizations" (175; emphasis in original). I argue that theorizations of diaspora have a role to play in this more self-conscious, provisional revisioning of regionalism as it pertains to Newfoundland, as they contribute to the heterogeneity of regions as "socially-produced spatializations" (Chalykoff 175). For Johnston, a diasporic subjectivity produces an understanding of a collective Newfoundland identity centred on Newfoundland as homeland, rather than hinterland.

Come from Away
The concern of critics like Pierson is not just with Johnston's *ability* to represent the island accurately from away, but of his *responsibility* to represent it accurately to an outside audience. But charging writers with such a responsibility merely perpetuates the notion that "regional" writers are incapable of postmodernism. As we have seen, Johnston deliberately shirks this responsibility in order to subvert the (first-solitude) regionalist tendency to read marginal spaces as real, authentic, and homogeneous. As Johnston uses his imaginary homeland to actively resist the regionalist tendencies of many of his readers and their limited conceptions of place, he also resists notions of literary authority itself.

But this stance does raise important ethical questions about the representation of place. In his article on "Truth and Fiction" for *Newfoundland Studies*, Gordon Inglis also expresses what he admits is a conservative expectation that writers depicting real places "get it right" (69). Inglis's article references many writers whose careful research inspires "confidence" in the reader that the settings are reflected "correctly" (70). While Inglis does not mention the fact that Johnston lives in Toronto, he brings his critique of *The Colony of Unrequited Dreams* together with a critique of American Annie Proulx's widely successful novel *The Shipping News* (1993), which has also been extremely controversial in the province. The comparison is apt since both novels have been similarly criticized for inaccurately depicting Newfoundland. But the comparison also raises deeper questions about the identity of the author, since critiques of Proulx's novel often point out that she is an American. *The Shipping News* depicts a harsh and backward Newfoundland, rampant with incest and sexual abuse, whose characters' voices are peppered with archaic words and whose accents are ventriloquized in sometimes nearly indecipherable phonetic spellings. Tracy Whalen writes that critical responses to the novel, "whether they call for geographical, cultural, or linguistic change, speak of a search for the true, a desire for narrative felicity with actual experience or real culture in Newfoundland" (52). But they also raise the issue of cultural appropriation, pointing out not only the inauthenticity of Proulx's portrayal but her lack of authority since she is a "CFA" or "Come From Away." For people like Inglis and Pierson the charge of cultural appropriation is key to combatting a representation of Newfoundland and Newfoundlanders that many find offensive. But it is the representation itself, rather than her personal lack of cultural authority due to her American identity, that must be called into question. Otherwise the debate centres around Proulx's national identity, rather than the social and cultural implications of her representation. While the idea of cultural authenticity in this context has significant ethical import, then, it is also not always easily defined. As Gunew puts it, "in the struggle for minority rights and the battles over who controls representation there are those who take the position that only members of such minority groups have the authority, or at least moral right, to represent themselves. But who, institutionally speaking, decides the group membership and who interprets and legislates whether this authenticity has been achieved?" (*Haunted* 69). How does one *define* an "authentic" Newfoundlander in the first place? And more to the point: are *diasporic* Newfoundlanders insiders or outsiders?

Newfoundland poet and novelist Michael Crummey claims that when he was living in Kingston, Ontario, he felt like a "faux Newfoundlander" ("Being There"). Writing, he claims, was his way of feeling more connected to his homeland, but his return to St. John's has made his writing feel more "authentic." Crummey, then, understands the negative reaction to books like *The Shipping News*, explaining that "in some ways that feeling [of resentment] was generated by communities of people who knew their stories hadn't yet been told and were just finding their own voice. So having somebody from the outside come in and start telling those stories when they had their own storytellers who were just in the process of doing that was a loss for them" (Interview with Leo Furey). These concerns are reminiscent of the "appropriation of voice" debates of the 1990s, initiated by protests against the appropriation of the stories of aboriginal peoples and people "of colour" by white Canadian writers. But while Crummey understands this reaction and feels the pressure himself to write "authentically," he rejects the notion that place of residence or historical fact should determine the value of literary work. Rather, Crummey expresses his respect for *Colony*: "for me, the liberties that [Johnston] took there served the purpose of his speaking about Newfoundland. So the historical facts took second place to his idea of what Newfoundland was and how it worked" (Interview with Furey). As Crummey's comments suggest, the notion that geographical or historical accuracy is a measure of the "authenticity" of the writer impedes the writer's creative freedom. Crummey's return to Newfoundland is thus a personal choice rather than a moral mandate.

Johnston also recognizes the proprietary impulse behind critiques of *The Shipping News*, but believes that preventing outsiders from writing about a particular identity is a slippery slope that can become paralyzing ("Afterlife" 125). He prefers to judge Proulx's book, which he admires, on its artistic merits.[2] In his own work, then, Johnston not only plays with the knowability of place, he also subverts the idea of the writer as authority. As I will discuss in detail in the next chapter, Johnston constantly subverts the authority of the historiographer, rendering Judge D.W. Prowse, author of the mammoth *History of Newfoundland* (1895), a decaying elderly man suffering from dementia and obsessively revising his book and the mistakes that he has found in it since its publication. Dragland notes that Johnston "seems to be pre-empting some of his critics" (194) when he has Smallwood publicly claim that he does not "get" Fielding's ironic newspaper editorials and cannot understand "the popularity of a writer so given to 'romancing,' which in Newfoundland simply meant not talking or writing about things as they really were" (*Colony* 500). This metafictional moment also hints at the fact that Johnston himself is "romancing" throughout his novel, subverting the accuracy of history and geography, even as he takes part in the Newfoundland cultural tradition of the tall tale.

Johnston's 2006 novel, *The Custodian of Paradise*, which revives the character of Sheilagh Fielding, continues this project of subverting literary authority: in this case, his own. In an admittedly maddening fashion, the novel seems to clash with the facts and events of *Colony*. Johnston does not correct the "errors" of *Colony*, but rather compounds them. The plot centres around the notion that Dr. Fielding, the man who raised Sheilagh, is not her real father, a suspicion that obsesses both her and the doctor. Yet nothing of this important fact is even suggested in the first novel. Fielding writes a newspaper column under the byline "Fielding the Forger," which consists of satirical letters supposedly written by prominent local figures. Yet this persona is not mentioned in *Colony*, in which Fielding's satirical voice is heard in her column Field Day. *The Custodian of Paradise* is not as successful a novel as *Colony*; the novel's focus on Fielding's personal struggles with finding her true father and giving up her own children for adoption are drawn out, and seem to evacuate the character of the strength that made her so compelling when we first met her. Yet reading the two novels together emphasizes the deliberate manipulation of facts and chronology and the playful shirking of narrative fidelity that ultimately expose the fictionality of Johnston's place and his characters. Johnston self-consciously rejects, then, the tendency to privilege narrative authenticity and its concomitant policing of cultural borders. In this manner he implicitly subverts the tendency to read diasporic authors either with suspicion, on the one hand, or as delegates for an authentically rendered region, on the other; what he offers instead is a somewhat sly reclaiming of both a playfully imagined Newfoundland and his own identity as a Newfoundlander in diaspora.

Sea-Seeking Rivers
Johnston ends his novel with what at first appears to be a romantic assertion of the enduring power of geography on the body, as Fielding reflects:

> From a mind divesting itself of images, those of the land would be the last to go.
> We are a people on whose minds these images have been imprinted.
> We are a people in whose bodies old sea-seeking rivers roar with blood. (562)

Such an image can easily be read as a first-solitude regionalism that posits that "to exist within the region is to feel its essence, and thus to be part of a regional community" (Chalykoff 165). The essence of Newfoundland, it seems, runs through the Newfoundlander's very arteries. But Johnston's image concludes a novel that constantly upsets the authenticity of place, so that while the arteries may be sea-*seeking* rivers, they never quite get there; there is a sense of removal from the physical landscape, an unrequitedness, that brings the novel's tone of loss full circle. While Johnston's novel is often read for a regionalism that is seen as quintessentially Canadian, such readings distort the very subject of his book: Newfoundland's tumultuous and even suspicious entry into Confederation and the ongoing sense of distinct identity that is defined in *national* rather than regional terms. Turning our attention to the diasporic aspects of Newfoundland literature is one means of upsetting the clear lines drawn between the centre and the hinterland, and of challenging the essentialist representations of an unchanging, "authentic" Newfoundland culture. In Part IV, I return to this novel, examining how Johnston's imaginary homeland contributes to the construction of an Andersonian "imagined community" that addresses head-on the legacies of Confederation and the ongoing conflict of the province with the rest of Canada.

PART FOUR

IMAGINING THE NEWFOUNDLAND NATION

 **SIX**

"THIS IS THEIR COUNTRY NOW": DAVID FRENCH, CONFEDERATION, AND THE IMAGINED COMMUNITY

> Newfoundland is no artistic utopia. I know that. But I was struck almost as soon as I got here by how much of the nation remains, and I've come to see how persistently it's growing in a massive communal project of recovery and creation in which many people toil alone, some of them offshore.
>
> Both history and fiction are wanted to keep this paradoxical country of no country growing.[1]
>
> —Stan Dragland, "*The Colony of Unrequited Dreams*: Romancing History?"

Wayne Johnston's *The Colony of Unrequited Dreams* is just one example of a number of recent Newfoundland literary texts that take the island's history, and the story of Confederation in particular, as their subject. The moment of Confederation has often been represented in these works as what historian Jerry Bannister calls a "debilitating psychic wound" leading to "a type of post-traumatic stress disorder" (182). The loss brought about by Confederation is therefore similar to the loss brought about by out-migration, as both are frequently depicted with this tone of grief, as a rupture of identity and of connection with homeland. For Confederation-era migrants, then, this loss is a double wound.

In the work of David French, this double loss leads to the construction of Newfoundland as an "imagined community" that resists what is regarded as the assimilating influences of Canadian citizenship and identification. French, in his cycle of plays about a Newfoundland family in Toronto, creates an imagined community for diasporic imaginaries abroad and a second generation of Newfoundland migrants. French's narratives also reveal the usefulness of the concept of diaspora to understanding Newfoundland displacement, by highlighting the group identity that is still bound by nationalist feeling even after the possibility of the Newfoundland nation has been foreclosed.

The Diasporic Imaginary and the Preservation of Identity
In French's Mercer cycle, five plays originally produced by Toronto's Tarragon Theatre over a period of three decades, audiences encounter a family of Newfoundlanders relocated to Toronto. Two of these plays, *Salt-Water Moon* (1984) and *Soldier's Heart* (2001) take place prior to the migration, when Jacob Mercer and his wife-to-be, Mary Snow, are young. But the three remaining plays, *Leaving Home* (1972), *Of the Fields, Lately* (1973), and *1949* (1988), take place entirely in the Mercer family home in Toronto and set the personal trials of Jacob, Mary, their two sons Ben and Billy, and other members of their extended family and community against the broader cultural clashes of Newfoundland with the rest of Canada. In this chapter I focus on *1949*, which takes place over the three days leading up to Confederation, as this play in particular exhibits the crucial link for the Mercer family between Confederation and their own emigration. The personal family conflicts, while touching and genuine, can also be read as allegories for the relationship between Newfoundland and its new host country. *1949* has by far the biggest cast of the cycle, which comprises not only family members, but old acquaintances from back home and figures in the local Toronto community who together encompass many differing perspectives on the Confederation issue. *1949*, then, unlike the other four very intimate plays, is a play about community, and the permeability between the private and the public.

The Mercer family live and work among other displaced Newfoundlanders in Toronto, who together form an ethnic enclave, or in Vijay Mishra's terminology, a "diasporic imaginary." Mishra defines a "diasporic imaginary" as "any ethnic enclave in a nation-state that defines itself, consciously, unconsciously or because of the political self-interest of a racialized nation-state, as a group that lives in displacement" (423). The formation of such communities is a major aspect of diasporic subjectivity. The Mercer household is the centre of such a diasporic imaginary. Jacob's mother lives with the family, and Mary's sister Dot and her husband Wiff live down the street, representing the common pattern of "chain migration" whereby family members or friends follow each other to the new city, benefiting from a shared network of contacts and knowledge (Bella 2). The Mercers also board Ned, a young Newfoundlander, in their home. Jacob works in construction with other men from the same part of Newfoundland, continuing old friendships and rivalries. Within this enclave they share a manner of speaking, memories, traditions, and prejudices. Thus the adult Newfoundlanders are distinguished in the written script by the phonetic spellings of many words to indicate the Newfoundland accent, such as "t'ink" for "think," or "j'in" for "join," as well as grammatical idioms like a first-person pronoun with a third-person plural verb form, such as "I gets." From the moment these characters open their mouths they are distinguished from the Canadian characters like Doctor Hunter or the teacher, Miss Dunn; Ned's girlfriend, April, in fact mistakes Jacob's accent for Irish (*1949* 86). In their study of the term "Newfie," sociolinguists Ruth King and Sandra Clarke argue that Newfoundlanders constitute a "minority group" within Canada, in part distinguished linguistically (538). Even outside of their home province, then, the Mercers are audibly part of a distinct cultural group.

Although they have lived in Toronto for several years, and could not even vote in the referendum, the Mercers refer to Newfoundland and Newfoundlanders with the personal pronouns "us" and "we" and "ours." The distinct accent and references to "back home" establish the Mercer home as a kind of Newfoundland outpost, where the functioning of the household seems defined by its "Newfoundlandness." Many of the interactions with Canadian characters centre upon this cultural difference. Ned's argument with April derives from the fact that he lied about his origin, claiming to be Irish. Ben's conflict with the teacher Miss Dunn starts when she singles him out as a Newfoundlander, leading to cruel teasing from his classmates. Both the neighbour, Norman, and the family doctor arrive concerned that Rachel is wearing a black armband, never dreaming that she wears the sign of mourning not for a person but for her country. Rachel explains to Doctor Hunter, "I'm afraid you'd have to be a Newfoundlander, my son, to understand. It's not your fault you was born in Canada" (17). This light-hearted teasing reveals the insular quality of knowledge, experience, and identity within French's Newfoundland diaspora. Thus the ethnic enclave, and its interactions with the neighbours who live outside it, expose the cultural distinctiveness of Newfoundlanders, both as immigrants to Canada and as citizens of a province joining Confederation.

The family is initially divided on the Confederation issue; while Rachel expresses her grief over the outcome of the referendum, her son Jacob is pleased. His motivations for supporting Confederation are the same as his motivations for leaving home: his kids "never saw fresh milk or fresh fruit till they come here," and he points out that the outports "have the lowest standard of living of any place in the English-speaking world" (78). He therefore welcomes the social welfare that Confederation with Canada promises. "Why are there more of us, Wiff, living in New York City than live on the island?"

he asks. "Why did I bring my own family here if it wasn't to find work and a better life for my kids?" (78). But Rachel shames her son for his support of Confederation by comparing him to his father: "Oh, your father may not have had two cents to call his own, but by God, he knowed who he was. He'd never have put his mark on a ballot that gave away his birthright. The way some did last summer, just to get the baby bonuses and old age pensions" (44). Jacob's response that the impoverished people who voted for Confederation couldn't afford their own funerals does not faze Rachel, who compares the betrayal of the confederates to that of Judas Iscariot (44). Rachel's passionate arguments against Confederation are balanced by the logic of Jerome, an old acquaintance, now a journalist in St. John's who comes to the Mercer home to do a Confederation Day story on the family. Jerome backs up his anti-confederate sentiments with political facts: that the confederates lost on the first ballot, that they won the second ballot by only two percent, and the promise that Britain had made to restore responsible government—which was suspended in 1934 by the Amulree Royal Commission—once the island's finances returned to order. Jerome admits that the poverty of his homeland is dire, but he articulately expresses his concern over "what we're losing […] Like our sense of ourselves. The pride of an independent people" (78). The complexities of the issue are slowly teased out as Jerome and Jacob debate, with Jerome admitting that his rich father voted against Confederation to "keep his power," while Jerome voted against it to "keep our identity. It's the sort of issue that makes for strange bedfellows" (79). French does not allow his audience to take one side or the other easily, as the debate seems to fall into a conflict between philosophical issues of identity and practical economic concerns. Jerome, as the non-migrant, represents loyalty to cultural and national identity. For Jacob, the pragmatist, Confederation and out-migration go hand in hand, as both are seen as paths to a better life for his family. Individual immigration to Canada, then, is a small-scale version of Newfoundland joining the Canadian federation.

But French deftly reveals that migration also leads to alienation and assimilation. Ben's troubles at school originate when his teacher, in anticipation of Confederation, asks him to point out on a map the place where he was born. He is unable to do so, having left when he was just six years old. But Ben's inability to point to the place where he was born is a sign of both the erosion of identity in the second generation and of impending assimilation. Rachel argues that "he should know where he comes from and be proud of it" (45). Jacob responds by showing Ben his birthplace in an atlas. But there is a sense that the locating of place on a page cannot make up for his overall loss of identity. Billy, the younger of the boys, is excited to go to school on Thursday because he will get a medallion in honour of Confederation and his school will sing "The Ode to Newfoundland." But when asked by his grandmother, Billy does not know the meaning or significance of the song, nor the words (32). As members of the second generation of the Newfoundland diaspora and the first generation of Newfoundland Confederation, Billy and Ben are warning signs of a potential loss of identity. Confederation and diaspora are thus dual forces of assimilation; French's drama reveals that Newfoundland is not simply another province of Canada, but a failed nation with a distinct culture. The transition from citizen of the Dominion of Newfoundland to citizen of Canada, whether effected by Confederation or by diaspora, is not smooth, but rather a moment of rupture and loss. This idea of citizenship-as-loss gestures towards Lily Cho's concept of "diasporic citizenship," a term whose inherent "dissonance" references "the losses which enable citizenship" ("Diasporic" 108). While Newfoundlanders may not have experienced the same racialized violence as the Asian and African diasporas to which Cho refers, the concept is useful here in that it simultaneously identifies the loss of home involved in becoming Canadian and indicates that for these new Canadians "citizenship" is a qualified term. For Cho, embracing the concept of diaspora and its attendant emphasis on cultural memory "allows us to be up against citizenship, to embrace it even as we hold it at some distance, to recognize it as both disabling and enabling" (108). For French's characters, diasporic memory means that their new Canadian citizenship is provisional, in ways that are both productively resistant to cultural assimilation and psychologically and emotionally damaging.

The adult characters encounter ignorance and resentment in their new home of Toronto. Ned's girlfriend's mother, not knowing where Ned is from, laments the joining of the tenth province: "'Isn't it awful,' she said, 'the expense that Newfoundland will bring on the Canadian taxpayers?'" (88). Jacob meets a man in a bar, who asks where he is from. When Jacob replies "Newfoundland," the man asks him if he knows an O'Leary from Red Rocks. Jacob's reply is impatient: "'For Christ's sake, man,' I said, 'Newfoundland is the sixteenth largest island in the world with a coastline of six t'ousand miles. You might as well ask me if I knows Norma Sludge from Dildo.' The damn fool!" (39). These moments serve to bolster what French, in an early interview with Peter Neary, identifies as the "feelings of inferiority" (27) of this generation of immigrant Newfoundlanders. All of these incidents in *1949*, as precursors to the Confederation moment, cast a tone of foreboding upon the upcoming union. The prejudice and ignorance that these immigrant Newfoundlanders have felt on a personal level foreshadow what will become an uneasy transition from nation to province of Canada.

But these incidents are rather mild compared to Ben's experiences at school. One of Ben's classmates recalls the sign at Sunnyside Swimming Pool during the recent World War that said "No dogs or Jews allowed," and adds that "the only mistake they made [...] was not adding Newfies to the list" (61). This shocking abuse stands out for its disturbing undertones of violence. In this moment the audience is prevented from regarding Newfoundlanders as easy Canadians or as possessing white privilege. Rather, it is confronted head-on with Newfoundland's difference, defined here in almost racial terms. Ironically, this same classmate is called a DP and a Wop by other kids. Jacob explains to his son that "a Wop is someone without papers. A DP is a displaced person. There was at least a million people like that in Europe after the War. Poles. Estonians. Jews. People like that. [...] You'd see them at Union Station, with tickets in their lapels. The Jewish kids had tickets around their necks, on a string with a lead seal" (61). This description of the hardship of displacement and ethnic otherness prompts Ben to ask, "Which were we, Dad? DPs or Wops?" (61). The question evokes Jacob's pride, and he declares, "We come from Britain's oldest colony. Four hundred and eighty-one years old" (62). Jacob, here, attempts to align Newfoundland with Britain in what Daniel Coleman has termed the project of "white civility." Coleman argues that in colonial Canada "non-English Celts used Britishness to infiltrate colonial privilege" (87).[2] In Jacob's rendering, the island is not just a British colony, but its "oldest," a fine example of how the "trials of colonial settlement were a kind of crucible that refined the civility inherited from Britain" (Coleman 24). Newfoundland, then, both is aligned with "pan-ethnic British cooperation" (Coleman 19) and exceeds "British Britishness" (24) through the hard work of building a colony and several centuries of progress. This scene between Jacob and his son thus highlights Jacob's ethnic insecurities; he seems to protest too much as he uncomfortably asserts his superiority over other European immigrants. Despite Jacob's claims to white civility and his laughter at the child's innocence, Ben's question reveals the child's sense of inferiority or alienation as an immigrant to Canada. For young Ben, this prejudice is internalized. Ned finally reveals to Jacob the full extent of what happened between Ben and his classmate: "Junior was sitting on his chest, screaming, 'You're just a Newfie, Mercer! Say it! Say it!' and Ben was screaming back, 'I'm not a Newfie! I'm not! I'm not a fucking Newfie!' [...] Maybe it wasn't what you thought, Jacob. Maybe it wasn't that Junior insulted Newfoundlanders. Maybe Ben was just upset that Junior called him one" (91). Ned makes the connection between Confederation and the alienation of out-migration clear when he asks Jacob, "What kind of pride are you teaching [Ben]? What the hell does Ben know about Newfoundland except that his own father can't wait to give it away?" (91). This revelation becomes a moment of crisis for Ben's father. For the Mercer family, the condition of diaspora lays bare the prejudice directed by Canadians against Newfoundland in general; this moment of violence not only exposes immigrant alienation, but also the alienation of Newfoundland as a whole as it is metaphorically displaced into Canada, and the failure of Newfoundlanders' claims to white civility.

The event leads Jacob to completely reverse his opinion of Confederation, and to join his mother in donning the "trappings of mourning" in the hours leading up to the union. Mary remains in favour of Confederation and for the sake of the kids opposes her husband's theatrics: "This is their country now, Jacob, their new home, and it's a little late in the day to be draping a black flag on the porch for some place they hardly even remembers. At their age they just wants to fit in." Jacob's response completely contradicts his earlier comments about their British citizenship: "It's not right to make them feel ashamed, either. Oh, they may not have come here with tags on their necks, but they'm no different than any other immigrants" (120). The contradiction is humorous and adds to Jacob's construction as a comically unreliable and melodramatic character, but it also emphasizes the extreme impact that Ben's fight at school has had on Jacob and his sense of self. The statement also seems closer to the truth, given the experiences of not only Ben, but Ned, and Jacob himself. Mary's response is cool: "I wants them to have what we never had, a chance in life. Isn't that why we came here?... Remember what I told that Immigration man who almost turned us back? 'If you sends us home on the next boat,' I said, 'I'll take the kids and leap overboard'" (120; ellipsis in original). Mary's response confirms their immigrant status but also prevents the audience from reading the play as a clear protest against Confederation. Like Jacob in the first half of the play, Mary's motivations for immigrating and her motivations for supporting Confederation are the same and cannot be separated in her mind. She sees both Confederation and migration as equivalent steps towards the better life that Canadian citizenship can provide, with more employment opportunities and economic stability.

The upcoming union between Newfoundland and Canada is mirrored by a proliferation of personal unions in the play: love is sprouting everywhere, as Jerome and Grace decide to marry, as Ned and April's relationship becomes more serious, and as chemistry even develops between the elderly neighbour Norman and the teacher, Miss Dunn. But the trope of relationships and marriage in *1949* does not just represent love and union, it also involves conflict, doubt, and sacrifice. While Mary does not realize it, her choice to marry Jacob echoes Jerome and Rachel's reasons for rejecting Confederation. One of the play's subplots is the tension arising from the fact that Jerome is an old flame of Mary's; Jacob in fact convinced her to break off her engagement with Jerome to marry him instead, even though Jerome came from a rich merchant family.[3] Jerome's return makes Mary nervous, Jacob and Grace jealous, and Jerome vulnerable as he asks her after all this time if she made the right choice. Mary's powerful speech to her son about why she married his father is informative:

> What do you suppose I saw in that man there, Ben? From the moment I decided to marry him I knowed there'd be no sable coats in my future. No expensive scotch whiskey in silver boxes. Those dreams belonged to another time... No, what I saw in your father from the first is what made him special. You see, I recognized that no odds what that man would always be there for me. Always be there for me and my kids. He'd sooner die first. [...] It takes courage to build a life, Ben. The courage to keep on against all the odds. And in the long run it may be the greatest courage of all. (163–64)

Mary's decision to marry a man for love and dependability rather than comfort echoes her own decision to do what she feels is best for her children, namely to sacrifice her national identity for diasporic citizenship, for a new home in a foreign country and the promise of better economic opportunities. While Jerome accuses her of choosing comfort over identity in the Confederation question, her choice to marry Jacob over him belies, or at least complicates, this assessment.

Wiff and Dot's marriage is in crisis throughout the play. Dot has moved out of the house and in with her sister's family, because Wiff refuses to take a fertility test. In the end we discover that Wiff had the test long ago but has kept it from Dot because his healthy result means that she is the one unable to bear children. Eventually we discover that this is likely because while Wiff was overseas in the war, Dot had an affair, became pregnant, and had an abortion. Wiff has always known this secret, making the depth of his sacrifice to protect his wife more profound. In his analysis of the Mercer cycle, Konrad Gross argues that the separation and reconciliation of Wiff and Dot "could be translated into a commentary on the relationship between Canada and Newfoundland" (261), since the couple stands on opposing sides of the Confederation issue. In the final scene, the reconciled pair dance a tango, and as Gross effectively argues, the scene takes on political overtones: "Now to dance the tango, Wiff, you have to keep this distance between us. See?... That means we don't ever get any farther apart than this. Or any closer" (*1949* 173, ellipsis in original). Gross argues that the distance maintained between them in the dance can "be read as a comment on the future relationship between Canada and the new province, which despite the union will be able to retain her regional distinctness" (262). But what Gross does not consider is that this union is barren. The dance freezes at the stroke of midnight, and the radio announces the King's Confederation message: "May the union that is now complete continue, under God's guidance, to grow in strength, prosperity, and happiness, and may it bring new benefits to its people from sea to sea" (174). The tableau of the dancers, narrated with the phrase "the union that is now complete," makes the symbolism of a reserved distance between the couple clear, and the audience is invited to consider Dot's infertility against the wish for growth and "new benefits" (174). The mistakes of the past may be forgiven, but they cannot be undone. The action "unfreezes, and the dance goes on," but it is a dance tinged with loss and doubt about the future. While the action in this scene is clearly allegorical, the national layer does not overshadow the literal layer that develops over the course of the play, the human pain of the couple's infertility and the strain on their marriage. The play does not reduce the relationships to a superficial allegory, but rather weaves together the intimate lives of this community of Newfoundlanders with the future of their nation.

"The Most Beautiful Story": Art and the Preservation of Nation
Amidst this loss and doubt, literary expression is the remaining hope for Newfoundland identity. Ned is an aspiring writer, but he begins the play having just had another story rejected. Simultaneously, Ned's relationship with April seems over when April discovers that he has been lying to her about his origins, pretending to be an Irishman instead of a Newfoundlander. His ability to write becomes intertwined with his vexed identity, as April confronts him over his deceit:

> APRIL: You think James Joyce ever denied his race? Or Yeats? Or any of those other writers you admire?
>
> NED: I don't deny what I am, damnit.
>
> APRIL: I think you do. I've never read your stories, Ned, but I'll bet there's not a trace of your homeland in a single one.
>
> NED: Listen, I've lived in this city now for four years. And if I choose to write about it, that's my business.
>
> APRIL: Keep telling yourself that, Ned. It may be why your stories never get published. [...] Joyce lived in Paris most of his life, Ned. Is that where he chose to set *Ulysses*? (89)

April's criticism leads Ned to write an autobiographical story, set in Conception Bay, "about how a young boy comes to be ashamed of his father. How he wants him to be like the American who stole his mother." He tells her, "maybe it'll help you understand me" (135). Ned's revelation that he is ashamed of his father is strikingly similar to the action in French's earlier play, *Of the Fields, Lately*, which is set twelve years later, in 1961. An adult Ben comes home to Toronto from the West and reflects on how he was always ashamed of his father, a shame that causes an irreparable rift between them. Both sons experience what Eve Kosofsky Sedgwick calls the "double movement shame makes" (37), as they both uncomfortably identify with the other, the father, and wish to separate themselves from him. In both relationships, it is the father's Newfoundlandness that is the source of shame: for Ned, his father cannot live up to the American rival; for Ben, the rift begins when Jacob shows up to his baseball game: "Twelve years old, and ashamed of my old man. Ashamed of his dialect, his dirty overalls, his bruised fingers with the fingernails lined with dirt, his teeth yellow as old ivory. Most of all, his lunchpail, that symbol of the working man" (*Of the Fields* 1–2). For Ben, his father's dialect, which marks him as a Newfoundlander, is intertwined with his working-class immigrant status, and Ben's desire to fit in with his Toronto friends seems to necessitate the repudiation of his family origins. For Ben and Jacob, the damage is irreparable, and at the end of *Of the Fields* Jacob dies, with "the wall" between them still there (112). In *1949*, however, Ned confronts, and perhaps even overcomes, his shame of both his father and his identity by addressing it through his art. His new story allows him to reconcile with April, who tells him "it's the most beautiful story I've read in years" (170). For Ned and April, reconciliation means the union of a Newfoundlander and a Canadian, but it is only possible once Ned comes to terms with, and celebrates, his own identity.

Thus at the moment that the nation of Newfoundland is dying, Ned's story becomes a way of reimagining both his own identity and his homeland at large, asserting the ongoing cultural identity of the "diasporic imaginary." Mishra writes that "diasporas construct homelands in ways that are very different from people of the homelands themselves. [...] At the same time the nation-state as an 'imagined community' needs diasporas to remind it of what the idea of homeland is" (424). Mishra's argument thus connects the "diasporic imaginary" with the larger "imagined community" of the homeland, suggesting that the diaspora not only imagines its own connections within and across communities in displacement, it also constructs itself as an extension of an imagined homeland. Diasporas, then, like nations, are "imagined" because their members do not know most of their fellow members, yet "in the minds of each lives the image of their communion" (Anderson, *Imagined* 6), and they are "communities" because regardless of the inequalities that may prevail within them, they are perceived as possessing "a deep horizontal comradeship" (7) both with and within the homeland. Thus Ien Ang argues that "the transnationalism of diaspora is actually proto-nationalist in its outlook, because no matter how global its reach, its imaginary orbit is demarcated ultimately by the closure effected by the category of the diasporic identity itself" ("Together" 144). Ang considers this proto-nationalist quality to be the limitation of diaspora in an increasingly globalized world (153), but in a situation where the nation no longer exists as a political reality—where it exists *only* in the imagination—diasporic literature can strategically construct alternative or subversive imagined national identities. In his more recent book *The Spectre of Comparisons* (1998), Anderson identifies the connection between the diaspora and the homeland as "long-distance nationalism" and is similarly wary of the phenomenon's potential for violence and extremism (74). He warns, in his chapter for Pheng Cheah and Bruce Robbins's *Cosmopolitics* (1998), that the "'diasporic' collective subjectivities that are imagined, census-fashion, as bounded series" problematically lead to "identitarian" conceptions of ethnicity, with serious "essentialist implications" (130–31). But while there is potential here for essentialist and violent ethnicization, long-distance nationalism is not, as Anderson admits, inherently extremist. Rather, the term is useful for bridging the concept of diaspora to the imagined community, remembering that the nation can be just as significantly "imagined" from a position of displacement as it can from within. For diasporic Newfoundlanders, reconstructing the homeland as an imagined community is a means of combatting the threat of assimilation and the persistent "feelings of inferiority," as French puts it ("Many Coloured" 27). It is a means of strategically preserving and celebrating a sense of identity and community within a sometimes hostile host environment.

The concept of the "imagined community," then, articulates the overlap between the ideological construction of nations and of diasporas. Anderson argues that print media are key to the development of the "imagined community"; the newspaper and the novel play important roles in allowing their readers to imagine a community of fellow readers in "homogeneous, empty time" (*Imagined* 24). The experience of simultaneous consumption is perhaps even more profoundly felt in theatre performances, in which the audience is acutely aware of the presence of other audience members, viewing and hearing the same performance at the same time.[4] Jonathan Culler argues that it is not the content of the text (or performance) itself, but the imagined communal act of its consumption that creates this community:

> The power of Anderson's thesis about the novel is that it makes it a formal condition of imagining the nation—a structural condition of possibility. Critics, who are interested in the plots, themes, and imaginative worlds of particular novels, have tended to transform that thesis into a claim about the way some novels, by their contents, help to encourage,

shape, justify, or legitimate the nation—a different claim, though one of considerable interest. The fact that Anderson's own examples involve some slippage from one claim to the other helps to explain the critical reception but does not excuse it. (48)

Culler argues that the difference between these claims must be maintained for the sake of "theoretical rigour" and the force of the argument, since the argument that "the novel, through its representations of nationhood, made the nation," places us on "shaky ground" (49). But acknowledging the slippage that occurs in Anderson's work, and the potential for "shakiness," I argue that in the case of Newfoundland, where the nation exists *only* in the imagination, Anderson's term is useful for considering the way in which the content of literary texts, and performances, *re*-construct the nation in the minds of its readers. Ned's story also performs the continued imagining of a community that has lost its opportunity to achieve political status as a nation and, should it be published, will connect its readers in a communal act of imagining, regardless of whether they identify as insiders or outsiders. In other words, it is not the act of reading alone here that could form the Newfoundland imagined community, but rather the act of reading about Newfoundland as a distinct, if troublesome, identity.

Precarious Belonging

Ned and the Mercer family have a key role to play on the front lines as Newfoundland begins to negotiate its own Canadianness. In her discussion of diasporic narratives, Sneja Gunew credits Anderson as she suggests that

> it may be time to consider the role of the writer as inventor of community where community is conceived not in the sense of the nostalgic return to the past and a lost place but as the impulse forward, the potential carried by the seeding of diaspora in hybridity. [...] The attempt here is to analyse the components and strategies of a kind of belonging that has not yet been established which [...] is assembled precariously out of the shards of individual lives and their "imagined relations" to genealogies (private histories) and public events, that is, global or national histories. (*Haunted* 109)

In *1949*, and in the two plays that catch up with the family several years later, we see the Mercers struggling to resolve their imagined diasporic community with the fact that their homeland is now also a part of Canada. By the late 1950s, when *Leaving Home* is set, Jacob is able to joke about his identity, which could be read as a coping mechanism for this ongoing struggle: "Harold, there's only two kinds of people in this world—Newfies and them that wishes they was. [...] Why else would Canada have j'ined us in '49?" (62). The joke that Canada joined Newfoundland, rather than the other way around, suggests a continuing national pride even as it pokes fun at his homeland's lowly status. It indicates the importance that his place of origin continues to have to his identity, and his diasporic citizenship. We discover in *Of the Fields, Lately* that young Ben, as a member of the next generation, is incapable of this "precarious" kind of belonging, as Gunew puts it. But where Ben eventually fails, we may hope that with his short story Ned has found a way to reconcile his ancestry with a new hybrid identity.

Ronald Rompkey also uses Anderson's term in reference to Newfoundland literature when he writes that "throughout the world, new political transformations, especially newly independent colonies, have found ways of symbolizing identity. A similar process has occurred for the past fifty years in Canada's newest province" ("Colonial" n. pag.). Where other post-colonies become "imagined communities" as independent nations, Rompkey asserts that Newfoundland's status as an "imagined community" is driven by its rebirth as a Canadian province.[5] I argue that Newfoundland literature's search for such "new ways of symbolizing identity" is motivated by the post-Confederation desire to preserve the nation in the imagination and to combat the ongoing effects of diaspora. While out-migration lays bare the passions and prejudices that accompany Confederation, out-migration itself clearly does not mean the renunciation of nation or identity. In *1949*, Jerome's last words to the family express this sentiment: "a country isn't just contained within its borders, Mary. It's contained within its people. It's what makes us special in our own eyes, and in the eyes of the world. Losing that sense of who we are is a high price to pay for comfort" (167). Even as Jerome laments the loss of identity that he fears accompanies Confederation, he privileges personal identification as the means of preserving the idea of the country. As he claims that "a country isn't just contained within its borders," he acknowledges the role that the diasporic imaginary has to play in constructing the country as an imagined community. The implication of Jerome's words, then, is that if Newfoundlanders are able to maintain that "sense of who we are" in spite of Confederation and diaspora, the "country" will live on as an imagined construct.

○●○●○●○ SEVEN

WRITING THE "OLD LOST LAND": JOHNSTON PART TWO

A more explicit privileging of art as the locus of the imagined community of Newfoundland occurs in Wayne Johnston's work. Here, as in French's play, diaspora and Confederation are often imagined as simultaneous, literal ruptures. But diaspora and Confederation are also often metaphorically intertwined, as both involve the loss of the Newfoundland nation and the threat of Canadian assimilation. Diaspora can also be, as we saw in Chapter 4, a useful authorial position from which to reimagine the Newfoundland nation. Johnston's *The Colony of Unrequited Dreams* and his memoir, *Baltimore's Mansion*, both use the distance of diaspora to reconstruct the nation of Newfoundland as it "might have been" were it not for the traumatic ruptures of Confederation. Each text uses the tropes of landscape and historiography to resist the assimilating influences of Canadian citizenship and displacement and to question historical narratives that consider Confederation the natural consummation of an *a mare usque ad mare* vision of Canadian unity.

Baltimore's Mansion and Newfoundland's "Grievous Wound"

Johnston's family memoir, *Baltimore's Mansion*, reflects on his family's Newfoundland identity, both before and after Confederation. The memoir centres around the relationships between three generations of Johnston men: Wayne, Wayne's father, Arthur, and Arthur's father, Charlie. Johnston is focused on unravelling the mystery of the falling-out that Arthur and Charlie had around the time of the referendum and Arthur's departure for the mainland. Though Johnston does not know why, he senses that this mystery is central to understanding what Confederation has meant for his family.

Throughout the memoir, the extreme passion and melancholy that the Johnstons feel both at the moment of Confederation and for decades afterward is conveyed. Johnston remembers one startling outburst from his father: "'My God Wayne,' he said once, his voice suddenly breaking with emotion. 'What a country we could have been. What a country we were one time'" (166). Johnston's aunt and uncle leave the room whenever "O Canada" is played, protesting against this symbol of a new adoptive citizenship. The extended family repeatedly and ritualistically mourn their country with evening-long performances during which Arthur rants about the conspiracy surrounding the referendum and the treacherous "closet confederates," Uncle Harold tearfully recites "The Lament for Newfoundland," and the whole family sing "The Ode to Newfoundland" (58–68). For these Newfoundlanders, the loss of the nation is a "grievous wound" (13), "something that had been done to us" (65). It represents an affront to Newfoundland identity and the termination of future possibility. The loss of the nation is most vividly symbolized by the death of Johnston's grandfather, Charlie: "For my father, as for all the Johnstons, it was not 'immediately before the expiration of March 31, 1949,' as set out in the Terms of Union, but with Charlie's passing that the old Newfoundland ceased to be" (202). Thus the Confederation moment is not simply a transferral from dominion status to provincial status, but is rather rendered as a death, a traumatic and irresolvable passing of both the country and the past. Johnston even suggests that Confederation was the cause of Charlie's death: "He had fretted himself to death as the countdown to Confederation proceeded, each day changing on a schoolroom slate that he hung on the wall in the kitchen the number of days left in the life of Newfoundland. Charlie died on January 14, 1949, the day after erasing the number 77 and hours after writing the number 76 on the slate" (200). Charlie's death and Confederation are entwined as parts of the same grief. For the Johnston family, Charlie's death is not so much an allegory for the loss of the nation as a metonym, a highly personal manifestation of a larger national mourning.

If, for the Johnstons, the Confederation moment is marked by the death of Charlie, it is even more so for Arthur, Charlie's son, who is away in Canada when both the death and Confederation Day occur. Johnston surmises that the last time Arthur and Charlie see each other becomes a traumatic memory for Arthur:

> It was to Canada that my father was going, to Canada at this of all times, the country he esteemed no more highly than Charlie did, but he had no choice, there being no college at that time in Newfoundland. To Canada, which Newfoundland would become part of while he was away. It must have seemed to Charlie like a betrayal. And when his father died while he was in Canada, how must my father have

felt? Somehow to blame perhaps. Against all assurances to the contrary—and there must have been many—somehow to blame. (201–02)

The death of Charlie and the death of the nation are conflated for all the Johnstons, but for Arthur, since both events occur while he is in Nova Scotia, the losses are not only conflated but compounded by the pain of diaspora. Arthur does not even have the money to return for his father's burial. When he does finally return, both the nation and his father are gone, and the "lifelessness" of his father's forge seems to embody the profound loss and change brought about by Confederation (251). The physical distance between Arthur and his home when both deaths occur exacerbates this sense of loss and contributes to a feeling of guilt that his physical abandonment of his father and his country has somehow led to their demise.

Diaspora and Confederation are coupled throughout the memoir. Johnston's Uncle Dennis's tentative contributions to his family's anti-confederate rituals are barely tolerated, for "he had gone away to Canada—as the Canadian mainland was still referred to by members of my family, though we had been Canadians for twenty years—and it had taken him seventeen years to see the error of his ways" (56). Dennis in fact returns in 1966, Newfoundland's "Come Home Year," a campaign orchestrated by Premier Joey Smallwood to celebrate the completion of the Trans-Canada Highway across the island and to encourage the tourism industry. Come Home Year saw the return of thousands of migrants, some for short visits, others permanently. But its association with Smallwood's industrialization schemes, upcoming Canadian centennial celebrations, and the completion of the nation-wide highway, all link Come Home Year with confederate complicity and, ironically, Canadian assimilation. Johnston observes that "these Newfoundlanders had been told by relatives or had read in ads placed in mainland newspapers that they were coming home to a new Newfoundland, the post-Confederation Newfoundland so different from the one they had left that they would hardly recognize it. They were told that once they saw that Newfoundland no longer lagged behind the rest of the world, they would want to stay for good" (52). For some, Come Home Year was an opportunity to assert the importance of a post-Confederation Newfoundland identity, to reinforce cultural ties across the diaspora. Arthur Scammell's commissioned promotional song, "A Newfoundland Come Home Song," expresses this sentiment that "distance may part us but never divide." The song assures returnees that:

> we are proud that you came—
> Some things have changed but the folks are the same. (115)

The lines gently allude to Confederation and the many changes of the 1950s and '60s, but assert that despite these changes a Newfoundland culture or identity remains constant—"the folks are the same." The sentimental optimism of the song effectively evoked nostalgia in many of the island's lost sons and daughters. But Johnston's take on the event is cynical. He writes, "it was a kind of amnesty, as if, on behalf of their relatives who could not bring themselves to do it, the government had declared to prodigal sons and daughters who had gone to the mainland to find work that all was forgiven, there were no hard feelings" (51). In *Baltimore's Mansion*, then, migration to the mainland is regarded as a kind of betrayal, a new way of voting for Canada even when it takes place following Confederation. Out-migration is perceived as complicit with the confederate cause, and by extension, with the foreclosure of Newfoundland identity. As a result, a full return is never possible, for former migrants are marked as outsiders.

Diaspora not only exacerbates the loss and guilt of Confederation, but also problematizes the citizenship that is a central part of identity. For the Johnston family, identity and citizenship are still thought of in pre-confederate terms, so that the label "Canadian" is synonymous with "outsider," even two decades after Confederation. But who qualifies as an outsider shifts; the layers of belonging and the factions of identity are complex and often self-contradictory. When Arthur is let go from his research position at the government's experimental farm, he is hired by the Department of Fisheries—the only viable career path in Newfoundland for a man with a degree in agriculture. Ironically, he is made a federal fisheries inspector and travels around the province to various fish plants. When he attempts to shut down a plant at a small community on the southern shore, which "reeks of fish gone or going bad" (152), he is met with extreme hostility: "In the shouting he makes out the words 'townies,' 'traitors' and 'Canadians.' There is no contradiction for these people, despite having voted for Confederation, denouncing feds as 'Canadians.' By Canadian, they do not mean confederate, they simply mean outsider, a kind of hyper-townie" (155). Johnston points out that for many outport Newfoundlanders in isolated communities, who had never seen Canada and knew nothing about it, a vote for Confederation was simply a vote for improved social programs, and did not change their perception of their own identity or citizenship. They see "Canadians" as interlopers who may have brought social programs but who also don't understand their way of life and attempt to interfere with their livelihood. For them, the terms "Newfoundlander" or "Canadian" have nothing to do with political citizenship but are entirely concerned with personal demarcations of identity.

But for those who, like Arthur, had already left Newfoundland or who were going to leave, diaspora highlights the profound change and loss associated with Confederation. The individual alienation that the diasporic Newfoundlander feels in mainland Canada reflects the larger alienation of the island within the Canadian state. For Arthur, this alienation is felt as a kind of physical trauma, when "at college in Truro, Nova Scotia, on April 1, 1949, induction day, the day Newfoundland joined Confederation, my father was set upon by a group of his mainland friends who hoisted him on their shoulders and, ignoring his protests that he would always be a Newfoundlander and the tears streaming down his face, carried him around the campus shouting, 'Three cheers for the new Canadian!'" (199). The Canadians' blindness to his distress, the physical restraint, and the forcible application of a new identity despite his contrary self-identification, mirrors what many Newfoundlanders regarded as the forcible co-option of the island as a whole by a colonizing nation that had "rigged the referendum" (56). While Arthur returns to Newfoundland, years after Confederation he still regards himself as "a man without a country" (176). The shift from citizen of Newfoundland to citizen of Canada is felt not merely as a change in political labels but as a kind of displacement from the nation of origin. Indeed when Arthur returns from the mainland it seems as though "all of Newfoundland had been resettled in his absence, its destiny as profoundly changed as if it had been floated on a raft across the Gulf" (252). Confederation is imagined as a physical dislocation.

At another point in the narrative, this idea that Confederation mimics displacement is literalized: Johnston describes the Newfoundland expatriates and travellers who left their country before the referendum with Newfoundland passports that did not expire until 1954, only to find themselves "itinerant citizens of a country that, since they saw it last, had ceased to be." He continues:

> In no sense were these people anything but Newfoundlanders until the first time they set foot on "native" soil, or until their five years were up. There were supposed to be some who neither came back home nor acquired new passports from the Canadian embassies in their countries of residence. Instead, they stayed away in protest, in self-exile from the country that now occupied their own. I loved the idea of these Newfoundlanders in the States, in England, Germany or France blending in among foreigners, still carrying their outdated passports. Citizens of no country, staging their futile, furtive, solitary protests that were at once so grand and so absurd. I wasn't even sure if there were such people, or if it was possible for anyone to live that way for long without detection. But it was a good story. (228)

For these "itinerant citizens," diaspora means the possibility of hanging on to citizenship as a form of imagined community, "imagined" not only because in the minds of each citizen "lives the image of their communion" (Anderson, *Imagined* 6), but also because of their nation's imaginariness, its non-existence.

A Citizen of Story

This idea of "a good story" is the central theme of Johnston's memoir; it even seems to shape life itself. As Johnston describes meeting his father in the yard the night before he is to go to the mainland for university, for example, he reveals both the constructedness of his story and a sense of inevitability about it. The circumstances of the moment are similar to those of when Charlie revealed his own secret to Arthur, the night before Arthur left for college:

> I know, before he begins to speak, that he is going to tell me. Everything favours it. If he does not tell me now he never will. I am leaving. He knows I plan to be a writer. He knows, or hopes, that someday I will write about him. He cannot get the story straight in his mind and believes that when I tell it he will understand it better.
>
> I do not know it yet, but there is a symmetry here that it would be pointless for us to resist. The time of the year is the same, early September, which in Newfoundland means early fall. Even the time of day is the same, almost twilight. (196)

Johnston's meta-memoir here points to the importance of story as a means of making sense of his family's lives. In an interview with *Quill & Quire*, Johnston makes the imagined quality of place in his narrative explicit: "I wanted to describe Ferryland [the outport where his father grew up] as a place of the mind—of my father's mind and of my own. [...] All the landmarks in Ferryland are capitalized, for example. Even if we're talking about the Pool, it's capitalized because, for my father, these places were kind of a template for everything that happened to him afterwards" (Pyper 20). For Johnston, Ferryland constitutes an "archetypal personal geography" (Pyper 20) whose imagined quality highlights both its importance in the construction of cultural identity and its ephemerality.

The imagined quality of Johnston's Ferryland can be extended to his Newfoundland as a whole. Johnston claims that "for someone who, like me, was born after 1949, the very existence of the country known as Newfoundland was just a story" (*Baltimore's* 228). While Johnston uses the diminutive "just," his memoir reveals that story is vital to the continuation of both personal and national identity. This story is not, as Tony Tremblay suggests, the recreation of "a pre-1949 'independent' Newfoundland" (273), but is rather the construction of an alternative Newfoundland that is not confined to the pre-Confederation era but rather continues to exist in the imagination. *Baltimore's Mansion* performs the reconstruction of Newfoundland citizenship as narrative, an ongoing connection to an "imagined community" that is imagined in part because it is forever relegated to the realm of what might have been. Stan Dragland draws a similar link between literature and the idea of the nation when he suggests that "Newfoundland is not a failed nation but a work in progress. [...] Newfoundland is very much alive *as an idea* and getting livelier with every book written on and out of the place" (189; my emphasis). As Dragland affirms, the nation exists not within the political arena, but within the culture and imagination of Newfoundlanders, and regardless of Confederation its story is still being written.

Diaspora, then, is a key plot line in this story of the nation. Throughout Johnston's memoir, we are inundated with people leaving: Johnston's great aunts who marry American servicemen, his Uncle Dennis, his own father who leaves for college, Johnston's siblings, Johnston himself. When his retired parents decide to leave Newfoundland for Alberta, the move is regarded with a sense of inevitability: "though they were in their sixties, the time had come, as it seemed it did eventually for all Newfoundlanders, to set out on their journey westward" (232). This journey is seen as one of "inscrutable necessity" (249). The organizing motif of the memoir, that of Lord Baltimore who established the settlement of Ferryland in 1628 and left with his fellow settlers after just one winter, sets up this inevitable pattern of diaspora: "theirs was the first casting-off, the first abandonment, the first admission of defeat. They were the first to pack up and leave everything behind. They blazed a trail of retreat that many after them would follow" (260). The book's title, *Baltimore's Mansion*, establishes this "trail of retreat" as a framing image for his family's story, reinforcing the connections between identity, Confederation, and diaspora. The mansion stands as a symbol of both ambitious hopes for the future, and abandonment. But as we are told of the archeological digging in Ferryland that is revealing the lost artifacts of Baltimore's mansion, the image also comes to stand for the careful uncovering of the past, and the reconstruction of that past, the reimagining of it, from the pieces retrieved. *Baltimore's Mansion*, then, the book, is also an archaeological site, a reconstruction of a narrative of the past from fragments of memory, second-hand stories, and historical facts. The text gives the impression of constant revision, as Johnston "the archaeologist"—in the Foucauldian sense of rejecting the authority of traditional historiography—uncovers new secrets, new pieces of the narrative, and jumps between decades to fill in the gaps.

While Baltimore's retreat from Newfoundland is one of defeat, for Johnston, diaspora is crucial to preventing the daily lived experience of Newfoundland from interfering with this imagined Newfoundland nation. Thus

Johnston wonders how to tell his father "that I have chosen the one profession that makes it impossible for me to live here. That I can only write about this place when I regard it from a distance. That my writing feeds off a homesickness that I need and that I hope is benign and will never go away, though I know there has to be a limit. And that someday it will break my heart" (236). The "distance" that Johnston needs enables his imagination to construct the nation not only as it was but as it "should have been" (186). Johnston calls the story of what might have been had Confederation been voted down a "ghost history": "Cashin as prime minister. The Pink, White and Green as the national flag. In that ghost history, the independents had won the referendum, the members of the national parliament of Newfoundland had been meeting since 1949, and it was Joey's and not Cashin's name whom no one under forty could remember" (241–42). Here, Johnston does not just construct a story of what might have happened, rather he constructs a ghost history that runs parallel to the "real" history. By using the word "history" to describe what *did not* happen, he suggests that history itself is just a story, and that remembering and imagining are closely linked. Johnston expands on the concept in his interview with Wyile, explaining that ghost history "has always been a theme in my work, the question of what is versus what might have been, and how the road of what might have been does still go on, at least people are aware of it all the time, so they have this parallel existence between their reality and their hopes and their dreams" ("Afterlife" 112). Paul Ricoeur contends that narratives that intertwine fiction and history serve to "free, retrospectively, certain possibilities that were not actualized in the historical past." He suggests that "the quasi-past of fiction in this way becomes the detector of possibilities buried in the actual past. What 'might have been'—the possible in Aristotle's terms—includes both the potentialities of the 'real' past and the 'unreal' possibilities of pure fiction" (3: 191–92). For Johnston, these imagined possibilities of the past include the *imagined* community of the Newfoundland nation. The fact that the "story" of the Newfoundland nation is configured in the creative imagination, however, does not mean that it is simply "unreal." As Ricoeur argues, the "naïve concept of 'unreality'" requires a systematic critique, as fiction can be productively revealing and transforming (158). In Johnston's work, this fiction reveals what he calls the "healthy obsession" in Newfoundland with the circumstances of Confederation, and what might have been had people voted emotionally rather than "bargaining self-reliance and self-definition, for material, if not wealth, at least security" ("Afterlife" 112). The alternative histories that might have been are "ghostly" not only because they have an ethereal, intangible quality, but because they haunt Newfoundlanders, even decades after the moment of their demise. They are not "unreal" but rather reveal the psychological impact of the Confederation legacy.

These themes are fleshed out in the section of the memoir in which a young Wayne and his father take a round trip across the island on the train in 1968, not long before the railway is set to be closed down by its new post-Confederation owner, the Canadian National Railway. As Johnston explains, the railway is endangered by the new Trans-Canada Highway and its faster buses, and the debate between the train and the bus becomes a revival of the old Confederation debate, with patriotic, nostalgic anti-confederate Newfoundlanders clinging to the train, and confederates extolling the progress of the bus. On the trip, Arthur encounters a man who represents the pro-bus side, who advises him, in an echo of confederate rhetoric, that he should "face the facts":

> "We're a country of fact-facing bus-boomers," my father said, grinning, looking out the window.
> "A province," the fact-facing bus-boomer said. "We're a province now, not a country. Never were a country, really. If you know your history." I heard in his voice a politeness that was meant to be transparently insincere, patronizing, the tone of someone who held in reserve a trump card he need never play. I could just see it. A riot on the train fought over a matter decided twenty years ago.
> "I know *my* history," my father said. (79; emphasis in original)

The semantic question of whether or not Newfoundland ever was a "country" (as opposed to merely a colony or dominion of Britain) becomes a conflict of multiple versions of history. Arthur's adamant assertion that he knows *his* history is also an assertion of patriotic feeling. His own version of national history, in which Newfoundland *was* a "country," goes hand-in-hand with his current claims to "country" status, claims based on culture and identity that continue to be asserted regardless of the political changes brought about by Confederation.

For Johnston, the way in which history is constructed and imagined as narrative is therefore central to the personal and cultural identity of Newfoundlanders. Ricoeur's concept of "narrative identity," postulated at the end of *Time and Narrative*, suggests this connection. Ricoeur writes that "the story of a life continues to be refigured by all the truthful or fictive stories a subject tells about himself or herself. This refiguration makes this life itself a cloth woven of stories told.... Individual and community are constituted in their identity by taking up narratives that become for them their actual history" (3: 146–47). The "story" of the Newfoundland nation is not just a fiction, or a history confined to the past, but a key thread in the fabric of Johnston's and his father's identities. For Arthur, Newfoundland's unique history and its elusive independence are central to his own self-definition as a Newfoundlander. For Johnston, it is both the island's history and *this* story, the story of his father's troubled relationship to his own citizenship, that become key to a complex and often conflicted Newfoundland identity negotiated from the position of diaspora.

As a Newfoundlander living in Ontario, Johnston actively evokes the island's unique history as one of the main loci of Newfoundland difference. Elsewhere, Johnston writes: "There is a misconception, by some people much encouraged, by others simply allowed to go unchallenged, that Newfoundland was 'born' in 1949, that in 1949, Canadian history retroactively became our history. That, for instance, 'our' first prime minister was Sir John A. Macdonald. The same misconception is applied to pre-confederate Canadian literature. Our actual history and literature now exist in a kind of limbo where not even many archivists set foot" ("*History*" 140). Johnston implies that remembering and celebrating a unique past prevents Newfoundland culture from assimilation within the Canadian nation. To combat the historical "limbo" of which Johnston warns, many Newfoundland writers reconstruct a distinct Newfoundland past in their historical novels, plays, or memoirs.[1] Johnston goes on to extol the importance of Judge D.W. Prowse's *History of Newfoundland* (1895), a text that is central in Johnston's novel *The Colony of Unrequited Dreams*. In *Baltimore's Mansion*, pondering the decision of many outporters to vote for Confederation, Johnston wonders "in how many homes or even classrooms was there a copy of Prowse's *History of Newfoundland*? Time was local, personal and even then less enduring than their experience of space, the circumscribed geography of 'home'" (89). Johnston suggests that had these outporters known more about their country's history, fewer would have voted for Confederation. Thus history is perceived as central to the idea of the nation, and Confederation enacts a "sudden severance from the past" (143), a fundamental rupture between pre- and post-Confederation identities. By returning to that pre-Confederation past, continuously, almost compulsively, in both the memoir and his novels, Johnston attempts to mend that rupture, writing a narrative of Newfoundland identity that stands separate from Canadian history, and that accommodates multiple perspectives, alternative possibilities, and archaeological fragments.

The imagined community of Newfoundland, for Johnston, is also intimately connected with landscape and geography. "The land," Wayne's father tells him, "is more important than the country. The land is there before you when you close your eyes at night and still there in the morning when you wake. No one can make off with the land the way they made off with the country in 1949" (227). While the nation as a political entity has been lost, the land still functions as the physical locus for the imagined community. The importance of physical space is revealed in an anecdote about Wayne's parents later in life. In 1992, Johnston's aging father and mother move to Alberta, where some of their children live:

> "The Newfoundland I knew is gone," my father said.
> He said it regretfully, but it also sounded a little like wishful thinking—wishful thinking that it might not be too late to escape the pull of the past. He was hoping that space would do what time had not. [...] It might not be too late for him, for them to not mind that nationality was obsolete, that it no longer mattered where they lived because the Newfoundland they loved, *their* Newfoundland, did not exist. (229)

But a few weeks after they arrive "abroad" (248), Arthur has a heart attack; four years later, one day after returning to Alberta after a visit to Newfoundland, he has a stroke. Clearly the stress and emotion of leaving his home, and likely the physical impact of travelling, lead to serious consequences for his health. Six years after moving to Alberta, Johnston's parents return to Newfoundland. Nationality is *not* "obsolete," it *does* matter where they live because while they can never return to the past, the place itself still has a firm grip on their sense of themselves. Newfoundland, then, is not a lost nation relegated to the past but an imagined community with an ongoing "sense of nationhood" (Johnston, "Afterlife" 119). Johnston argues that "for a person to go from Saskatchewan to Manitoba is simply to go from one province of this country to another; for a person to go from Newfoundland to anywhere else in the world is to leave a country, not literally, but in every other sense" ("Afterlife" 119–20). I do not believe that Johnston means to suggest that the Saskatchewanian would not feel a sense of loss or homesickness in leaving his or her home, but his statement reveals the extent to which Newfoundland's recent independent status continues to animate Newfoundlanders' constructions of their own identity in diaspora.

The vastness and mysteriousness of the landscape justifies its nation status. The symbol of the train, so important to Arthur, is linked to this perception of geography, since the vast landscape of the interior can only be appreciated by the train as it cuts a narrow swath through the wilderness. Young Wayne reflects that "my father had wanted me to see all this. How much land there was, how like a country Newfoundland was in its dimensions and variousness" (*Baltimore's* 88). "The point of this journey," Johnston adds, "was to get me away from the sea so that when I went back to living within two miles of it, I would know the land was there, land whose capacity to inspire wonder in all those who beheld it was in no way diminished by its being coloured the colour of Canada on maps" (88–89). Arthur suggests that it is the inability to comprehend the vastness of this unknown landscape that led many fishers to vote for Confederation: "they had conceived of Newfoundland as a ribbon of rock, a coast without a core, a rim with water outside and nothing, a void, inside. [...] They had had no idea when they cast their votes what they were voting for or what they were renouncing. They had not known there was a country" (89). Here the question of whether or not Newfoundland was ever really a "country" recurs, and the source of the conflict is identified not as the nuances of political definition, but rather as a problem of the knowledge of geography. "Country," here, is a term whose definitions of "rural landscape" and "nation" are not different meanings but are rather coterminous. For Arthur, the existence of the nation literally depends on one's ability to imagine the country.

For Johnston, Newfoundland's island borders are key to its continuing identity as a separate culture. The clear borders that separate Newfoundland from the rest of Canada are central to the imagined geography of cultural identity. Johnston recalls his impressions upon first seeing the gulf separating Newfoundland from mainland Canada as a boy:

> The other side of *this* gulf was remoter than the moon, on which men had just landed and which I had seen with my own eyes countless times. Only on TV and in photographs had I ever seen the world alleged to exist beyond the shores of Newfoundland. I had read about it in books, but any book not set in Newfoundland was to me a work of fiction. Anywhere but Newfoundland was to me as fabled a place as the New World must have been to Cabot or Columbus. (94; emphasis in original)

The rest of Canada is not visible and seems so different from his own experience that he cannot even comprehend it. According to Johnston, "an island until you leave it is the world" (120). This phrase is repeated, with a small variation, emphasizing the mantra: "Any place between you and which there is land is more real than a place from which you are separated by the sea. An island to someone who has never left it *is* the world. An island to someone who has never seen it does not exist" (218; emphasis in original). These phrases connect the geography of Newfoundland as an island with its identity as an imagined community, physically and therefore cognitively isolated from the country that has adopted it and the continent alongside which it sits. Once Johnston does leave it, it becomes possible for him to imagine his homeland as a construct, to make it a place of fiction, and therefore to preserve it as a possible nation.

The final lines of the text illustrate how story works to preserve the nation by stopping time. Johnston imagines his grandfather at the moment of his death: "As he looks out at the sea, everything is as it was before he crossed the stream, before he crossed over into Avalon. The House, the Gaze, the Beach, the Downs, the Pool, Ferryland Head, Hare's Ears, Bois Island, Gosse Island and the sea. All are fixed in a moment that for him will never pass" (272). David Williams argues that this moment in the memoir is a means of preserving "the world in a moment of fixity." The text is therefore a way "to fix the 'nation'" in a manner that will endure (130). I would add that the distance of diaspora is crucial to preventing daily life from interfering with this fixing of the nation in story. Yet as Ricoeur avers, story by definition implies a conclusion: "to follow a story is to move forward in the midst of contingencies and peripeteia under the guidance of an expectation that finds its fulfilment in the 'conclusion' of the story." This conclusion "gives the story an 'end point,' which, in turn, furnishes the point of view from which the story can be perceived as forming a whole" (1: 66). The nation of Newfoundland is a story in that it ends. Telling stories preserves the lost nation in the imagination as a completed whole, but ironically also preserves and re-enacts its inevitable demise in a melancholic repetition.

The Colony of Unrequited Dreams and the Diasporic Imaginary

The importance of history and geography to the imagined nation is paralleled in *The Colony of Unrequited Dreams*, to which *Baltimore's Mansion* has been called the "nonfiction counterpart" (Dragland 188). The books were published a year apart, with *Baltimore's Mansion* appearing in 1999, the fiftieth anniversary of Confederation. The texts were thus being written and published at a time when Confederation had returned to the forefront of Newfoundlanders' consciousness, when the upcoming anniversary cast light on the fact that, as Bruce Porter notes in the anniversary issue of *TickleAce*, "the same anxiety that marked the vote of 1948 pervades its cultural psyche still" (7). In Chapter 5, I showed how Johnston uses his diasporic position to construct Newfoundland as an "imaginary homeland" that combats the tendency to read Newfoundland literature for an exotic depiction of a remote region of Canada. But like *Baltimore's Mansion*, *Colony* also couples diaspora with Confederation, and the displacement of both Smallwood in his early life, and Johnston himself, are key to the construction of not only an "imaginary homeland," but an "imagined community."

Colony depicts several examples of the Newfoundland diasporic imaginary in early twentieth-century New York. As a young man, Smallwood moves to

New York in order to pursue his socialist ambitions. His reasons for leaving are entirely personal, but as he boards the ship that will take him to the mainland he places his departure within the context of the diaspora that had already been in progress for decades: "To leave or not to leave, and having left, to stay away or to go back home. I knew of Newfoundlanders who had gone to their graves without having settled the question, some who never left but were forever planning to and some who went away for good but were forever on the verge of going home" (144). In New York, he moves in to a boarding house nicknamed "the Newfoundland Hotel" because so many Newfoundlanders live there. Within the building, the residents leave their doors open to welcome visitors from other rooms in the tradition of small outport communities. Fielding, the love interest who follows Smallwood to the city, sums up the boarding house with characteristic acerbity: "have you ever seen so many island-pining, mother-missing, sweetheart-I-left-behind-bemoaning, green arsed Newfoundlanders in your life?" (158). But Smallwood remains an outsider to this imaginary, closing his door and refusing to participate in the evening socializing and parties, refusing to become a part of the community. His choice of residence is not motivated by any desire to become part of the diasporic community. Rather, "it was convenient," he explains, "aside from the fact that I could afford it, because it was about a block from Fifth Avenue and five minutes' walk from Union Square" (136). His place of residence serves only to emphasize his difference, by juxtaposing the tight-knit community with the isolation in which he chooses to live. Smallwood's self-imposed exile from the community foreshadows the tenuous relationship that he will have with his country as the father of Confederation. He is a man who dreams of becoming the Prime Minister of Newfoundland but who holds himself apart from his compatriots. He is in some circles considered a "representative" Newfoundlander, and proclaims his identity proudly, but at the same time can pass for a Jew, because of his nose, or an Irishman, because of his accent, when circumstances make such passing beneficial to his project of campaigning for socialism. This self-isolation and shifty identity are key to the characterization of a man who will, as much out of personal political ambition as for ideological reasons, drag his country into Confederation against the will of 48 percent of its citizens; he will later tell us that "I decided I would be [Confederation's] champion in part because it was the one cause that, far-fetched and unlikely to succeed, had no champion" (433). While he tells us he believes in the cause, his personal motivations cloud the moral and economic reasons for Confederation.[2] Throughout the book, Smallwood continues to be a man whose identity stands separate from the rest of the nation. His initial isolation from the tight-knit diasporic imaginary is important background to his complex and contradictory vision of his country.

The diasporic imaginary is extended when Smallwood, unemployed and reduced to sleeping in a park, is recognized as a Newfoundlander by the brand of his boots. Hines is a fellow expatriate who periodically wanders the parks on the lookout for Newfoundlanders. He publishes a newspaper for diasporic Newfoundlanders called the *Backhomer*, and Smallwood goes to work for him, writing articles on Newfoundland subjects and editing the "lost Newfoundlanders" page, comprised of letters searching for long-lost friends and family. "We were always homesick; we could not help it, since all we ever wrote or read about at work was Newfoundland," Smallwood tells us. "We were at once homesick and sick of home, sick to death of hearing about it, writing about it, sick of keeping tabs on and interviewing other homesick Newfoundlanders" (190–91). Newfoundland becomes central to Smallwood's day-to-day life, but it exists for him only as painful loss, as a homeland just out of reach.

The *Backhomer*, as a text distributed to Newfoundland readers in forty different countries (185), connects its readers in a diasporic imaginary.[3] Benedict Anderson places great importance on newspapers as a means of constructing imagined communities, as "each communicant is well aware that the ceremony he performs is being replicated simultaneously by thousands (or millions) of others of whose existence he is confident, yet of whose identity he has not the slightest notion" (*Imagined* 35). The *Backhomer*, which is probably not a daily and which would have taken some time to distribute to other cities and countries in the 1920s, does not constitute quite the same sort of daily ritual that Anderson has in mind, nor is it consumed on such a large scale. But the knowledge that the same issue is being read almost simultaneously by other displaced Newfoundlanders constructs the diaspora as an imagined community. Hines periodically publishes the abroad subscription lists, "putting asterisks and exclamation points after the names of the farthest-flung subscribers" (191), emphasizing to the readers that they are a part of such a community, and making that community more intimate by giving names to some of the fellow "communicants" he or she imagines. Since the paper is also read by Newfoundlanders at home, it also connects the diaspora with the homeland in one imagined community. But rather than identifying with this community, Smallwood fantasizes about more extreme alienation from it, imagining himself as one of his "Lost Newfoundlanders," "dropping out of sight and coming across thirty years from now, in a paper like the *Backhomer*, a picture of me as I was when I was twenty-four. [...] For a clean getaway, I would have to do little more than change my name" (192). Smallwood's fantasy again emphasizes his alienation from his own community.

Hines also keeps a boarding house called the Coop and rents out the rooms at a reduced rate to anyone who can prove himself to be a Newfoundlander. The Coop is free for two weeks, after which time if the resident finds a job, he can stay on indefinitely. Hines's charity is part of the diasporic network and is extended only within a group defined by national parameters. Here Smallwood finds himself forcibly a part of, rather than isolated from, the diasporic imaginary. But the community is a place where imagining the homeland is a painful, rather than productive, creative process, and seems to take him farther from home rather than closer to it.

Hines is the minister of a church he calls the Pentecostal Church of Newfoundland, which features a large wooden carving of Newfoundland on the pulpit. He prints his sermons in the *Backhomer*. In his column, Hines "forever likened Newfoundlanders to the Jews, pointing out parallels between them. There was a 'diaspora' of Newfoundlanders, he said, scattered like the Jews throughout the world. He saw himself as their minister, preaching to his flock from his columns, most of which began with epigraphs from the Book of Exodus" (191). He is fond of telling his reporters in lofty, biblical language to "remember [...] thou art a Newfoundlander and unto Newfoundland thou shalt return" (191). While Hines is an eccentric, even ominous character, and while Johnston's rendering of his church is rather hyperbolic and satirical, the ties between religion and nationality are nevertheless striking and serve to emphasize the strong feelings of ethnic identity and difference that Newfoundlanders tend to share in displacement. Where in *1949* the comparison between Newfoundland out-migration and the Jewish diaspora highlights the hardship and prejudice experienced by newcomers to Canada, here the comparison serves to sanctify Newfoundland identity, giving the island an other-worldly, almost heavenly, character. The place takes on an imagined quality that renders it just out of reach. The distant, sacred quality of the homeland is fleshed out in the only sermon that Smallwood attends:

> Some of you who left that new found land were drawn here by prideful ambition. Some, like me, were driven here by shame. But most of you came here because you had to, and you believe yourselves to be as undeserving of your exile as Jonah was of being swallowed by the whale. But you are wrong, for because you are sinners, you deserve much worse than this.
>
> Homesickness. What is that compared with hell-fire and damnation? You were homesick before you left home. You were in exile when you lived in Newfoundland. Homesickness is but the yearning for salvation. Newfoundland is but the place your body came from. Your true home is the birthplace of your soul, the place where it began and to which, when you have breathed your last, it will return. Remember, man, thou art a Newfoundlander and unto Newfoundland thou shalt return. (198)

In this odd sermon Newfoundland is at first merely "the place your body came from." But as he ends the thought with the statement "unto Newfoundland thou shalt return," Hines suggests that "Newfoundland" in fact represents the Garden of Eden, or heaven, that it is the "birthplace of [the] soul." Newfoundland thus becomes spiritual, ethereal, but also a place of dramatic and irreparable loss. This loss is felt not only within the diaspora, but even as Smallwood returns home.

The "Old Lost Land"
Smallwood's time as part of (or disconnected from) the Newfoundland diaspora lays the groundwork for a more metaphorical intertwining of diaspora with Confederation. After five years in New York, Smallwood approaches Newfoundland by sea:

> It was as if I saw, for a fleeting second, the place as it had been while I was away, and as it would be after I was gone, separate from me, not coloured by my past or my perceptions, but strange and real as towns seem when you pass through them on your way to somewhere else, towns that you have never seen before but that seem remindful of some not-quite-remembered other life. A kind of hurt surged up in my throat, a sorrow that seemed to have no object and no cause, which I tried to swallow down but couldn't. It was the old lost land that I was seeing, as if, like fog, the new found one had lifted. How long I stood there staring at it, I'm not sure, seconds or minutes. When I came out of whatever "it" was, the new found land was back and tears were streaming down my face. (212)

This image of Smallwood as an outsider to his homeland echoes the isolation he felt from the Newfoundland diasporic community in the Newfoundland Hotel, and from Newfoundland itself as a homesick writer for the *Backhomer*. But it also foreshadows his destiny as the father of Confederation with Canada. The phrase "old lost land," a play on the island's colonial name, at once conjures the homeland lost to the Newfoundland diaspora, and an ancient land separate from the place's political history, and its inevitable political future. Smallwood is terrified that his life will not make an impact on his nation's history, yet most readers know that he will go on to engineer Confederation, the most profound political change the island will undergo. That inevitable future looms in this scene; it is implicit in the phrase "on your way to somewhere else." And yet in this instant Smallwood sees the "old lost land" as a country estranged from him, "not coloured by [his] past or [his] perceptions." The "new found land" carries with it a ghostly other, its mirror image, the "old lost land." The country's political future is haunted by its alternate ghost histories, its "not-quite-remembered other [lives]." It is Smallwood's departure and return, moreover, that makes this ghost visible. Although he is returning, he views the island with nostalgia, as though he can never fully return. This diasporic perspective will continue to colour the characters' relationships to place throughout the rest of the novel.

The phrase "old lost land" recurs throughout Johnston's work, often explicitly associated with the losses of Confederation. The phrase initially appears at the beginning of the novel, when Smallwood's father rants "they should have called it Old Lost Land, not Newfoundland but Old Lost Land" (17). Here the phrase reads as the nonsensical ravings of a drunken man. But as Smallwood regards the land from the ferry the phrase takes on a significant meaning for him, suggesting both past losses and those yet to come. The phrase appears again much later in the novel when Smallwood has dinner with his parents a few days before the second referendum. Charlie Smallwood once again is driven onto the deck to yell at the city below: "'OLD LOST LAND,' he roared. [...] 'A country that might have been but may never be because of one of mine'" (480). Charlie's phrasing captures the loss already inherent in the idea of the nation of Newfoundland — it is merely a colony, but "might have been" a country were it not for Confederation. The "old lost land," then, is the loss of possibility for this "country of no country" (*Baltimore's* 228).

The image of the "old lost land" also appears elsewhere in Johnston's oeuvre. In *Baltimore's Mansion*, Johnston's parents and aunts and uncles long to forget the pain of Confederation, and hope that the defeat of Smallwood in the 1971 provincial election will help as they will no longer be "daily reminded by his face and his voice and his name in the paper of their father's Old Lost Land" (186). Here, the "old lost land" is explicitly the island before Confederation and before the legacy of Smallwood's rule. The "old lost land" exists in the memories of this generation of Newfoundlanders, separate from the political realities of the new Newfoundland. Its memory is painful, but it captures the essence of Newfoundland's "greatness," its physical geography rather than its colonial and political history. The phrase also appears in the title of Johnston's Henry Kreisel Lecture, "The Old Lost Land of Newfoundland: Family, Memory, Fiction, and Myth," delivered at the University of Alberta in 2008 and published by NeWest Press and the Canadian Literature Centre. In this anecdotal lecture, Johnston does not elaborate on the concept of the "old lost land," but as his title the phrase frames a meditation on the disjuncture between Newfoundland's impressive geography and history and its underwhelming political fate.

The only component term not made its opposite in transforming "Newfoundland" into "Old Lost Land" is "land"; the phrase serves to call attention to the importance of "land" in the cultural imaginary of the place. In *Colony* the same idea noted in my discussion of *Baltimore's Mansion*—that the greatness of the land is commensurate with status as a nation—prevails. Johnston makes the parallels between the two texts obvious, not only with the repetition of similar phrases, but also with the recurrence of an identical scene. The first passage below is from *Baltimore's Mansion*, when a young Wayne asks his father how big Newfoundland is, and his father tries to show him on a map. The second passage is from *Colony* and appears in Fielding's journal at the beginning of the "Old Lost Land" chapter. Fielding recalls asking her father the very same question as a child.

> "We're here," my father said, pointing at the tiny star that stood for St. John's. "Now last Sunday, when we went out for our drive, we went this far." He moved his finger in a circle about an inch across. Then he moved his hand slowly over the rest of the map. The paper crackled beneath his fingers. "Newfoundland is this much bigger than that," he said, making the motion with his hand again. "All this is Newfoundland, but it's not all like St. John's. Almost all of it is empty. No one lives there. No one's ever seen most of it." (*Baltimore's* 88)

> "We're here," my father said, pointing at the tiny encircled star that stood for St. John's. "Now last Sunday, when we went out for our drive, we went this far." He moved his finger in a circle about an inch across. Then he moved his hand slowly over the rest of the map, the paper crackling expansively beneath his fingers. "Newfoundland is this much bigger than that," he said, making the motion with his hand again. "All this is Newfoundland, but it's not all like St. John's. Almost all of it is empty. No one lives there. No one's ever seen most of it." (*Colony* 128–29)

Johnston does not just recycle a similar image, but rather repeats the passage almost word for word. For those readers who have already read one of the texts, reading the second becomes an experience of déjà vu, even if one does not immediately or consciously recognize the passage.[4] The identical passage also appears in Johnston's Kreisel lecture. This repetition makes the moment seem almost obsessive. The overall effect is to ritualize the first awesome discovery of the landscape. But in all versions this ritual discovery is tinged by loss. In *Baltimore's Mansion*, the scene prefaces Wayne and Arthur's pilgrimage across the island on one of the last train trips. In *Colony*, the scene opens the chapter entitled "Old Lost Land," in which Smallwood announces that he is moving to New York. This opening scene, and the chapter's title, not only emphasize the importance of physical geography in the construction of place, but also orient Smallwood's diasporic experience toward the homeland he has left behind, rather than the new home at which he will arrive.

In her journal entry Fielding goes on to reflect on the lyrics to "The Ode to Newfoundland," written by Sir Cavendish Boyle while he was governor of Newfoundland from 1901–1904:

> Though they are anthem-like, there is something indefinably sad about the words, resigned, regretful, as if Boyle imagined himself looking back from a time when Newfoundland had ceased to be. It is the sort of song you might write about a place as you were leaving it by boat, watching it slowly fade from view, a place you believed you would never see again. He was governor of Newfoundland for only a few years, so he must have written it in the knowledge that he was soon to leave. (129)

In this passage, Confederation is foreshadowed with the image of Boyle looking back "from a time when Newfoundland had ceased to be." This sense of impending loss is brought together with the image of leaving, so that Newfoundland "ceasing to be" and the physical departure from the island are felt with the same sadness and resignation. Fielding's sense that Newfoundland's anthem has a tone of loss and a subtext of departure is telling; even the trappings of nationalism seem to foretell the losses of both Confederation and diaspora.

This tone of loss seems to permeate every reference to Newfoundland as a country. Upon crossing his first land border, that between New Brunswick and Maine, Smallwood reflects how arbitrary the border seems, since the landscape is identical on either side. He muses:

> Perhaps we Newfoundlanders had been fooled by our geography into thinking we could be a country, perhaps we believed that by nothing short of achieving nationhood could we live up to the land itself, the sheer size of it. It seemed so nation-like in its discreteness, an island set apart from the main like the island-nations our ancestors left behind. Perhaps it was not patriotism that drove us on, so much as a kind of guilt-ridden sense of obligation. Yet no sooner had these thoughts occurred to me than I felt guilty for thinking them and chased them from my mind, telling myself I was only looking for an excuse to justify my leaving home, about which I was also feeling guilty. (154)

Although this moment in the text occurs decades before Confederation, long before the idea of Confederation has even occurred to Smallwood, long before even responsible government is given up to the rule of a British Commission, the past tense in the passage suggests that it has already occurred, that the nation's fate has already been sealed, as our narrator reflects back on his life from far in the future. Here, guilt over his thought that Newfoundlanders had been "fooled" into thinking themselves a nation is intertwined with guilt over leaving home; again, Confederation and diaspora are coupled as similar or related griefs, for which Smallwood feels guilty.

After Confederation, this guilt is made more explicit. Smallwood reflects, "I did not solve the paradox of Newfoundland or fathom the effect on me of its peculiar beauty. It stirred in me, as all great things did, a longing to accomplish or create something commensurate with it. I thought Confederation might be it, but I was wrong" (552). In this moment Smallwood becomes an almost tragic character; despite the fervour with which he campaigned for Confederation, and the despotic arrogance with which he governed the new province for the following two decades, ultimately, secretly, he feels that he was wrong in pushing Newfoundland into Canada. His dreams of greatness for his country are left "unrequited," and the country can never move beyond its status as a "colony" of somewhere else. Johnston is devious in deflating his Smallwood in this way, but he makes the regret that many Newfoundlanders feel over the fate of their country profound by putting it into the very man who orchestrated Confederation in the first place. Johnston argues that a "sense of grievance" over the loss of the nation has become a culturally foundational "animating myth" of Newfoundlanders" ("Afterlife" 119). The tragic irony of Johnston's Smallwood is that he has succeeded in constructing a cultural myth that "brings people together and holds people together," by creating a legacy of loss and grievance. In this moment he becomes the quintessential Newfoundlander, the origin of what Johnston sees as an overwhelming "legacy of guilt" over the loss of the nation, a guilt that "distinguishes Newfoundland from the other parts of Canada" ("Afterlife" 113).

This sense of grievance is manifested in Fielding, for whom displacement also becomes a metaphor for Confederation. Paul Chafe astutely observes that

> while Johnston's novel deals only briefly with the "Newfoundland diaspora" [...] it does deal extensively with the notion of Newfoundlanders "leaving" their colony/nation and "arriving" in a strange new country. In the opening lines of the novel, Sheilagh Fielding states that "[t]he past is literally another country now," and she again expresses the anxiety generated by the loss of "cultural identity and cultural belonging" brought on by such a unique "diaspora" near the end, when she claims, "[w]e have joined a nation that we do not know, a nation that does not know us." ("Scuttlework" 323)

The line "the past is literally another country now" (written in her journal seven months after Confederation) sets a tone of loss that will colour the entire text. Indeed Fielding's journal entry goes on to read "in this journal I write to people as if I am bidding them goodbye, as if they are asleep in the next room and will read what I have written in the morning when I'm gone" (*Colony* 8). Even though Fielding is not leaving, her engagement with her country and with Smallwood feels like a departure, as it is impossible to live in the "old lost land."

What Might Have Been

The physical geography of the island is therefore powerfully linked to its political status: its identity as a "country" and its future as a province. Alexander MacLeod contends that there is something quintessentially Canadian about this relationship between geography and the course of history in this novel: he argues that in *Colony* Newfoundland "remains, resolutely, a Rock, a 'hard' Canadian place where the forces of environmental determinism continue to shape the subjectivities of inhabitants" (80). Of the avalanche that stuffs Smallwood's neighbour's mouth with snow early in the novel, MacLeod writes "a more iconic 'Canadian' death would be hard to imagine" (72). Connecting the novel to the pillars of Canadian thematic criticism, Margaret Atwood's "survival" and Northrop Frye's "garrison mentality," he anachronistically identifies Johnston's Newfoundland of the 1920s as a "naturalized, starkly physical Canadian landscape" (76), decades before Newfoundland becomes part of Canada. What MacLeod's comments do not consider is the way in which the persistence of this physical geography in fact *resists* assimilation into the Canadian nation. The island's vast interior and clearly defined borders suggest a Newfoundland "nationhood" (Johnston, *Colony* 154) that cannot be subsumed into a broader Canadian identity. MacLeod's attempt to fit the novel within "the familiar spatial epistemologies consistently used to interpret Canadian [...] cultural geography" (76) merely homogenizes Canadian space, obscuring Johnston's treatment of the Newfoundland nation as an uncomfortable fit within the Canadian state and as an entity with a distinctive identity prior to Confederation.

Throughout the novel Johnston plays with this distinctive history, and with alternative possibilities to Confederation, effecting what Wyile aptly calls a Frostian "allegorical meditation on 'the road not taken'" (*Speculative* 126). MacLeod's environmental determinist reading, which, as he points out, reflects many of the novel's reviews and other scholarly articles, misses the fact that the "road not taken" is also embedded in this local environment. Rather than a single, deterministic geography, Johnston creates a doubled geography, represented by the division between the "old lost land" and the "new found land." In this dichotomy, Johnston represents the fork between the road not taken and the road taken, the nation of Newfoundland and Confederation. It is the disjuncture between Newfoundland's impressive geography and its fate as a have-not province of Canada that provides the space for the construction of the nation as imaginary, as a meditation on what "might have been." Johnston's text questions the very notion of a pan-national geography and focuses his attention on the particularities and possibilities of Newfoundland space.

In the final section of the novel, in one of Fielding's editorials dated 1959, Fielding alludes to the choice she made as a young girl to give up her children, connecting this event with the event of Confederation. Here, the "roads" taken and not taken are refigured as rivers, an image that further emphasizes the importance of physical landscape to the Newfoundland nation:

> We have joined a nation that we do not know, a nation that does not know us.
> The river of what might have been still runs and there will never come a time when we do not hear it.
> My life for forty years was a pair of rivers, the river that might have been beside the one that was.
> On the day this country joined Confederation, I was hiding out from history, mine, yours, ours. (560)

The image of the "river of what might have been" also appears in *Baltimore's Mansion*, where Johnston reflects on the bewilderment of his parents' generation at the loss of their nation, and their inability to let go of their other, ghost history. He writes "they had followed the river of what should have been, knowing it led nowhere" (186). Here, the "might" is transformed into "should," and the image takes on a darker tone of irreparable and unjust loss. The novel, then, is perhaps a lighter and more optimistic version than the memoir, but in both texts Newfoundlanders are haunted by ghost histories. Johnston ends his Kreisel lecture with the same statement, again slightly modified. Here his parents and their friends "followed the river of what should have been though they knew that it led nowhere. Or that it led to nowhere but the Old Lost Land of Newfoundland" (44). With this new addition it becomes clear that the "Old Lost Land" is not only what has been lost—the Newfoundland before Confederation, the Newfoundland lost to its many out-migrants—but also what might have been, the ongoing ghost history that continues to haunt Newfoundlanders.

In Chapter 4, I showed how diasporic distance enables Johnston to play with geographical and historical details in meaningful ways, and to challenge regionalist visions of Newfoundland by constructing it as an "imaginary homeland" that eschews the limitations of environmental determinism. But we can also take this argument further. Johnston not only rejects regionalist readings of Newfoundland as marginalizing visions of place, he also rejects the way that regionalist visions of Newfoundland define the island in relationship to the rest of Canada. Johnston here is constructing not only an imaginary homeland, but an imagined community, a nation of Newfoundland that lives on in the mind if not in reality. As James Clifford writes, "positive articulations of diaspora identity reach outside the normative territory and temporality (myth/history) of the nation-state." Therefore, "resistance to assimilation can take the form of reclaiming another nation that has been lost, elsewhere in space and time, but powerful as a political formation here and now" (307). As Johnston uses his own displacement to construct an imaginary homeland, he reclaims a nation that has been doubly lost through diaspora and Confederation—space and time. He thereby resists the easy assimilation of Newfoundland into the Canadian nation-state.

The theme of historiography is central to this reconstruction of the imagined Newfoundland nation in this novel. In conversation with Noah Richler, Johnston explains that "when Shelagh [sic] Fielding says that after the referendum, there will always be the people and the place of Newfoundland, it is a way of countering historians trying to fit the place into patterns" (Richler 305). Newfoundland does not fit easily into the "pattern" or fantasy of Canadian union from sea to sea. Its pre-confederate history does not naturally lead to Confederation, but rather combats it, as "Newfoundland is already outside whatever patterns there may or may not have been" in Canadian history and literature prior to 1949 (Johnston, qtd. in Richler 303). Johnston writes against traditional history by satirizing historiography and manipulating the historical record, creating a history with intentional changes or "errors" that highlight the constructedness of historical narratives, and by extension, of nations.

Prowse's *History of Newfoundland* frames the novel, with excerpts from it serving as epigraphs to each of the novel's parts. The novel's first epigraph introduces its technique of historiographic metafiction from the first page: "The history of the Colony is only very partially contained in printed books; it lies buried under great rubbish heaps of unpublished records, English, Municipal, Colonial and Foreign, in rare pamphlets, old Blue Books, forgotten manuscripts…" (vii, ellipsis in original). By opening his historical novel with this admission, Johnston signals that his own historiography is similarly scattered. The epigraph acts as a sort of caveat or warning of the suspect history to follow. Prowse himself is a character in the novel, reduced by a stroke to delusions and confusions, writing "revisions" of his book that amount to nonsensical scribbles. Prowse's *History* also takes a central role in the plot of the novel. It is an object of obsession for Joe's father. When Joe's mother throws it down the hill in frustration, it causes a fatal avalanche that becomes her and young Joe's devastating secret. The *History* is also the object of Joe's downfall at school, since the letters cut from another copy of the book form a letter sent to the newspaper designed to frame him. Joe retrieves his father's copy when the snow melts, and he seems fated to carry the book with him throughout his life, taking it to New York and carrying it despite its heft on his long, arduous walk through the interior to unionize the sectionmen of the railway. He reads it over and over again with impressive zeal, until "it began to seem that this, and not the walk, was the epic task that I had set myself, to read the history of my country non-stop, over and over until I had committed it, word for word, to memory, as Hines had done with the Bible, the one book that remained unopened in my suitcase" (214). The parallel of the *History* with the Bible evokes Hines's sanctification of the Newfoundland diaspora, further elevating Newfoundlandness as a meaningful identity rather than an accident of colonialism. But this obsession with history, both as an authoritative document and as an ambition, is Joe's fatal flaw. His obsession does not leave room for alternative interpretations, perspectives, or futures. Johnston, then, makes fun of the privileging of history, rendering it a physical object that can be powerful, that represents Newfoundland's colonial past and class divisions, but that also can be manipulated in the recovery of the nation. Prowse's *History*, in 1895, identifies Confederation with Canada as "a consummation devoutly to be wished" (qtd. in Johnston, *Colony* 429); it is the part of the historical narrative that has not been written yet, but that seems inevitably imminent. Johnston's historiographic metafiction, as a challenge to the historian's authority and "the traditional causal, closed, linear nature of narrative history" (Hutcheon, *Canadian* 14), resists the assimilation of Newfoundland history into a teleological narrative ending in Confederation with Canada. By playing with and questioning Prowse's teleological narrative, Johnston puts the outcome of Confederation itself into question, paving the way for an alternative perspective on Newfoundland's place in Canada.

Like French's Ned, like Wayne Johnston himself, Johnston's Smallwood also has literary ambitions: we are told that as a boy he "fancied that [he] would one day write a book that did for Newfoundland what *War and Peace* had done for Russia, a great, national, unashamedly patriotic epic" (40). Smallwood does go on to write, as a journalist, as a radio storyteller, as the editor of Newfoundland's encyclopaedias, as a political orator, and finally as an autobiographer. But he does not write a novel. Following his success on referendum night, he thinks, "I didn't have to write about others any more. From now on, others would write about me. I would make history, had made it. I no longer had to write it" (484–85). By changing the course of Newfoundland history, Smallwood *becomes* that national epic, becomes history. But as we have seen, Smallwood eventually admits that this history does not "live up to the land." He goes on to muse that "perhaps only an artist can measure up to such a place or come to terms with the impossibility of doing so. Absence, deprivation, bleakness, even despair are more likely than their opposites to be the subject of great art, but they otherwise work against greatness (552). Once again, art is privileged as the locus of the nation. Smallwood seems to concede that Confederation has done little to combat "absence, deprivation, bleakness" and "despair"; rather these problems have overshadowed what he had hoped would be his legacy. Johnston strategically undermines the significance of Smallwood's achievement. In the process, Johnston opens up the possibility that his own epic achieves what Smallwood could not—for Dragland, the passage "surely invites us to consider whether Johnston himself has risen to the challenge of holding the greatness of the place" (201). Dragland answers that "*The Colony of Unrequited Dreams* builds a vision of Newfoundland large enough and compelling enough and playfully original enough to earn a place alongside other nation-making epics" (208). But Dragland's praise comes with full awareness of the irony of writing a "nation-making epic" for a nation that is no more. Johnston's novel constantly plays with the idea of what "national epic" might mean for a colony that is now a mere province of Canada. By distorting and deflating historiography Johnston both reveals Newfoundland's difference from the rest of Canada and resists the traditional narrative in which Newfoundland's difference is resolved in a tidy union with Canada. Historiography can be questioned and manipulated, and as in *Baltimore's Mansion*, the nation of Newfoundland lives on in the alternative narratives created.

While Smallwood sees history as a single narrative to be "made," Fielding sees it as a construction that can be imagined. Where Confederation threatens to sever Newfoundlanders from their own past, Fielding recuperates this past, adopting it as a basis for national imagining, but refusing to allow it to become a single narrative. Throughout the book, we are given excerpts from the viciously funny *Fielding's Condensed History of Newfoundland*. Her book constitutes a parody of Prowse's in both its structural elements and its content. The fact that hers is a "condensed" history gently pokes fun at the verbosity of Prowse's eight-hundred-page text, which Smallwood as a boy thinks contains "not a record of the past, but the past itself, distilled, compacted to such density that I could barely lift it" (46). Fielding's book works against this laudatory impression by showing that Prowse's book is emphatically *not* history, but rather one interpretation subject to critique and even ridicule. Her text satirizes historical documents, writing an alternate version of Boyle's "Ode to Newfoundland" to represent his "love/hate" relationship with the place:

> When rotting sculpins line thy shore,
> When capelin swarm thy strand,
> The stench is such one hears men roar,
> "Thou reekest, wind-swept land." (475)

With this rewritten, irreverent ode Fielding undercuts the sentimentality that she privately expresses towards the real ode earlier in the novel. Fielding titles this chapter "The Ode Not Taken" (474), playfully alluding to Frost's poem, as well as to the dichotomy between the river of what "might have been" and what was. The two odes form two possible histories, two possible but conflicting perspectives. This moment is juxtaposed with Smallwood's account of the pre-referendum campaigns, reinforcing the link between the two "odes," and the two "roads" of Confederation and Responsible Government. The final verse of the rewritten ode, then, seems a meditation on the possibility of the ruptures of Confederation. The line "As lived our fathers, we live not" suggests the dichotomy between the pre-Confederate past and the post-Confederate future. The final assertion, "With God nor King to guard our lot, / *We'll* guard thee, Newfoundland" (475; emphasis in original), is a claim of both loyalty and ownership; it suggests resistance to both the Commission of Government and the confederate cause. The two roads, the two odes, continue to run parallel. While Fielding's politics can never be pinned down—she is actually exposed as writing conflicting columns for rival newspapers under various pseudonyms—her voice never allows Smallwood's first-person narration to have complete control of the novel. His vision for Newfoundland, in turn, is consistently undermined. While Smallwood's life is devoted to earning his place in the history books, Fielding's satirical versions of history belittle this ambition, emphasizing the constructedness of historical narratives and, by extension, of nations.

Fielding is also given the final lines in the book, but here they take a much more serious tone as she describes a train conductor celebrating on Confederation night by blowing his whistle:

> I have often thought of that train hurtling down the Bonavista like the victory express. And all around it the northern night, the barrens, the bogs, the rocks and ponds and hills of Newfoundland. The Straits of Belle Isle, from the island side of which I have seen the coast of Labrador.
> These things, finally, primarily, are Newfoundland.
> From a mind divesting itself of images, those of the land would be the last to go.
> We are a people on whose minds these images have been imprinted.
> We are a people in whose bodies old sea-seeking rivers roar with blood. (562)

Although the land endures, and the bogs and rocks do not care about Confederation (560), it is as though Newfoundlanders have been physically severed from this landscape, so that the images even of the physical topography exist not around them, but nostalgically imprinted in their "minds." The rivers of what was and of what "might have been" have been placed within Newfoundlanders' very bodies. These rivers of blood seek the sea, as though they have been distanced from it and long to return. As Chafe puts it, "a peculiar form of immigrant, the Newfoundlander occupies the in-between space of identity" ("Scuttlework" 343). There remains "always a longing for a return to what never was—the colony of Newfoundland *if only* things had turned out differently" (344). As the novel concludes, diaspora again operates as a metaphor for Newfoundlanders' severance from an imagined colony of the past.

The Country of Newfoundland

In *Against Race* (2000), Paul Gilroy reflects on the complex relationship between diaspora and nationalism: "Diaspora identification exists outside of and sometimes in opposition to the political forms and codes of modern citizenship. [...] Diaspora yearning and ambivalence are transformed into a simple unambiguous exile once the possibility of easy reconciliation with either the place of sojourn or the place of origin exists" (124). I argue that the converse is also true; reconciliation with the "place of sojourn" can be strategically resisted through diaspora identification. Since diaspora identification resists the easy adoption of new citizenship, identification with the Newfoundland diaspora is a means of resisting assimilation into the post-Confederation Canadian state. For Newfoundlanders, reunion with the nation-state of origin is not possible because of the fundamental rupture of Confederation. But maintaining the idea of Newfoundland as an imagined community in diaspora prevents the erasure of Newfoundland as a distinct identity. In *Baltimore's Mansion* and *The Colony of Unrequited Dreams* the nation of Newfoundland exists as a product of the imagination, as a fiction, a story. And in both texts diaspora plays a key role—as a chapter in that story, as a motivation behind it, and as the location from which the story is written.

Toward the end of *Colony*, in a 1949 journal entry, Fielding claims that with Confederation "nationality, for Newfoundlanders a nebulous attribute at best, will become obsolete, and the word *country* will be even more meaningless than it was before" (493). But her own work, and that of Johnston, David French, and others belies this pessimistic attitude. While the word "country" may no longer have political reality, it is far from meaningless, for it signals the post-Confederate and diasporic imagined communities constructed by Newfoundland literary texts.

PART FIVE

POSTMODERN ETHNICITY AND MEMOIRS FROM AWAY

EIGHT

HELEN BUSS / MARGARET CLARKE AND THE NEGOTIATION OF IDENTITY

In Part III, I argued that Newfoundland nationalism is a central part of both a distinct Newfoundland identity and a diasporic consciousness. But Helen M. Buss / Margaret Clarke's 1999 *Memoirs from Away: A New Found Land Girlhood* raises the question of how Newfoundland diasporic identity can be understood outside of the discourse of nationalism.[1] For Buss/Clarke, her pre-Confederation Newfoundland origins do not preclude a Canadian identity, but rather mark it; in her memory, the occasion of her country joining another is a moment of positive self-declaration and performance.

Many diaspora theorists argue that the concept of diaspora in fact subverts nationalism. David Chariandy summarizes that "an impulse to worry the nation" is fundamental to articulations of diaspora by writers and theorists who are concerned by "the patriarchal, classist, ethnocentric and homophobic aspects" of ethnic articulations of nationhood (n. pag.).[2] "Diaspora," then, challenges the dangerous conflation of the nation-state with clear ethnic boundaries; this is what Jonathan and Daniel Boyarin call the "powers of diaspora." The Boyarins write that "diaspora offers an alternative 'ground' to that of the territorial state for the intricate and always contentious linkage between cultural identity and political organization" (10). Diaspora, then, necessitates group identities that exist outside of the place of origin. Diasporas are therefore usually unified by a common genealogical kinship rather than a common territorial homeland. Yet Newfoundlanders are defined by an identity grounded in place, rather than racial or religious commonalities. How, then, can a Newfoundland identity continue to exist once its subjects are removed from that place of origin? In other words, if not by place of residence, how is Newfoundlandness defined and demarcated?

Frequently, diaspora connotes "ethnic" identification. In her influential 2000 book, *Scandalous Bodies: Diasporic Literature in English Canada*, Smaro Kamboureli does not in fact differentiate between "diasporic" and "ethnic" literature. "I have refrained from joining the ongoing debate about the semantic and political differences between diaspora and ethnicity as concepts," she writes in her preface; "although they are different, their genealogies overlap, and I have decided to work with their intersections rather than to offer definitions that could at best be provisional" (viii). While many diaspora theorists have proposed definitions of diaspora that are not dependent upon ethnic identification, in Canadian contexts the terms are often inextricable. Chariandy asks, among a litany of other crucial questions, "are racial and ethnic groups automatically diasporas?"—a question prompted by the work of several key diaspora theorists that reveals the extent to which "ethnicity" and "diaspora" are coupled. Vijay Agnew, in her introduction to *Diaspora, Memory and Identity*, acknowledges the multiple and shifting definitions of the term, but also indicates that diasporas "create an understanding of ethnicity and ethnic bonds that transcends the borders and boundaries of nation states" (4). I have argued that an important connotation of diasporic subjectivity is a feeling of difference and marginalization in the new home, a condition that implies ethnic subjectivity. If Newfoundland out-migration can helpfully be considered a "diaspora," are Newfoundlanders, then, "ethnic"?

In this chapter, I first work through the complex and shifting relationship between diaspora and ethnicity. I then move into a close analysis of Buss/Clarke's memoir, which has also informed her academic work on the memoir form, particularly her book *Repossessing the World: Reading Memoirs by Contemporary Women* (2002). Throughout *Memoirs from Away* Buss/Clarke deploys a postmodern memoir form to highlight the shifting nature of diasporic identity as an affiliation based on ethnic rather than national or territorial ties. Finally, I use Buss/Clarke's work to attend to the implications that discourses of race and whiteness have for the concept of a Newfoundland diaspora.

Are Newfoundlanders "Ethnic"?

Applying the term "ethnic" to Newfoundlanders does create discomfort with some academics who work on issues of ethnicity and race, as well as with some Newfoundlanders, and the potential arguments against it require careful consideration. Such a claim to ethnicity threatens to erase the history of colonization, substituting Irish and English settler heritage with a myth of indigeneity. For some, it suggests homogeneity and ethnic absolutism, erasing the presence of First Nations and recent immigrants, as well as the long conflicts between classes, religions, and rural and urban dwellers. It could be interpreted as an attempt to increase the cultural capital of members of a perceived dominant white majority. As James Overton warns, the idea of a Newfoundland ethnicity has been largely invented and commodified by a growing tourism industry (49). It thus often allows what Kamboureli calls the "performative manifestations of heritage" (*Scandalous* 106) — the exotic cod-tongue-eating, fiddle-playing performance of "Newfoundlandness" — to stand in for actual experiences of identity.

Despite these dangers, for those who study Newfoundland out-migration, "ethnicity" has been a helpful concept for articulating Newfoundlanders' community formations and sense of difference in the hostland. In her sociological study of Newfoundland out-migration, Leslie Bella argues that "Newfoundlanders 'away' in Canada are a distinct ethnic group. Many Newfoundlanders can trace their roots in Newfoundland further back than most mainland Canadians. Newfoundland has its own dictionary. The Newfoundlanders participating in this study belong to a 'true ethnic group,' associating together because they view themselves as alike in important ways, such as common ancestry, experience and culture. However, Newfoundlanders are invisible in Canadian literature on ethnicity and multiculturalism" (vi). While the criteria that Bella uses to define ethnicity here may be contestable, clearly Newfoundland ethnicity is, for her, a helpful and important claim to make to further her understanding of the experience of out-migration. Similarly, Harry Hiller and Tara Franz, in their study of online diasporic communities, claim that "the intense loyalty which Newfoundlanders feel to their homeland has produced a nascent or emergent ethnicity that is rooted in distinctive speech patterns and word meanings, vibrant myths and folklore about the past, a strong sense of history and a pervasive group consciousness." This nascent ethnicity has emerged "in the context of economic underdevelopment and dependency and frustrations over political and economic control" (736). For Hiller and Franz, then, Newfoundland ethnicity is demarcated not only in diaspora, but also at home, in Newfoundland's relationship to the rest of Canada. Sociolinguists Ruth King and Sandra Clarke define Newfoundlanders as an ethnic group based on "emic" grounds (539), a self-identification that is meaningful to both resident Newfoundlanders and "expatriates." The notion of a Newfoundland ethnicity also has value for members of the diasporic community themselves. In her study of the Newfoundland diasporic community in Cambridge, Ontario, Karen Dearlove quotes Dick Stoyles, known as the "mayor of Cambridge Newfoundlanders." "Some people think Newfoundlanders aren't an ethnic group. But we are," Stoyles argues. "We have our own language, our own food, our own music" (qtd. in Dearlove 10). Ethnicity, then, is a way of articulating Newfoundlanders' sense of difference at home and abroad, in terms of both positive differentiation and negative marginalization, and in both academic and popular contexts.

Some Newfoundlanders are perhaps inclined to claim "ethnicity" because, as Kamboureli, Enoch Padolsky, and others have noted, Canada's official multiculturalism policies privilege ethnic identification. Newfoundlanders, who feel that their heritage constitutes a crucial aspect of their personal identity, and who do not feel an easy identification with English or Irish origins, may claim ethnicity because that has become a dominant discourse of Canadian society, whether it is in the much derided sense of "song and dance" multiculturalism—"boutique multiculturalism" in Stanley Fish's term—or in the optimistic sense of anti-racist activism and awareness of the links between ethnic status and social power. Whether or not we agree with the ideology of multiculturalism, to deny that sort of claim to Newfoundlanders who want to make is not productive. Ethnicity is a dominant framework within which to articulate their feelings of difference and marginality. To be clear, I do not mean to suggest that for Newfoundlanders the adoption of "ethnicity" is always a matter of choice; the choice lies, rather, in whether or not to adopt the *term* "ethnicity" as a means of articulating their experiences of identity. As Margery Fee argues, responding to Werner Sollors' location of ethnicity on a sliding spectrum of "consent" versus "descent," "the more powerful our social group, the more likely we are to believe that our social relations are freely chosen, while the more powerless our social group, the more likely we are to believe, in part because a hard-edged ethnicity is forced on us, that our social relations depend wholly on descent" (274). Where Newfoundlanders might fall on such a spectrum varies according to individual experiences. But whether ethnicity is experienced as a chosen identity or as an imposed marker of difference, clearly for some Newfoundlanders "ethnicity" is the most appropriate term to describe their identity within a multicultural society.

At this point, then, it is necessary to consider exactly what is meant by the term "ethnicity." The connotations of "ethnicity" are shifting and often contradictory. "Ethnicity" has been used almost synonymously with "minority" or "race," suggesting experiences of prejudice and marginalization. This understanding of the term is key to Kamboureli's theorizing of diaspora. But elsewhere, "ethnicity" has been regarded as a term co-opted by the discourse of multiculturalism in order to circumvent issues of race; it has been associated with delineations of whiteness, and therefore relative privilege. Sneja Gunew notes that "'ethnicity' as a defining category was initially employed as a differential term to avoid 'race' and its implications of a discredited 'scientific' racism. Ethnicity was more easily attached to the European migrations which proliferated around the two world wars" (*Haunted* 16). Structured as a "choice," "ethnicity was of course not able to deal with the characteristics pertaining to visible minorities" (23). In still other contexts, "ethnicity" is meant to reference neither privilege nor marginalization, but rather the cultural heritages to which everyone may lay claim, so that English is just as much an ethnicity as, say, Chinese. Kamboureli argues that under the 1988 Multiculturalism Act, "treated as a sign of equality, ethnicity loses its differential role. Instead, it becomes a condition of commonality: what 'all Canadians' have in common is ethnic difference" (*Scandalous* 100). Kamboureli writes that this false image of ethnicity as equality elides histories of discrimination and hides the fact that a white majority still dominates the country.

I locate my analysis of the Newfoundland diaspora, then, at the juncture of these conflicting meanings of ethnicity. By straddling these contested and contradictory connotations of marginality, privilege, *and* equality, I reference the prejudice and feeling of difference that many Newfoundlanders experience in relationship to the rest of Canada, while simultaneously acknowledging the difficulties with marking a settler culture and province of Canada as "ethnic." What I am moving towards is a strategic ethnicity; many Newfoundlanders, at home and abroad, strategically lay claim to ethnic identity as a means of marking their difference as a distinct society within an officially multicultural state. It is therefore a *process* of identification, in Stuart Hall's terms, rather than a biological or cultural certainty ("Diaspora" 392). What I have in mind is similar to Ien Ang's concept of a "postmodern ethnicity": "This postmodern ethnicity can no longer be experienced as naturally based upon tradition and ancestry. Rather, it is experienced as a provisional and partial 'identity' which must be constantly (re)invented and (re)negotiated. In this context, diasporic identifications with a specific ethnicity (such as 'Chineseness') can best be seen as forms of 'strategic essentialism'" (*Not Speaking* 36). Drawing on the work of Gayatri Spivak and Stuart Hall, Ang proposes postmodern ethnicity as a means of acknowledging the various positions of power from which everyone speaks. I strategically invoke postmodern ethnicity as a means of theorizing the Newfoundland diaspora and its complex relationship to the rest of Canada as a particular position of power.

This nuancing of the term ethnicity with the political and aesthetic proclivities of postmodernism has particular value for understanding its articulations in literature. While the phrase "postmodern ethnicity" is Ang's, in her important 1988 work *The Canadian Postmodern*, Linda Hutcheon also links the two terms in a more literary context. Hutcheon argues that the postmodern takes a unique shape in Canada, citing the country's regionalist tendencies as well as its ethnic diversity as "ex-centric" impulses that lend themselves particularly well to a postmodern aesthetic (*Canadian* 3–4). Kamboureli criticizes Hutcheon's privileging of "ex-centricity" for appropriating marginalized identities into a new master narrative of postmodernity itself, erasing ongoing conditions of violence and grievance (*Scandalous* 168). I agree with Kamboureli's concerns over Hutcheon's erasure of important historical and current hierarchies of ethnic and racial difference. But while Hutcheon's use of the term "ethnic" as a sign of equality or of Canadian identity may be problematic, Kamboureli's recourse, to reserve "ethnic" for the literature of groups who feel marginalized by the dominant white majority, is also problematic. As Hall suggests, the deployment of ethnicity is crucial to anti-racist or other political work: "ethnicity is what we all require in order to think the relationship between identity and difference. [...] We cannot do without that sense of our own positioning that is connoted by the term ethnicity" ("Ethnicity" 18). In a specifically Canadian context, Fee shows the importance of this positioning in literary criticism: "Anglo-Canadians are seen as without ethnicity, as possessed of a 'Canadian' ethnicity (generally depicted as not much different from no ethnicity at all), or as possessing the national high culture, while ethnic minorities are permitted to have broken English, colourful costumes, exotic dances, and unusual food. Their writing, categorized as 'ethnic writing,' is instantly devalued as both less than national and therefore, less than literature" ("Ethnicity" 270). Fee suggests, then, that the universal application of ethnicity is crucial to combatting this devaluation: "the assumption of ethnicity may indeed be deployed to add to the privilege of the already-privileged, but it also has the potential to lead to an understanding of how that privilege has been ideologically constructed" (272). The universal application of ethnicity to all Canadian literatures is crucial to acknowledging, rather than erasing, the differences between them in terms of hierarchies of power. Ang's linkage of ethnicity with the postmodern, with its literary connotations of historiographic metafiction and a questioning of received histories and master narratives, of fragmentation, of invention, and of fluid or hybrid identities, becomes a useful discourse within which to think Newfoundland diasporic writing.

Buss/Clarke's Diasporic Double Consciousness and Postmodern Ethnicity

The title of Buss/Clarke's memoir immediately identifies the two poles of diaspora, that of the Newfoundland homeland, and the current location "away." Drawing from Paul Gilroy's memorable phrasing, Ang writes that for migrants "the relation between 'where you're from' and 'where you're at' is a deeply problematic one. To be sure, it is this very problem which is constitutive to the idea of diaspora, and for which the idea of diaspora attempts to be a solution" (*Not Speaking* 30). While Buss/Clarke's primary concern throughout the memoir is her experience as a woman and the development of her feminist ideology, this problematic disjuncture between the migrant's origins and new location colours the narrative; it is both the occasion for writing and the framework within which she negotiates the construction of her multiple identities as a woman, an academic, a writer, a daughter, and a Canadian.

Buss/Clarke's two names are emblematic of a fragmented postmodern identity. While she signs off her foreword with the statement that a "desire for the self that is joined to all the others and the otherness that makes me who I am, leads me to sign myself...Helen Buss / Margaret Clarke" (xiii, ellipsis in original), the effect of the slash is not one of fusion, but rather places emphasis on the fissure. The origins of her names—the maiden name of her childhood versus the married name of her adopted western home—also identifies the slash between them as the rupture of diaspora. Diaspora enables both identities to exist simultaneously, divided by space as well as the passage of time, so that Buss/Clarke imagines that returning to Newfoundland space will also enable a return to the past. Researching her memoir, she plans to "travel back over the territory of my life, all my Canadas, from my research into the past in Victoria, through the Calgarian present, to a month of reflection and preparation at the Manitoba cottage" (6), with the trip culminating in Newfoundland, the place of her childhood. In her chapter on diaspora in *Mirror Talk: Genres of Crisis in Contemporary Autobiography* (1999), Susanna Egan argues that "autobiographers of diaspora privilege space over time in order to retain all their possibilities. Space, as realized in these narratives, enables plural identities to coexist simultaneously despite their being contradictory [sic]" (158). But for Buss/Clarke, this privileging of space over time is precarious. Once those spatial distances are collapsed, Buss/Clarke's careful demarcations of identity are threatened. She writes that "the idea of walking in my old neighbourhood has, over the years, become mysteriously fearful. The memory of feeling like a ghost when I went there in my twenties, my refusal to set down my foot there when I had come a few years ago, had built a kind of anti-nostalgia in me: the dread that some carefully shaped identity would disintegrate by the very act of touching the ground" (15). Her identity as a Newfoundlander, (re)constructed from "away," depends upon that spatial distance, that diasporic location. While she longs to experience a "present moment in Newfoundland" (5), she recognizes that "I cannot construct a return to my homeland in the satisfying way you and I might want it. [...] I did not, and cannot return to my homeland. After four decades of living on the Prairies I am from 'away' and therefore cannot come home" (9–10). Buss/Clarke's precarious Newfoundland identity, then, is both claimed and thwarted within the introduction, rendering any assertions of identity that the speaker might make throughout the book suspect, or at least multiple. She adds that in Newfoundland "away" is the word they use to explain the crass, the ignorant or the merely mysterious acts inevitable to the condition of being foreign to a place: "Never mind the girl, she's from away," they would say with compassion. And I will always be from away. [...] The truth is, dear reader, that wherever I am I will always be from away. What happened to me in Newfoundland in that summer of returning was something between déjà vu and tourism, short moments of familiarity, small glimpses of people I might have been. (10)

Buss/Clarke's evocation of the people she "might have been" were it not for the rupture of diaspora is reminiscent of Johnston's reflections on Confederation in *Baltimore's Mansion*, but for Buss/Clarke, what "might have been" refers not to the alternative possibilities for the island, but to her own multiple subjectivities. The condition of diaspora means that identity is perpetually multiple and constantly being constructed.

The specificity of the state of "awayness" to Newfoundland culture highlights the insularity of the place and Newfoundlanders' propensity to fiercely cling to Newfoundland identity in the face of the perceived threats of Canadian assimilation. If Newfoundlandness is an ethnicity, Buss/Clarke cannot lay claim to it because of this barrier of "awayness." She can only lay claim, then, to a *postmodern* version of Newfoundland ethnicity, which allows her multiple identities to coexist, in all their precarious constructedness. While she does not use the word "ethnicity," Buss makes this claim to a particularly postmodern Newfoundland ethnicity through her memoir, by constructing her own past as a historiographic metanarrative, by strategically refiguring her own Newfoundlandness within the context of Canadian diversity, and by foregrounding her own body as a contested space of identity.

Making Stories

Metafiction has become a prominent postmodern literary technique. This self-referentiality is also widespread in postmodern memoir, where the story the author is telling is more intimately entwined with the processes of constructing that narrative. Buss/Clarke deploys meta-memoir throughout her text, sometimes ad nauseam. In her review for *Canadian Literature*, Claire Wilkshire writes that "the dogged exploration of Buss/Clarke's at times conflicted motivations constitutes one of the book's main weaknesses" (131). But while it may be "relentless," even "self-absorbed" (Wilkshire 131), the meta-memoir is a key strategy in the construction of Buss/Clarke's postmodern ethnicity. These self-reflexive elements occur on almost every page; the text in fact reads as though it was not subjected to any revisions. "I have just read these last paragraphs aloud to my husband" (7), she writes, creating a sense of immediacy and intimacy, as though we are reading a journal or a work in process. Elsewhere she pauses to tell us "it is harder to do this than I imagined. Real people keep getting in the way. Between this paragraph and the last, between yesterday and today I have heard from two of my three children" (32). By foregrounding the constructedness of the memoir, reducing it to the creation of specific paragraphs and highlighting the difficulty of the process, Buss/Clarke reveals the constructedness of her very identity, exposing the gaps in memory and the invention necessary to the recreation of her Newfoundland.

The recollections of her childhood neighbourhood, for example, include a two-page memory of discussing with another little girl the fact that the French eat snails.

> "Would you eat snails?" I asked.
> "Oh no," said she. "What would the garden do without them? They turn the soil you know." Sometimes, even if you are only six years old, you have enough sense to know when you are in the presence of poetry. (16)

But Buss/Clarke interrupts her own tale: "Now that I reread what I have recounted to you as my memory of the snails and the little girl (whose name I still cannot remember), I realize much of it may be invented out of mere fragments of actuality" (17). She goes on to explain that "the part about turning the soil and realizing poetry—well—that's just what decades of education in the literary tradition makes you do. [...] After an hour or so at my word processor, language just takes over, has its way with me. I'm sorry. I apologize" (18). The direct address to the reader implicates him or her in this metafictional moment; as Hutcheon writes, metafiction makes "us aware of the active role of the reader in granting meaning to texts" (*Canadian* 17). The moment alerts us to the literary conventions and expectations that creep into the construction of narratives; by identifying and disrupting these expectations Buss/Clarke questions the way in which narratives operate to construct particular identities.

As Buss/Clarke negotiates these moments of invention, of fiction, she grapples with her own feelings of imposterhood and discomfort with an invented identity. She feels "unreal" in Newfoundland (5), like "a ghost haunting a former life" (4). Part of this feeling of unreality is connected to narrative, and her inability to locate a Newfoundland identity within her life story: "Every place I looked, I found the stories belonged to someone else; they were not mine. Cousins were kind, hospitable, but I did not feel at home. They had lives in this place; I did not" (4). She is "a woman haunted by unmade stories" (5). The memoir, then, is her opportunity to make her own stories, but her feelings of disconnection cause her to foreground their making, their invention. Hutcheon suggests that such a postmodern process of invention can be inspiring: "Postmodernist 'recording' and 'inventing' are clearly processes, not products. They are not fixed, closed, eternal, and universal. Instead of feeling threatened by this un-fixing of certainties, postmodern culture tends to find it liberating and stimulating. Perhaps the loss of the modernist faith in fixed system, order, and wholeness can make room for new models based on things once rejected: contingency, multiplicity, fragmentation, discontinuity" (*Canadian* 19). In her academic work on memoir, Buss explicitly connects these processes of recording and inventing with her autobiographical form: "Memoir's acts of survival are restoration, reformation, and reinvention. Through making the old alive in the new, we can perform acts of repossessing the self and the world" (*Repossessing* 34). Instead of being "haunted" by her precarious identity and lack of stories, Buss/Clarke finds that a postmodern invention of Newfoundland ethnicity is an important way of negotiating her place in the world. This may be why Buss/Clarke's title refers to a "New Found Land Girlhood" rather than a "Newfoundland girlhood": by splitting the name up into its component parts, she restores the place of her childhood as a "new found" location of identity. Buss/Clarke's process of reinventing her own identity thus resonates directly with Ang's concept of postmodern ethnicity as an identity that is constantly "(re)invented and (re)negotiated" (*Not Speaking* 36).

Buss/Clarke begins her narrative with the memory of Confederation, an event that her family supported and that became a key moment in her construction of self. She remembers watching her father debate Confederation with other men from behind a set of glass-panelled doors, reflecting that "these are the kind of moments memory's imagination shapes for its myth of the self; all the time delays, all non-essentials of character and plot fall away and only the archetypal necessities of identity remain" (2). Here, while Buss/Clarke foregrounds the imagined or invented aspects of the memory, she nevertheless emphasizes the importance of the memory to her identity. Buss/Clarke places this "mythology" of self within the context of citizenship and diasporic location:

> Spending an extended time in Florida, I found myself writing about the Canadian identity that I adopted, or that adopted me, as a seven-year-old Newfoundlander; the American difference reminded me constantly of what it was to be Canadian. Being Canadian is real in Florida, because you know you are not American, whereas here in Victoria, in my own country so to speak, I often find myself uncomfortable, as if

I were a Newfoundlander from the old-time outports in a merchant's town parlour. (1)

This analogy, oddly, renders her Newfoundland origins as a metaphor; she is not from an "old-time outport" but rather grew up in St. John's. It is unclear, then, whether her feeling of discomfort is derived from her Newfoundlandness, or if Newfoundlandness and the implied class hierarchies are simply analogous to a less tangible feeling of alienation. Buss/Clarke in fact goes on to identify this discomfort as a key component of *Canadian* identity:

Some days now I feel like the only Canadian. Some days I feel like the last Canadian. Some days I feel that being a Canadian is impossible. I like to think that all of these feelings are essential to being a Canadian. Every Canadian must feel this alone. All Canadians must feel that their own personal history is the one that makes them Canadian and since no one else has had quite the same history, they live alone in their Canadian identity. When we talk of being Canadian we speak not of national myths, but of our own lives. To be a Canadian is to be an autobiographer. (2)

While Buss/Clarke suspects that this strange relationship to Canadian identity is experienced by all Canadians, the way in which this paragraph is introduced, through the memory of Newfoundland Confederation, suggests that the simultaneous feelings of impossibility, of uniqueness, of singularity, are derived from her Newfoundland origins and a resulting diasporic hybridity. Moreover, she identifies the project of autobiography as the space in which to negotiate her personal feelings of nationality with the imperfect experience of citizenship. Her Canadian identity, in fact, is explicitly an "invention" (1); she describes standing as a little girl on the eve of Confederation beneath the maple trees in her childhood backyard (the symbolism of the maple is also noted), ritualistically declaring "I am a Canadian; I am a Canadian; I am a Canadian; I am a Canadian" (2), as though the performance will close the gap between the fact of the words and the personal experience of identity. From the second page, then, we are made aware of the contingency of Buss/Clarke's Canadianness, and the fluidity of her national or ethnic origins. While she is Canadian by citizenship, she is not Canadian by birth; her Newfoundland origins therefore occupy the place of ethnic identity, as a modifier of her nationality.

In *Memoirs from Away*, then, moments of meta-memoir are usually deployed in reference to the construction of her personal history. But there are also important moments where this meta-memoir or metafiction turns to historiography. "There is always a history," she writes. "You just have to find it and shape it to your needs" (34). Historiography is one means by which diasporic subjects reconstruct their own ethnic identities. Janice Kulyk Keefer connects the Hutcheonean form of historiographic metafiction to ethnicity specifically in her reformulation "historiographic ethnofiction." For Keefer, "part of the aesthetics of writing ethnicity is the writer's ethical need to confront and struggle with the history, both private and public, of her 'ethnos'" ("Historiographic" 101). This process involves the "Janus-faced" vision of writers both engaged in the "invention of ethnicity" in the new home and invested in a relationship with the country of origin and its history ("Historiographic" 85). For Keefer, history is key to an understanding of ethnicity, history "in a twofold sense: personal and public, private and collective" (84). Buss/Clarke delves into such a twofold history as she describes exploring a now-deserted Newfoundland outport, and reading "its story in the language of the graveyard's headstones" (13). The narrative that she constructs for the settlement is made representative of the island as a whole: "These bleached-white testaments tell the history of so much of Newfoundland, the brave, tenuous communities of interconnected families, the generations of lives spent in these small worlds of the coves, their ultimate diaspora. It would not be surprising if we were to meet someone from Sudbury or Seattle or Singapore climbing up through the underbrush to see her ancestor's graves" (14). Buss/Clarke thus locates her own private diasporic identity within the public history of Newfoundland as a whole and identifies the search for one's ancestors as an important part of that diasporic experience. Genealogical historiography, then, as an archaeological process, creates a narrative of identity out of fragments of memory and the artifacts of place, and Buss/Clarke transforms this historiography into a self-reflexive "ethnofiction."

As a child, Buss/Clarke's negotiation through history class becomes a negotiation of citizenship. She writes of her grade six *Story Workbook in Canadian History*, which was "like my own personal Canadian citizenship papers, sent by Uncle Louie [Prime Minister St-Laurent]. The *Story Workbook* taught me that the history of New France was my history also, that Cartier, Champlain, and the Jesuits at Long Sault were all mine. This concept had to be held inside my head with the opposite idea that, as obviously illustrated by *The Story of Newfoundland*, the French were our sworn enemy, the armed raiders that were hellbent on killing my ancestors" (129). As she moved through the grades, these conflicting accounts of history were complicated by the contradictory representations of both England and the United States. Buss/Clarke writes,

> History worked its way around all this confusion and finally came up with a correct story that went something like this: Newfoundlanders were a strong and free people who, with little help from anyone, had

achieved one hundred years of independence which had to be given up because of some hard-to-understand money matters. We came again under the wicked rule of the Colonial Office. Now, however, we did not need independence or money, because we would be part of the great Canadian nation where the French were no longer our enemy, a sea-to-sea nation which had showed those pushy manifest-destiny, slave-owning Americans a thing or two in the War of 1812. (130)

This simplified, tongue-in-cheek version of Newfoundland's place in the world is carefully constructed out of a multiplicity of conflicting histories; Buss/Clarke's facetious historiography here locates Newfoundland at the centre of an invented Canadian identity. Hutcheon writes that postmodern texts "re-narrate and re-conceptualize the past, both literary and historical, and thereby re-formulate the possibilities of subjectivity narrated in them" (*Canadian* 9). Buss/Clarke uses this "re-narration" to identify her own Newfoundland subjectivity as a contested site. It also contrasts the alternative narrations of Newfoundland Confederation that identify Newfoundlanders not as a "strong and free people" who complete the Canadian nation, but as a charity case dependent upon Canada's goodwill.

The "Multiple Origins" of Canadian Identity

Buss/Clarke's historiographic metafiction (or ethnofiction), then, is one of the means by which she locates her own diasporic Newfoundlandness within the context of Canadian diversity. At the end of the memoir, Buss/Clarke recounts a visit to the Museum of Civilization. She describes how

> the European first-comers to Newfoundland were pictured in the museum in the form of a diarama [sic] of those tough Basque sailors surviving the fishing season on the Grand Banks of Newfoundland, and a few hard winters in Placentia. I admired them and was very willing to share origins with them, but my people's early arrival was not noted. [...] I was beginning to feel the loneliness of my Canadian identity again. My ancestors—unlike the First Nations peoples, unlike the Basque fishermen, unlike the Acadians, unlike the Québécois, my ancestors—with their fish flakes and their cabbages—were not part of the origins this national museum chronicles. (152)

While Buss/Clarke's Canadian identity includes her Newfoundland history, it is a "lonely" identity; the Canadian identities described by the official histories of the national museum exclude her origins. Newfoundland does not enter into the museum's "story of Canada" until Confederation, and while this omission may be appropriate to someone like Johnston, who resists the appropriation of Newfoundland history into Canadian history, for Buss/Clarke, the omission is alienating. The phrase "my people" immediately references Buss/Clarke's own ancestors, but it also asserts that Newfoundlanders as a group form an identity equal in importance to the Acadians or the Québécois—in other words, an ethnicity. Buss/Clarke wants the museum "to collect a multitude of histories, a plethora of voices, a whole babble of memoirs and organize it all in some clever multimedia way so that when my children and grandchildren come to the museum they can seam together their multiple origins." She imagines her niece attending such a museum, being able to "take up all the threads of her history and pattern them as she wants with the history of many others in the museum [...] She should be given many possibilities of identity so she can make her own story" (153). In this moment, Buss/Clarke locates her heritage, and in fact her own memoir, within the context of Canadian multiculturalism; she privileges her memoir as having the potential to locate Newfoundland history within the larger narrative of Canadian history, and to therefore become one of the postmodern ethnicities that make up an imagined Canadian mosaic.

As she inserts Newfoundland identity into this mosaic, Buss/Clarke counters her marginalization. In *Repossessing the World*, Buss theorizes that "the memoir is increasingly used to interrogate the private individual's relationship to a history and/or a culture from which she finds her experience of her self and her life excluded." She adds that women most often use the memoir to revise such "cultural contexts," and "in doing so, these women are changing the ways in which we tell our stories as human beings; they are bringing female gendering to bear on our previously male-gendered narratives of the self and culture" (3). Buss thus equates her exclusion as a woman with other forms of exclusion, such as the marginality of her home province. But her references to "making" an identity out of many "possibilities" is a decidedly postmodern vision of how Canadian identity might be both performed and represented for marginalized or "excluded" subjects. Hutcheon argues that "the textuality of history matches that of literature: that is, the only way we can know the past today is through its traces, its texts. This is one of the lessons of the postmodern" (*Canadian* 14). This postmodern vision of identity and historiography is in sharp contrast to Buss/Clarke's experiences of Canadian education as a young diasporic Newfoundlander: "we were way ahead of the prairie kids, but lost out in the end because they laughed at our Newfoundland accents and we felt inferior" (126). In this brief moment, Buss/Clarke references the popular definition of ethnicity, that of marginality. She does not dwell on this moment of prejudice as an audible minority. But her vision of a museum that would celebrate her own history and legitimate her place within Canadian society acts as a response to such moments of prejudice and erasure.

The Autobiographical Body
Buss/Clarke's vision of a postmodern, pluri-ethnic museum ends with a feminist emphasis. She writes that while "I trust my nation's continuing propensity for revision to bring us around to the early settlement of Newfoundland sooner or later," she is "not so sure that the larger revision of culture will come so quickly around to the gender consciousness I would want" (152–53). Throughout the memoir, Buss/Clarke emphasizes her experiences of patriarchy and her own identity as a feminist; despite the title of her book, this identity takes precedence over her relationship to Newfoundland. But Buss/Clarke's feminist attention to her gendered body is helpful in understanding her relationship to other identity formations.

For Buss/Clarke, her female body is what Sidonie Smith calls a site of potential homelessness: "the body functions as a powerful source of metaphors for the social. It offers itself up, in bits and pieces, in its blood, immune system, organs, in its topography and pathology, for use in constructing the social environment and assigning persons their places in that environment" (269). Buss/Clarke describes this process of "assigning persons" to particular social roles with characteristic anger:

> puberty is not a physical fact so much as it is a political fact. In today's world puberty begins with the assault of a sex-drenched, reproductively starved ideology mounting a little girl's mind with masochistic images of her body as object of desire. In my day things worked a little differently. No television existed to shape our imaginary selves, but instead we had the hands of men protected by the terrible positivism of a society that said all dads were good guys. (137)

She thus has learned what she calls one of the lessons of civilized identity: "You do not need to live inside a body so powerless that anyone can use it. You can tend that body, use that body, eventually learn to protect that body, even, if you have a mind to, take pleasure from that body. But you do not have to live there" (144). This profound disconnection between the self and the body is a result of her generation's refusal to speak of the realities of sex and gender, of her painful socialization as a woman, and of her own experiences of childhood sexual abuse, all of which taught her that it is male authority figures, not herself, that possess the control of her body. For Buss/Clarke, the process of memoir writing in many ways mimics the extensive psychological therapy that she has undergone, and the postmodern fragmentation, lack of linearity, and blurriness of "truth" are all part of what she has elsewhere termed making "memory work to help heal the past" (*Repossessing* 153).

If the literary techniques of postmodernism can recreate the therapeutic work of coming to terms with the trauma of sexual abuse, they can also be useful in coming to terms with the ruptures of diaspora. Buss/Clarke's "homelessness" in the gendered body also extends to a sense of homelessness in the ethnic body. Reflecting on an earlier trip to Newfoundland, she writes that she "felt like a ghost haunting a former life. I remember not liking that feeling. It was the beginning, I think, of being overly conscious of my disconnectedness from my own lived life, the uneasy way you have to feel in order to be driven to words, driven by desire for those small moments when, writing, you live inside your own experience, your own body" (4). Her inability to place her foot on the ground in her childhood neighbourhood further emphasizes the rupture, the irreconcilability that diaspora has caused between the homeland and the physical body. For Sara Ahmed, the feeling of being at home is like inhabiting a "second skin," and thus the ruptures of migration are often felt as physical discomforts. Diaspora entails a split between home as place of origin, and home as bodily experience, "the sensory world of everyday experience" (90). For Buss/Clarke, this uneasy disconnection from the body becomes a driving force behind her writing. As a diasporic figure, her moment of writing becomes a moment of reconnection with her body and her homeland, a resolution of the multiple and "unreal" identities that occupy her. But these moments of reunion with the body are necessarily fragmented, experienced as temporary sensory memories rather than a coherent narrative where home and body coexist in perfect union.

Often, such feelings of diasporic homelessness are attributed to the alienation of the racially marked body. But how do migrants who are racialized as "white" understand their own experiences of homelessness? It *could* be argued that Newfoundlanders like Buss/Clarke, who describes being laughed at for her accent, are victims of racism despite their prevailing visual "whiteness." Leslie Bella tentatively makes this move, pointing out the negative impact of "Newfie" jokes and stereotypes (xiv). Bella also cites many Newfoundlanders' deliberate attempts to lose their accents as possible "internalised racism" (xv). Clearly these examples constitute prejudice and discrimination, but are they "racism?" Is the postmodern ethnicity that I have laid out merely a euphemism for racialization? And if not, how do "white" identities fit within the phenomenon of diaspora?

The White Body

Newfoundland is characterized by an overwhelming whiteness and Anglo-Celtic heritage; 5,720 people in the province, a mere 1 percent of the population, considered themselves "visible minorities" in the 2006 census (Statistics Canada). While Newfoundland identity is not exclusively or definitively white, the movement's demographic make-up raises some important questions.

A case could, and often has been made, that Newfoundlanders as a group are subject to "racism." In an interview with CBC's Debbie Cooper, former federal Finance Minister John Crosbie called a Margaret Wente article disparaging Newfoundlanders as "surly Islanders" on employment insurance "the worst type of [...] racism I've seen in a long time" (*Canada Now*). In his novel *The Nine Planets* (2004), Edward Riche satirizes this kind of move in a conversation between two teenage Newfoundlanders, one of whom, Chuck, is about to move to Toronto with his family:

"People are always calling me Newfie and shit. It's horrible."
"That's racist," said Cathy. She wasn't sure it was. She was echoing a sentiment she'd frequently heard voiced by her father in an effort to boost Chuck. One of the few things she knew about boys and men was how fragile their egos were, how in need of constant support. (165)

This humorous moment points to Newfoundlanders' ambivalent position in relationship to identity and race. While they have certainly been the brunt of discrimination, "racism" is a strong term. Racism suggests the way in which "visible minorities" are immediately identified as Other by perceived physical markers. Racism has been used to justify institutionalized inequalities, as well as the worst historical violences—slavery, colonial conquest, apartheid, genocide. Applying "racism" to Newfoundland seems to deflate the term of its visceral power. Where "whiteness" is usually a code for "privilege," then, what tools do we have for understanding movements like Newfoundland out-migration, that account for both their whiteness and their dislocation?

The theoretical concept of diaspora has been ill equipped to accommodate white racial identities. When "White Diaspora" as a category is considered it is usually as a form of colonial expansion, such as Gillian Whitlock's definition of "white diasporas" as the "distinctive and highly organized programmes of migration which were a feature of nineteenth century Anglo imperialism" (91), or Catherine Jurca's "ironic" usage of the phrase to highlight white American suburbia's self-representation as victims (8). These usages, regardless of their intended ironies or awareness of privilege, problematically obscure diaspora's connotations of uneven power relationships with the new "host" society. Canadian historian Donald Harman Akenson carefully works through the etymology and theoretical development of the term "diaspora," yet he also abandons many of the useful definitions that have developed in recent decades in order to locate the colonial settlement of English-speaking

Canada within a wider British ethnic and cultural nexus. But I remain unconvinced that applying the term "diaspora" adds any useful or appropriate nuances to this history. Rather it seems to form the opposite of the precise and "textured" view of history that he advocates (395), by suggesting that the migrations of every group to Canada can be considered in parallel terms. If the category of diaspora were to become so capacious, why not simply call it "dispersal?" At what point does the term become meaningless? Akenson cites the Armenian diaspora as an example proving that the term can apply to "white" groups, but by considering "diaspora" merely as a label to be applied rather than as, in Cho's useful terms, a "condition of subjectivity" ("Turn" 11), he quickly slides down a slippery slope to the conclusion that any movement, including the colonial invasion of Canada, can and should be considered diasporic. The "whiteness" of the Armenian diaspora cannot be easily compared to the "whiteness" of British imperialism.

While the work of writers like Akenson, Jurca, and Whitlock raises troubling questions about the capaciousness of "diaspora," and about how both the words "diaspora" and "white" should be defined, many other theorists in fact define diaspora in racialized terms, where "racialized" refers to the problematically drawn categories of "visible minorities" or groups "of colour." In such a context "the two terms in the phrase, 'white diaspora,' almost seem antithetical" (Kalra, Kaur, and Hutnyk 105). Cho, for example, contends that "in order for diaspora to retain its purchase as a critical term, I cannot help but feel [it] must be reserved for racialized subjects connected to histories of dislocation" ("Affecting" 119). But the connection between race and diaspora is more often implicit, so that even traditional diasporas such as the Irish are often discussed in terms of their racialization, their tenuous and shifting relationship to whiteness (Ignatiev). Indeed, thinking of diaspora as not just a movement but a condition of marginalized subjectivity seems to preclude whiteness, since whiteness itself is often conceptualized as, in Virinder S. Kalra, Raminder Kaur, and John Hutnyk's phrasing, a "passport of privilege" (111). Theorists like Cho and Kamboureli find the concept of diaspora crucial to addressing the place of race in Canadian society; Cho's concept of "diasporic citizenship" is one means of addressing the relationship of racialized "minority" literatures to the "majority" ("Diasporic" 108). The adoption of the concept of diaspora in anti-racist discourse means that applying "diaspora" to "white" identities causes discomfort and serious ethical reservations. While few diaspora theorists explicitly exclude white identities from diasporic identification, we must address head-on the question of whether applying the concept to white identities undermines such crucial anti-racist work.

In order to answer this question, I want to linger, for a moment, on the definitions of "whiteness." It is, as Gargi Bhattacharyya, John Gabriel, and

Stephen Small argue, a shifting and self-contradictory concept, an "imaginary" rather than an ontological state (12). Daniel Coleman persuasively argues that whiteness has been tied to a Canadian national project of "white civility," which manages different identities through the learned performance of normative colonial manners and behaviours. While whiteness *suggests* the biological markers of skin tone, it is for most theorists a marker of privilege. It is therefore possible for a diaspora to "become white," as Noel Ignatiev famously argues in his study of Irish immigrants to the US, or as Myrna Kostash describes as a Ukrainian-Canadian who has been differently racialized within her lifetime. David Roediger and others outline how historically there has been a lot of anxiety about the racial identity of the Jewish diaspora as well, despite the group's diversity. If whiteness is pure privilege, then we are forced either to consider marginalized "white ethnic" groups as being somehow outside of whiteness or to simply include them in a homogeneous category of privilege. Himani Bannerji makes the latter move in an essay on Canadian multiculturalism. She writes: "In the presence of contrasting 'others,' whiteness as an ideological-political category has superseded and subsumed different cultural ethos among Europeans. If the Ukrainians now seek to be ethnics it is because the price to be paid is no longer there" (144). This kind of homogenizing of European identities as white privilege and supremacism undermines Bannerji's otherwise important anti-racist intervention. Ironically, if part of the power of whiteness is its very invisibility, or as Bhattacharyya, Gabriel, and Small put it, its "naturalization" as being not a race but a norm, then Bannerji's move to homogenize whiteness merely reinforces this naturalization. We must, then, both acknowledge the privileges of whiteness and highlight the fact that whiteness is a shifting, arbitrary, and constructed category that does not always guarantee that privilege or possess a monopoly on it. We must acknowledge that "white" does not mean the same thing to everyone and that people are not *naturally* white, but rather also undergo a process of racialization, a process of attributing white racial characteristics to groups (Bhattacharyya, Gabriel, and Small 1). By defining whiteness exclusively as a form of privilege we merely reinforce its ability to appear, in Patricia Williams' word, "un-raced" (qtd. in Bhattacharyya, Gabriel, and Small 24).

Yet Robyn Wiegman, in response to studies like Ignatiev's and Roediger's, persuasively writes that history "rescues contemporary whiteness from the transcendent universalism that has been understood as its mode of productive power by providing prewhite particularity, which gets reproduced as prewhite injury and minoritization" (137). Wiegman thus warns against the manoeuvres that Ignatiev and Roediger make as they seem "unable to generate a political project against racism articulated from the site of whiteness itself" (139).

The project of making whiteness particular, then, must not simply make claims to marginality or victimization, a kind of "empathetic otherness" (Fee and Russell 188), but must acknowledge the privileges of whiteness even as it attempts to explode white universalism and invisibility.

It is crucial to carry this work of making white identities visible into the realm of diaspora studies. Equating "diaspora" with "racial minority" in Canada serves to reinforce the notion of a homogeneous, dominant white majority, so that racialized "others" are always outsiders, always from elsewhere. This move threatens to refigure experiences of racism as a problem of integration, rather than of systemic, institutionalized racism. Ang argues a similar point when she writes that the idea of diaspora may be used as "a ploy to keep non-white, non-Western elements from fully entering and therefore contaminating the centre of white, Western culture" (*Not Speaking* 34). These concerns lead Ang to question the usefulness of diaspora as a concept. But we can reject this kind of racist move without abandoning the concept of diaspora altogether. By beginning to disentangle race from diaspora we expose the fact that racism is endemic in Canada, and that marginalization does not always hinge upon identification with an origin outside of Canada. The "Newfoundland diaspora" is one concept that resists the ways in which the term can reinforce a false binary between an indigenized, universalized white monolith, and racialized others perpetually asked "where are you *really* from?" (Ang, *Not Speaking* 29). I am committed, then, to Wiegman's call for interventions that are "not simply rendering whiteness particular but engaging with the ways that being particular will not divest whiteness of its universal epistemological power" (150).

Buss/Clarke's contradictory relationship to identity illustrates how I want to deploy the concept of Newfoundland diaspora as a particular but sometimes powerful whiteness. Buss/Clarke in fact reveals anxiety about her own whiteness. She describes her childhood fantasy of living in mid-nineteenth-century Newfoundland and befriending the last Beothuk. In her fantasy, she escapes with the captured Shanawdithit, just after Shanawdithit contracts the consumption that will kill her. The fantasy, she tells us, takes various forms:

> I used to like the learning-to-survive-in-the-wilderness plots the best: how Shanawdithit teaches me to use snowshoes and chew deerskins until they are soft leather and how I brew up a secret tea that my grandmother taught me to make on the Scottish moors, tea which cures Shanawdithit's illness. [...] We live in a teepee of course and hunt in the winter and live off berries in the summer. [...] In my stories we never seem to make much effort to find her people or mine. We live outside of history. (134–35)

Buss/Clarke admits that "nowadays I realize that this fantasy is merely an appropriation of someone else's tragedy, honed into story to make me feel less shame" (135). But despite this self-consciousness, the moment nevertheless reinforces stereotypes and a problematic power relationship between the white woman and the colonized Beothuk. Shanawdithit is helpless and needs to be saved by the white woman. She is idealized, yet silent. While Buss/Clarke admits, "I know I have no right to make such a story, that I have to live with sadness and shame as part of my share of history" (135), her fantasy nevertheless distances her from colonization. Her "shame" becomes directly equated with the shame she feels following sexual abuse; shame "was what I felt when the father of the boys next door walked up to me while I was skipping and put his hands between my legs, pinching me where I peed. Shame was the feeling that something terribly wrong had happened, something deeply forbidden, something you did not dare tell your parents about, because it was bound to be your fault" (133–34). By using the word "shame" to signify both sexual abuse and the white shame of colonization, she defines "shame" as a guilty feeling on the part of the victim. Buss/Clarke's story is not only "an appropriation [...] to make [her] feel less shame," it is appropriation disguising an absolution of racial guilt.

Buss/Clarke's childhood fantasy is thus an appropriation of a story about colonial violence, distorted into a story about feminism. By rewriting history with a feminist goal, by indigenizing herself into a constructed matriarchal tribe, she denies Shanawdithit's history as a victim of colonial invasion and forces her into a story that has little direct relevance to her plight. Instead it serves Buss/Clarke's own feminist agenda. Her suggestion that a matriarchal society would not have exterminated the Beothuk people is a way of not talking about the real issues of colonial power. She writes: "it seems obvious to me as an adult feminist that what I should have been feeling then was neither shame nor sadness at the fates of my heroines. What I should have felt was robbed: robbed of a fuller history, robbed of the very moral values my culture told me it abided by" (134). The tragedy is centred on Buss/Clarke herself, and her feminist disappointments.

Buss/Clarke's narrative, then, reveals anxiety and self-consciousness about her own whiteness, even as it reinforces the privileges of whiteness; she, and not Shanawdithit, is in a position in which she is able to reimagine the outcome of history. The unsettling suggestion that her victimization as a woman may equal, or at least be comparable to, the victimization of colonial genocide, exposes Newfoundland ethnicity as a site of relative privilege. This privilege, then, this unequal power dynamic that continues even more than a century since the "last Beothuk" died, reveals why the Newfoundland diaspora must not be racialized outside of whiteness. Diaspora as a concept must be able to accommodate both the pain and marginalization of the Newfoundland migrant in displacement, and the relative advantage of Newfoundlanders in relation to groups that do not benefit from the privileges and histories of whiteness.

A New Found Land Ethnicity

Buss/Clarke's gendered and raced body is thus emblematic of the contested positionings of postmodern ethnicity. She embodies both the marginalization of womanhood and ethnicity and the privileges of whiteness, often occupying both positions simultaneously. Her body, then, is a site of multiple strategic essentialisms that mark her as a diasporic figure; indeed her diasporic condition does not necessitate an essentialized, minoritized ethnicity, but rather enables the postmodern invention and multiplication of identities as she moves between various spatial and conceptual "homes."

 NINE

THE "HOLDIN' GROUND": DAVID MACFARLANE AND THE SECOND GENERATION

If most diasporic Newfoundlanders are "white," physically marked only by their accents, one may assume that their children, born outside of Newfoundland, do not feel marked by a particular Newfoundland ethnicity. Indeed, even diaspora theorists "of colour" wonder about the affiliation of their own children in the new homeland. Rajagopalan Radhakrishnan distinguishes between first-generation immigrants, "emotionally committed to India," and the second generation: "It would be foolish of me to expect that India will move my son the same way it moves me" (208). But he goes on to admit that "it would be equally outrageous of me to claim that somehow my India is more real than his; my India is as much an invention or production as his" (208). Is the second generation's invention of an imagined homeland really lacking in "emotional commitment?" And is it driven by that generation's being "*marked* as different by virtue of their skin color, their family background, and other ethnic and unassimilated traits" (Radhakrishnan 206; emphasis in original)? In other words, to what extent does the "white" second generation retain ethnicity?

For second-generation diasporic Newfoundlanders, ethnic affiliation may be embraced, rather than imposed by experiences of racism, but Newfoundland nevertheless does evoke strong feelings of identification and a significant "emotional commitment." Ted Russell's classic radio play, *The Holdin' Ground* (1954), creates a powerful metaphor for the affiliation of the children of Newfoundland out-migrants:

> I'm sittin' on my stage head lookin' out at where Skipper Joe Irwin's schooner is ridin' at her moorin'. And lookin' at her, I've noticed how she's always on the move. Swingin' this way and that with the tide and

the baffles of offshore wind from the hills; fallin' back till her chain brings up taut, then shootin' ahead to slacken it. Always and forever on the move. A stranger not knowin' the difference'd think she was adrift. That is, if he didn't know about her chain and her anchor — and her holdin' ground. (1)

Initially, this metaphor stands for the "people along this part of the Newfoundland coast. And most likely [...] people everywhere," who differ in opinion but are nevertheless held together by a common bond. But as the play goes on, the swinging and moving of the schooner come to stand for diaspora. The play tells the story of Michael, the son of an outport family that left for the mainland before he was born. Michael returns to visit the place, and though he has not been there before, he knows the location of all the hidden rocks in the cove and cries as he surveys the abandoned houses of his family. The common expression "you can take a man out of the Bay, but you can't take the Bay out of the man" (37) recurs throughout the play, revealing that an emotional connection to place can exist even for those who have never lived there. Michael is attached to his homeland, then, despite his birth abroad and worldwide travels, like the schooner anchored to the "holdin' ground" below.

This image of the "holdin' ground" as the tie of the second generation to their Newfoundland ancestry is a helpful starting point for an analysis of Newfoundland ethnicity. While the second generation are not marked by physical traits that identify their heritage, they often feel a genealogical link to place that becomes an important aspect of identity. In their study of online diasporic Newfoundland communities, Harry Hiller and Tara Franz found that "second-generation migrants possessed a sense of rootedness that was based on Newfoundland being a parent's place of birth" (746). Whiteness, then, does not necessarily mean that individuals live easily as part of an ethnically neutral majority. In her study of Ukrainian Canadian literature, Lisa Grekul asks:

> What does ethnicity mean to us, the children of multiculturalism and the grandchildren of assimilation, who are many decades removed from our ancestral roots? We pass. We are not called upon to explain where we come from, as racialized minorities often are: it is assumed that we come from here. We are not "read" as different, anything other than "Canadian," because we wear no outward signs of difference: most of us don't speak our ethnic languages, we don't speak accented English, we don't practice customs and traditions that make our ethnic identity visible. But many of us nonetheless *feel* different, and that feeling is legitimate. (xxiii; emphasis in original)

That feeling of difference is often manifested in literary works, particularly, as Grekul's study shows, in family memoirs. David Macfarlane's family memoir of Newfoundland, *The Danger Tree* (1991), reveals that whiteness does not prevent a feeling of difference, of ethnicity, of being tied to a homeland by a strong "holdin' ground." Like Wayne Johnston, Macfarlane emphasizes the importance of story in the construction of his identity; story becomes his claim to a Newfoundland ethnicity. And like Buss/Clarke, his is a particularly postmodern ethnicity, characterized by metafiction, fragmentation, invention, and a constructed link between personal identity and national history.

Come-From-Away or Emergent Ethnic?
As a native of Hamilton, Ontario, Macfarlane has an uneasy identification with his Newfoundland heritage: "When Newfoundlanders resent the rest of Canada, they zero their resentment on exactly the part of Canada from which I come. Up-Along, they call it. And strangers, like me, are called Come From Aways. My uneasiness has never prevented me from feeling proud of my Newfoundland connection, however" (38). The American edition of Macfarlane's memoir was in fact published under the telling title *Come from Away*. But while southern Ontario is the place where he grew up, and also his father's birthplace, Macfarlane establishes his Newfoundland connection by outlining his maternal genealogy, as the descendant of the prominent Newfoundland family the Goodyears. The memoir devotes a lot of attention to Macfarlane's great-grandmother, Louisa Goodyear, and the four generations of Newfoundland heritage seem to justify his position as a "well qualified" observer (Staveley 42). Throughout the book he is positioned as both insider and outsider to Newfoundland culture; he describes both personal memories and events that happened long before he was born. Newfoundland is first described in the book through the eyes of his ancestors on his father's side, the Scottish immigrants that he imagines coincidentally landing on the Newfoundland coast before making their way inland to settle in Ontario. Yet even as he takes on the perspective of the stranger, seeing Newfoundland for the first time, he pauses to let us in on an inside joke: "the lakes are called ponds—the oldest joke about the Newfoundland accent being that a pond is an inland body of water, no matter how big; a leak, pronounced 'lake,' is what's wet in your boots" (12). Like any inside joke, it loses something in the explanation; one must be able to imagine the Newfoundland accent, and to picture an outsider making the mistake of calling a pond a lake, to find it funny. Macfarlane thus occupies a liminal space between inside and outside, the liminal space of diaspora.

This diasporic identity is at once passively inherited and actively performed. Helene Staveley argues in her article on *The Danger Tree* for *Newfoundland*

Studies that "while the discomfiture [of his dual heritage] does bring unease, apparently it also permits Macfarlane a certain clearness of eye. Raised with whatever advantages a metropolis can offer [...] if he can nevertheless passionately love a place and a people so seemingly different from his Hamilton home and its people, then it is implicit that this love must be a result of choice" (43). While Macfarlane's decision to venerate his Newfoundland ancestors in his memoir is certainly a choice, his feeling of identification with his Newfoundland heritage, his feeling that parts of his personality can be easily traced to his Newfoundland roots, suggests that there is more at play here than simply choice. Macfarlane recalls first hearing as a boy the unlikely story of how his parents met and feeling a moment of existential panic. He writes:

> I realized suddenly that the odds stacked against my existence had been overwhelming. I stared from the window of our car and wondered whether I was actually a boy in the back seat of a turquoise Pontiac or somebody else. [...] How was I to know? And at that precise, unnerving moment I didn't know, but over the years I learned the awful truth: it had been a long shot, but I was the boy in the Pontiac all right. I am who I am because inside me is wedded the discomfiture of two societies as distinct from one another as night and day. (20)

The phrase "awful truth" emphasizes that Macfarlane's identity is not chosen, but is rather a hybrid identity composed of what he sees as two very different cultures. Ang argues that this third space of hybridity can be a very creative space, and it is key to her concept of postmodern ethnicity. Hybridity accommodates the heterogeneity of diasporic "imagined communities," their "internal differences and particularities" (*Not Speaking* 36). The recognition of hybridity is a recognition of the fact that while the diasporic subject can never return to his or her "origins," "the cultural context of 'where you're at' always informs and articulates the meaning of 'where you're from'" (35). For Macfarlane, hybridity is not an easy blending of two identities, but rather a state of constant tension between two parts. But this tension is what makes him "who he is," and it locates him in a creative liminal space where Newfoundland and Canadian heritages meet. Throughout the text, then, these heritages remain in tension, and as we will see, reflect the ongoing conflict between Newfoundland and Canada as a whole in the new federation formed shortly before Macfarlane's own birth.

This negotiation between what is inherited and what is chosen, and between the new home and the old home, recalls Stuart Hall's concept of "emergent ethnicity":

> If you ask my son, who is seventeen and who was born in London, where he comes from, he cannot tell you he comes from Jamaica. Part of his identity is there, but he has to discover that identity. He can't just take it out of a suitcase and plop it on the table and say "That's mine." It's not an essence like that. He has to learn to tell himself the story of his past. He has to interrogate his own history, he has to relearn that part of him that has an investment in that culture. ("Ethnicity" 19)

For Hall, then, the position of the second generation necessitates that identity be imagined and constructed. But the idea that one may "relearn" something one has never actually experienced reveals that while emergent ethnicity may need to be constructed, it is also inherited. He writes, "we tell ourselves the stories of the parts of our roots in order to come into contact, creatively, with [the past]. So this new kind of ethnicity—the emergent ethnicities—has a relationship to the past, but it is a relationship that is partly through memory, partly through narrative, one that has to be recovered. It is an act of cultural recovery" (19). The concept of emergent ethnicity, with its emphasis on processes of identification and the construction of narrative, links an Angian postmodern ethnicity with the specific condition of the second generation. It is in this process of recovering the stories of his Newfoundland roots—his "holdin' ground"—that Macfarlane engages in his memoir.

"Homebred Bumpkins": Out-Migration to the Mainland

Macfarlane's emergent ethnicity is informed by an inherited sense of Newfoundland's uneasy fit within the Canadian federation. While the Americans invented the term "Newfie" during the Second World War, the "Newfie joke," Macfarlane notes, was a "Canadian invention": "This was because Newfoundland was poor—a quality that American servicemen, interestingly enough, hadn't found particularly funny. It was because the province had the lowest per capita income, and the highest rate of emigration and unemployment. Probably it had the worst teeth" (158). For Macfarlane, Newfoundland's marginal place within Canada is a direct consequence of poverty and its companion, out-migration:

> In the 1950s, '60s, and '70s many young Newfoundlanders with gaps in their yellow grins were unable to afford educations or technical training, and they showed up in Toronto, in Hamilton, and in Alberta looking for work as laborers. And it was because Newfoundlanders had distinctive accents—Protestant West Country, Catholic Irish, broad, unintelligible expressions from the Bay, and thick colorful turns of phrase that were unique to St. John's—that Newfoundlanders became

Newfies. Canadians needed a homebred bumpkin to emphasize their own prosperity and sophistication. (159)

To anti-confederates, like Macfarlane's grandfather, Canada was responsible for "kidnap[ping] the sons of Newfoundland families for labor in the automobile factories and the steel plants of Ontario. [...] People watched their sons and daughters leave for Ontario and Alberta, and they wondered whether confederation had actually made things better for Newfoundland, or, in fact, had made things worse" (31). Macfarlane internalizes this conflict, so that "[my] grandfather's opposition to confederation, and the fact that I was the first issue of a marriage that began not in Newfoundland, where by custom it should have, but in Ontario—a wedding that was almost precisely coincidental with the island's union with Canada—has made me feel a little uneasy all my life" (37). For Macfarlane, his parents' marriage parallels the union of Newfoundland and Canada, and his own dislocation from his motherland parallels the wave of out-migration that Confederation seemed to cause.

Macfarlane's affiliation with two such migrant Newfoundlanders, with whom he shares shifts at a Hamilton steel plant during summers off university, is thus both natural and poignant. The two self-identified "Newfies" live up to the stereotypes that Canadians held of their province: "George and Danny knew the requirements. For starters, they were both hard drinkers. [...] They were also good fighters. [...] Still, they were nice guys. There was something gentle and friendly beneath all their self-destructive bluster. They shared a wry, fast-paced sense of humor, an instinctive distrust of authority, and an amazing inability to save money" (161–62). Macfarlane spends his shifts with the Newfoundlanders, smoking pot and telling stories, but his descriptions of them make it clear that his relationship to them is one of an outsider. He sympathizes with their circumstances: "The Newfies hated Hamilton and they hated the coke ovens, and they felt no particular gratitude to anyone for having to spend seventy hours a week in such a hellhole. They weren't going to leave in September for sherry parties in the quad and seminars on *The Waste Land*. They were there forever—or at least until they were laid off—because they had car payments and pregnant girlfriends and because there was no work for them in Newfoundland" (163–64). Macfarlane is acutely aware of his own class position here, as the son of a dentist who labours for the summer but is able to return to post-secondary education in the fall. While he is a product of diaspora, he is not a member of a family forced to leave by economic hardship; he is not the son of a George or a Danny, working their whole lives in the steel plant. Yet Macfarlane also reveals that while diaspora is often a class issue, it is also an issue of the uneven relationship between Newfoundland and the other provinces. By linking diaspora with the failures of post-Confederation development, and with the condescending attitude of the rest of Canada, Macfarlane shows how Newfoundlanders as a group have been characterized as "bumpkins" in relationship to the mainland—as an ethnic stereotype, rather than a class stereotype. Macfarlane's liminal or hybrid position allows him to be both self-reflexive about his own class positioning and indignant about the marginalization of Newfoundlanders, at home and abroad.

"The Stories Found Their Way Back"
Macfarlane negotiates this second-generation identity with the help of storytelling, a tool that he inherits from the Newfoundland side of his family early on. He describes how one year, at the age of eleven, he modified the annual school social studies project on Hamilton to a comparison between Hamilton and Newfoundland. While his descriptions of the project are cute and amusing—"in a paragraph entitled 'Recreation,' Hamilton was credited with having the YMCA and an exceptional football team, while Newfoundland had the Atlantic Ocean" (38–39)—the anecdote reveals the equal importance of his hometown and his mother('s)land in his young mind. It also marks the beginning of his using the written word to mark a connection to place.

Macfarlane's memoir does not concentrate on his own memories and experiences, but rather tells the stories of his grandparents, great-grandparents, great uncles and great aunt. All of these people have passed away; by giving voice to their stories he becomes their delegate, adopting their voices as part of his own. For Macfarlane, the biggest difference between the Ontario and Newfoundland sides of his family is that, while his father's family are famous for their silences, his mother's are famous for their stories. Macfarlane takes this trait not just as differences in family personalities, but as representative of the cultures from which they originate. By becoming a storyteller himself, then, Macfarlane has assumed this all-important ethnic trait of Newfoundlanders.

The form that Macfarlane's stories take imitates the oral, circular form that his family used. He tells us:

> It was as if Newfoundland contained all the best stories in the world. [...] What I liked best was that they talked in great, looping circles. I was used to people who spoke in straight lines, darting from subject to subject like foxes looking for winter cover. But my Newfoundland relatives set their stories going and then let them roll from one tale to the next until I—sitting on the steps of the veranda—was certain they had no idea where they had begun. [...] Tales were abandoned in the telling in favor of other tales, but one story led seamlessly to another,

spiralling like drifting pipe-smoke, farther and farther away from the conversation's beginnings. Yet somehow, without so much as a where-were-we, the stories found their way back, hours later, to where they had started. (41–42)

This spiralling form is a model for the chapters of Macfarlane's memoir. The chapter in which he recounts his time at the steel plant in 1973 is a prime example. It begins with Macfarlane recalling that the last time he saw his great-uncle Roland was in 1973. But instead of launching into this last meeting, Macfarlane digresses into a description of the job he had at the time and of the two "Newfies" he worked with there. He goes on to inform us of the origins and connotations of the term "Newfie," which leads into the long history of the American influx during World War II. The tale spirals back to the two young steel workers, and several anecdotes about their time together at the plant, before he finally returns, twelve pages later, to the afternoon that he last saw his Uncle Roland in 1973, by the side of his parents' pool. By imitating this spiralling structure, Macfarlane employs the storytelling form that he has identified as a particularly Newfoundland trait. Storytelling, then, becomes a means of embracing his "emergent ethnicity" as a Newfoundlander, by, as Hall puts it, telling himself (and us) the stories of his roots and doing so with a particularly Newfoundland voice.

But Hall notes that the "recovered" stories of emergent ethnicities are necessarily invented and constructed, emphasizing that identities are not biological or cultural givens, but always negotiated. Like Buss/Clarke, Macfarlane uses the postmodern technique of meta-memoir to highlight the construction of his text. In addition to retelling the stories of his family, he also writes about what he does not know. As he tells us the story of the last time he saw his Uncle Roland, he laments: "That afternoon, by the pool, I could have sat down with Kate and Roland and found out about Ladle Cove and Grand Falls and Ray and Stan and Hedley. Roland and Kate were both born when Queen Victoria was on the throne. [...] We could have talked for hours. They might well have enjoyed my curiosity" (167). He goes on to list the many questions that he could have asked, about the family business, the relationships between the brothers, the source of his great-grandparents' money. For an entire page we are inundated with scraps of detail that lead only to mysteries and questions, not stories. But as a young man Macfarlane did not have the same interest in his family's stories, and while it "haunts [him] now," he recalls how he spent that afternoon long ago: "I am floating on an air mattress. I am listening to the radio, half asleep. I am doing my best to ignore the old people at the end of the pool" (168). The meta-memoir points to the active recovery and (re)construction required in the making of postmodern ethnicity.

Elsewhere, Macfarlane makes up for these lost stories by recounting events as though he has the first-hand knowledge required to tell the tale. He imagines, for example, the time that Roland took a stuffed caribou to London for the Exhibition of the Empire, to promote investment in Newfoundland: "He stood in the silent ranks on Pall Mall with the glass eyes of a dead caribou staring out from underneath his black armband, marvelling at the size of the crowds around him and dreaming of the pit props and the gold bullion and the acres upon priceless acres of Newfoundland that the Goodyears would some day sell to them" (49). But Macfarlane interrupts this narration with a metafictional moment: "Or this, at least, is what I imagine, for these stories—the ones that precede the First World War—are almost completely lost now" (49–50). While we know that Macfarlane cannot know what Roland was thinking as he stood on a London street, we get caught up in the fictional mode and accept the story. But Macfarlane does not allow us to easily accept his authority; rather, he upsets it in order to emphasize the negotiation required in the construction of his heritage. He lets us in on the research process:

> Someone—my mother's cousin—told me about the caribou only because he had come across it by accident, hanging above a door in a shop near Piccadilly after the Second World War. Someone else—my aunt—had heard the story of Miss Manuel and Susie Green. People I asked about those days could remember a stuffed white seal in Louisa Goodyear's parlor, and her bell-jar. My great-uncle Roland left some notes in his trunk about his father's adventures on the seal hunt. I could look at old photographs and guess at the stories. I could even use lines from an opera for dialogue if I wanted to: no one would know the difference. I called a dozen Manuels in the Newfoundland phone book. Up to my knees in snow and almost frozen by a coastal gale, I found Susie Green's tombstone, near a white frame church with a single silver spire, one January afternoon in Newtown. But long before I became interested, there was almost nothing left to hold these relics together. They had become isolated from one another, like the remnants of memory left by old age. The family had lost the story. (50)

Here, Macfarlane reveals how he has reconstructed the stories from fragments of knowledge and family documents and artifacts. But he also informs us that his power of reconstruction involves the power of invention as well, since "no one would know the difference." While he seems diligent about admitting the gaps in his knowledge and the luck involved in recovering the fragments, he also renders his reconstruction unreliable. We are not privy to all of the details that inform the memoir. The recovery of his heritage, then, is a creative, postmodern act that invites us to question the ways in which we may tend to privilege ethnicity as the seamless inheritance of identity.

At other times the stories Macfarlane tells are fictionalized without metafictional comment. But the fragmented nature of the memoir, and the metafiction we have already read, mean that these moments simply emphasize the invention. The opening scene enters the head of Macfarlane's grandmother, suffering from Alzheimer's in a nursing home. The scattered and confused stream of consciousness is a fitting way to begin a book that emphasizes not only memories but the gaps of forgetting between them. Between fragments of memory, Macfarlane's grandmother is vaguely aware of the comings and goings of visitors: "they come in from somewhere. […] They put in like schooners on a coast of arms and legs. She used to try to find out where inside her they belonged. Don't you remember? No, she doesn't. She's asleep. That's all" (2). The line "they come in from somewhere" is repeated several times throughout the scene, emphasizing the distance between the world inside her mind and the visitors like her grandson who seem to belong somewhere else. From the opening pages, then, Macfarlane simultaneously attempts to enter the private space of his grandmother's mind and memory, and emphasizes the impossibility of doing so, of overcoming that distance.

"No Escaping Them": Narratives of Postmemory

The memories and histories that Macfarlane seems most interested in penetrating, however, are his grandfather's and great uncles' experiences in the First World War. The memoir details the deaths of three of the Goodyear brothers, his great-uncles, and the lasting impact that the deaths have on the family, including future generations: "It was the dead who would loom over the Goodyear family," he writes. "There was no escaping them" (292). For Macfarlane's great-aunt Kate, the loss of three of her brothers during the war is a trauma that for another seven decades would still render her helpless against a "sudden avalanche of sadness" that "seared past her eyes, took her breath and her voice away, and then ended its descent in the same inconsolable hollow where the news had first settled years earlier" (245). But for Macfarlane, the trauma of his grandparents' generation is distanced by time and space; he can only begin to imagine it through the memories of his grandfather, and Aunt Kate's refusal to remember it. The trauma of the war for Macfarlane, then, is reminiscent of what Marianne Hirsch calls "postmemory," which is "distinguished from memory by generational distance and from history by deep personal connection." Postmemory "characterizes the experience of those who grow up dominated by narratives that preceded their birth, whose own belated stories are evacuated by the stories of the previous generation shaped by traumatic events that can be neither understood nor recreated" (22). While Hirsch developed the concept in relation to the children of Holocaust survivors, she suggests that it is also applicable to other second-generation experiences. Postmemory, then, is not formed out of a direct connection to the past, but rather arises "through an imaginative investment and creation" (22). The concept thus evocatively legitimizes invention and creativity as a means of aligning oneself with one's family history, and it identifies the experience of hearing stories as a means of tapping into a collective form of memory. Macfarlane inherits, not Aunt Kate's trauma, but the postmemory of that trauma; he feels a "deep personal connection" to it that is nevertheless rendered distant. The postmemory of the war takes on a new significance in Macfarlane's treatment of his great uncle Ray: "When I asked Aunt Kate about him, she said he'd been too young to have left many memories behind. 'You'll have to imagine him' she said. 'He was just a boy'" (136). Here, the imagination of postmemory takes the place of actual memory, since Ray was so young that he had hardly lived long enough to leave memories behind for his family. Postmemory becomes the *only* way of memorializing him.

For Hirsch, photographs play a central role in postmemory: as representations of "what no longer is," photographs "affirm the past's existence and, in their flat two-dimensionality, they signal its unbridgeable distance" (23). Photographs bring the past into the present as a "ghostly revenant" (20), always referencing the past's irretrievability. The family photos that mark the beginning of each of Macfarlane's chapters, then, do not simply put faces to the characters that he writes about but also operate as signs of loss, of the "unbridgeable" disconnect between generations. In Macfarlane's text the photographs of the family's war dead haunt their survivors. We are told that "the photograph of Hedley Goodyear at Melrose Abbey stayed on his fiancée's mantelpiece for fifty years" (264). After Hedley is killed, his fiancée remains unmarried for the rest of her life, frozen in a state of unresolved engagement, haunted by the photo that represents the loss of both her lover and her past. This was the case for an entire generation of Newfoundlanders, following the devastating battle at Beaumont Hamel in France: "Their fiancées waited for them forever, their mail went unanswered, their deals never closed. Their plans were left in rough draft, their sentences unfinished" (189). This uncanny state of perpetual stasis continues to haunt future generations: "After the war, their pictures hung in the homes of their parents and their surviving brothers and sister. Then, remarkably, they continued to hang in the homes of relatives who had never known them, and could only guess at who they had been. The photographs were kept up by the next generation and the generation after that" (190). These subsequent generations, then, preserve the photos as representations of a lost past, and as testimonies to an inherited postmemory that continues to impact their lives.

While they represent an irretrievable past, these photographs also resonate powerfully in the present as representations of a turning point in Newfoundland's history. Macfarlane comes to believe that:

> The photographs were as modern as I was. They were the pictures of our failures. Somehow, in our present—in the disappearance of an innocence, in the bankruptcy of an enterprise, in the dimming of a country's political vision—I seem to know who these young soldiers are. They are the missing pieces. The three dead brothers kept their places in the family—gaps among the three brothers who survived them—and the century that carried on past the moments of their deaths was not what it might have been. (191)

Macfarlane writes that the balance upset in the family by the death of the three brothers is echoed in Newfoundland as a whole; while before the war "the island seemed to be on the brink of prosperity" (192), the war's devastating losses for Newfoundland, both human and financial, meant that "Newfoundland's role in the great War led inexorably to bankruptcy, to an unelected government, to the colony's abandonment by England, and, finally, to confederation with Canada" (193). World War I is often considered a defining moment of Newfoundland identity and nationalism; as Macfarlane reminds us, "the raising of their own regiment was a source of great national pride to Newfoundlanders. [...] Newfoundland had claimed its place among the nations of the Empire" (143). The decimation of that regiment, in turn, created a collective trauma that reinforced Newfoundland's national imaginary as a community in simultaneous mourning. But for Macfarlane, the war marks both Newfoundland's "great moment of nationalism" (193) and, ironically, the beginning of the end for the Newfoundland nation. Macfarlane locates his narrative, then, at the pivotal moment of Newfoundland identity. He aligns himself genealogically with the soldiers who defined Newfoundland identity with their deaths, and as he laments their loss he also laments the loss of the Newfoundland nation.

This sense of loss, as well as the "discomfiture" between Macfarlane's Ontarian and Newfoundland identities, are perhaps best captured in the final scene, as he visits Newfoundland on July 1st. Since World War I, July 1st had always been Memorial Day, in remembrance of the Newfoundland Regiment decimated in the battle at Beaumont Hamel. But July 1st, of course, is also Canada Day, and since Confederation the coincidence of the two dates has caused many Newfoundlanders consternation; for Macfarlane's grandfather, a veteran of the battle, it was "an appalling indignity" (193). Macfarlane visits his mother's hometown of Grand Falls for Memorial Day ceremonies, only to find that they were held the week before. Instead, the town is hosting a Canada Day rock festival featuring the Beach Boys. Macfarlane's account of the influx of cars and tents, and the signs announcing "Surf City Discounts" (296), is sharply juxtaposed with his account of the infamous battle at Beaumont Hamel, the morning after which a mere sixty-nine soldiers from a regiment of eight hundred answered the roll call. This juxtaposition provides a poignant commentary on Newfoundland's uneasy fit within the Canadian nation, and Canada's jarring disregard for one of Newfoundland's identity-forming tragedies. The image of Newfoundlanders themselves replacing memorial services with celebrations further complicates the idea of ethnicity; while Macfarlane, as an Ontarian, inherits a profound respect for Newfoundland's veterans and July 1st, Newfoundlanders born and raised in the province do not seem to place the same value on the rituals of commemoration. Their Newfoundland identities are secure and do not necessarily clash with their Canadian identities in the same way. For Macfarlane, born "away," the two parts of his heritage are in necessary tension and, represented by physical distance, they cannot be easily resolved.

The memoir's final image is fittingly haunting: as Macfarlane makes his way to his grandmother's nursing home for a last visit before he returns to Ontario, he hears a train. Puzzled, since there have not been any trains in Newfoundland for years, he stops to watch: "I looked down at the ground behind the wheels. The diesel was dragging two long, parallel lines of rusted steel along the railbed. The engine—perhaps the last in all of Newfoundland—was pulling up its own tracks" (304). These final lines of the book are haunting in their pathetic finality and act as a synecdoche for a changing post-Confederation Newfoundland. The Newfoundland of the Goodyear family is gone; the "country," as Macfarlane's grandfather always stubbornly referred to it, has been replaced by "the province of Newfoundland" (29). The defining tragedy of Newfoundland's history has been forgotten in the shadow of a Canadian holiday and an American rock band. And Newfoundland's train system, shut down after Confederation by Canadian National, its new owner, is engaged in its own final self-destruction. The final tone is one of profound loss. But Macfarlane's Newfoundland identity is maintained through postmemory; despite the loss of the Newfoundland nation, the death of his Newfoundland ancestors, and the threat of assimilation that his Canadian identity seems to pose to his Newfoundland identity, Macfarlane is dominated by the stories of his mother's family, of a place that seems to "sit at the center of the universe" (205), and he uses these stories to construct his own narrative of emergent ethnicity.

The "Holdin' Ground"

As Macfarlane interweaves his own memories with the memories of his family and the history of the island, he not only adopts his family's spiralling story structure, he also writes himself into these stories, demonstrating the intergenerational impact that stories have on diasporic identities. Sara Ahmed writes that in diaspora "generational acts of story-telling" are "bound up with—touched by—the forming of new communities. In this sense, memory can be understood as a collective act which produces its object (the 'we'), rather than reflects on it" (90–91). Even as Macfarlane reflects on his own disconnection from the Newfoundland community, his intergenerational stories serve to construct a Newfoundland diasporic community to which he belongs. Stories produce a second-generation identity that is fragmented, shifting, and self-consciously constructed, but that nevertheless provides a connection to a lineage, a home—a "holdin' ground."

Conclusion

WRITING IN DIASPORA SPACE

In 2002 I began writing my own family memoir of Newfoundland, collecting the voices of my parents, grandparents, and great-grandparents from interviews that I recorded and the poems, letters, and documents they left behind. I don't know where this impulse came from. Sure, their stories are fascinating—tales of shipwreck, war, the hardships of outport life during the Depression—but I felt as though I was writing towards something, staking claim to something. It was not just a memoir of my ancestors but an imagining of place. Newfoundland has always been more than the province my parents come from: it has been, strangely, an identity. It is an identity that defines my Canadianness, that colours it. In grade two, when we all had to bring in a recipe that represented our family's heritage for a classroom multicultural cookbook, I was sent to school with fish chowder.

I am still working away at this memoir, a decade later. I am listening to the tapes I recorded of my grandfather before he died, rewinding again as I strain to catch every word, to accurately transcribe every "um" and "well" in his low, accented speech. He tells me of the shipwreck his mother survived at sixteen, of his childhood on the farm outside St. John's, of the city during the Second World War. And he tells me of Confederation, how the buildings in St. John's were draped with black flags on 1 April 1949, of the conspiracy he swears was behind the referendum, and the dirty dealings of Joey Smallwood. The pride in the nation of his birth is still audible through the hissing of the tape. (Whenever we heard weather reports of storms and neck-deep snow in Newfoundland, and my mother phoned to ask him how they were doing, he always said the weather's not so bad, those damn mainlanders at the CBC are always making Newfoundland sound worse than it is.)

I call the memoir *The Bosun Chair*, after the chair that my great-grandmother supposedly rigged to help transport people from a sinking ship to the shore, in the middle of a storm, in 1906. It is, as Wayne Johnston might put it, a good story. But I feel like I have to explain how it could be mine. If I am an Albertan, what does this book mean?

The word "diaspora" seems like an answer to this question. "Diaspora" seems to explain why I feel this connection to Newfoundland, why I am compelled to write about a place where I have never lived. It seems to explain how I could grow up in Alberta and never feel like an Albertan, or why David Macfarlane, a boy from Ontario, wrote a memoir not just of his family, but of Newfoundland itself. And it explains why I identify with Janice Kulyk Keefer's journey in her memoir, *Honey and Ashes*, to reconstruct her mother's birthplace on the border of Ukraine and Poland, or with Denise Chong's fictionalization of her family's story in China and British Columbia in *The Concubine's Children*.

The present work does not insist that Newfoundland migrants and their descendants are automatically diasporic subjects, but rather considers the role that literary texts play in constructing diasporic identification through shared narratives of displacement, home, and identity. Lily Cho compellingly writes that "no one is born diasporic. Rather, one *becomes* diasporic through a complex process of memory and emergence" ("Turn" 21). The concept of diaspora both enables and is enabled by an understanding of differences and of the losses "shared across geographies and communities" (21). Cho's metaphorical spatialization of diasporic engagement suggests one way of conceptualizing how history and collective memory construct diasporic subjects into the second and third generation, and how these subjects come to identify with other experiences that may be worlds apart from their own.

My parents are about to leave for a trip "home," to visit my grandparents and the few siblings who have not left. They will return with a fresh supply of Newfoundland's Mount Scio savoury, an essential ingredient in turkey stuffing. When my mother asks her cousin, who lives around the corner from her, if she wants anything from home—Purity brand cookies, Newfoundland salt beef—the reply is "just kiss the ground for me." This connection to the very ground has been passed on to me, often resulting in a melodramatic sentimentality. But it also appears in other ways, like when my husband laughs at the way a "t" on the end of a word sometimes slips between my teeth.

...

I envision my memoir as part of a Newfoundland literary diaspora, a body of work by writers who write back to the place—writers including David French, Wayne Johnston, and Donna Morrissey. But writers who have stayed or returned also speak to this continual atmosphere of loss. Tom Dawe's haunting verses in *In Hardy Country* (1993) portray the gradual scattering of an outport's children, making the penultimate line of "Hide and Seek"—an offhand comment about "how small the world was"—painfully ironic. Bernice Morgan's novel *Waiting for Time* (1994) depicts a woman born in Ontario who, upon discovering her Newfoundland roots late in life, is pulled to the place and her history. Morgan dedicates the book "to young Newfoundlanders who must go away," including her own children (3). Paul Bowdring's short novel *The Roncesvalles Pass* (1989) follows a community of diasporic Newfoundlanders in the cold urban space of Toronto. Younger writers like Michael Winter, Lisa Moore, Michael Crummey, and other members of the Burning Rock Collective write stories and novels in which out-migration is a natural part of everyday life. In his introduction to *Essays on Canadian Writing*'s 2004 special issue on the literature of Newfoundland, Lawrence Mathews suggests that writers like Winter and Moore constitute a separate "literary culture" from writers like Johnston and Morgan and an older generation of novelists who are concerned with the thematic preoccupations of "collective identity" (12). But rather than a dichotomy of cultures, I see Newfoundland's as a rich and evolving literature in which defining social phenomena like diaspora are both explored in projects that explicitly construct collective identity, as well as simply captured in poetry and prose that tell the stories of everyday life.

Moore's short story "Azalea," in her 2002 collection, *Open*, is exemplary of how diaspora is being taken up by writers who focus on the cosmopolitan setting of contemporary St. John's. The story is an intimate portrait of Sara, a wife and a mother to a toddler. The prospect of moving to Montreal when her husband is offered a job there is intertwined with other reflections and everyday movements through the urban space of St. John's. The lush and sensuous details of daily life overwhelm the thread of narrative, imbuing Sara's surroundings with a mood of nostalgia simply at the prospect of leaving. These fragments of taste and sight—the farmer's market with its jars of "flaring" bakeapples, the street shiny in the rain, a cookie made with "table butter"—are not explicitly tied to a Newfoundland culture or identity but simply to the geography of home. Read within the context of a broader Newfoundland diaspora, however, Sara's dilemma becomes not just personal but culturally particular and poignant. After a century and a half of continuous out-migration, this simple story is now as much the face of diaspora as works that explicitly grapple with issues of citizenship and identity.

...

While I want to define my creative work in relationship to this literary diaspora, I do so tentatively, self-consciously. I have been called "Newfie" by well-meaning friends, and I get a feeling of intense discomfort, like I am impersonating a Newfoundlander and will be found out, though I have never claimed to be one. I am proud of my heritage but intellectually aware of the problems of appropriation, or worse, of allowing a whitewashed "we-are-all-immigrants" Canadian multiculturalism to obscure the power differentials of a society that in many ways has been built on a deeply entrenched racism.

Newfoundland, moreover, is just a province of Canada. I am descended from colonial settlers complicit in the eradication of the Beothuk people. My feeling of difference is tentative, almost sheepish, and sometimes, perhaps, strategic. Is diaspora, then, merely a dangerous "lure" (99), as Rey Chow puts it? Is it a form of cultural capital, a claim that obscures the privileges of economic migration, or that erases the class differences between my white-collar family members and the oil-rig workers of Fort McMurray? Does my own memoir blindly laud the ethnic absolutism of identity politics or neo-nationalism?

Claiming diaspora without a detailed interrogation of the term's histories, internal differences, and implications does risk erasing the important power differentials behind its dislocations. Yet restricting diaspora to a set of criteria including racialized subjectivity, a level of victimization, or lack of class privilege involves other risks, such as reducing identity to origins and territory, reifying ethnic and racial categories, and constructing bizarre hierarchies of victimhood. Such restrictions risk stratifying communities based on the conditions of migration, rather than recognizing the productive similarities and cultural and historical connections between the groups' members. I follow the influential work of theorists such as Stuart Hall, James Clifford, and Avtar Brah, who argue for definitions of diaspora as a concept involving complex and shifting processes of identification. As Brah puts it, "processes of diasporic identity formation are exemplars *par excellence* of the claim that identity is always plural, and in process. [...] The concept of diaspora refers to *multi-locationality* within and across territorial, cultural and psychic boundaries" (197; emphasis in original). Considering diaspora in these more flexible conceptual terms does not mean that the term should be applied willy-nilly to any movement of people. Rather, this usage of diaspora as a concept or a condition of subjectivity, rather than a concrete unit of study, accommodates a considered reflection of the conditions of diasporic movements, community formations, and identity construction, as these conditions relate to that of other groups.

• • •

Canada can therefore helpfully be considered what Brah calls a "diaspora space," the "intersectionality of diaspora, border, and dis/location as a point of confluence of economic, political, cultural, and psychic processes," which includes "the entanglement, the intertwining of the genealogies of dispersion with those of 'staying put'" (208–09). Brah uses England as an example of a diaspora space, within which "African-Caribbean, Irish, Asian, Jewish and other diasporas intersect among themselves as well as with the entity constructed as 'Englishness', thoroughly re-inscribing it in the process" (209). Formed in part through colonial encounters and imperial rivalries, the diaspora space of England is continually reconstituted by border crossings and cultural "traffic." Canada is similarly characterized by a multitude of colonial, indigenous, and diasporic identities, further differentiated by various "axes" of class, race, gender, or sexuality. Brah's formulation does not posit everyone within a diaspora space as necessarily diasporic, but rather articulates how diasporic identifications are constructed by interactions with other cultural identities within a given location, in turn constructing that location as a place of shifting identities, and continually reconfiguring received notions of "Englishness" or, in this case, "Canadianness" (210).

Much of this book has considered Newfoundland in "national" terms, resisting the tendency to anachronistically appropriate historical representations of pre-Confederation Newfoundland into restrictive, thematically defined visions of Canadian identity or Canadian literature as an institution. But post-Confederation constructions of the Newfoundland nation are, ultimately, inseparable from the Canadian space of which Newfoundland has become a part. The concept of diaspora both highlights the vexed position of Newfoundland within the federation and intimates the relationship between diasporic Newfoundlanders and other Canadian identities. While Newfoundlanders do, of course, move to other countries, and in the late nineteenth and early twentieth centuries formed large diasporic communities in the eastern United States, the vast majority of Newfoundland migrants today move to other parts of Canada. This relationship between homeland and hostland informs the relationship of Newfoundland as a whole with the rest of Canada, contributing to feelings of difference, subordination, and sometimes resentment over Confederation. But as the concept of "diaspora space" suggests, Newfoundland identities also reconfigure notions of "Canadianness." What Brah calls the "interesectionality" of the Newfoundland diaspora with other diasporic and immigrant groups, with First Nations peoples, Québécois, white Anglo-Canadians from various regions, long-standing communities of Africadians or Japanese Canadians, and countless other identities, constantly challenges and redefines traditional representations of Canada as the home of "two solitudes," as a place bound by a "survival" or "garrison mentality," or as a multicultural "mosaic."

Much of this reconfiguration occurs within the body of narratives that may collectively be termed "Canadian literature." In 1990, Linda Hutcheon and Marion Richmond's important anthology, *Other Solitudes*, attempted to revise the "two solitudes" vision of Canada by acknowledging the country's "multiracial, pluri-ethnic nature" (Hutcheon, "Introduction" 2). Yet invoking the image of "solitudes" further entrenches the old binaries at the centre, with "minority literatures" on the outskirts. As Donna Bennett puts it, "we assume a mainstream against which 'other solitudes'—a minority collectively struggling against a dominant culture—define themselves, and our official attempts to legislate more complexity into Canadian culture collapse back into the Us–Them dialectic these policies [official multiculturalism] sought to escape" (11). More recent critical work draws on theories of diaspora, post-colonialism, and critical regionalism to formulate new paradigms for thinking through "Canadian Literature" as a concept. Bennett, for example, in her 2005 article "Getting Beyond Binaries," contends that "identity in Canada resides neither within some unitary construction of nation nor in the binary nature of the doubled immigrant experience but in the complex mixture that now arises when individuals from many groups come together" (14). She proposes the neologism "polybridity" as one way of getting at the "other ways of seeing" (12) offered by Canadian literature. In the preface to *Trans.Can.Lit*, the collection of papers from the first TransCanada conference in 2005, Smaro Kamboureli traces some of the problems of "CanLit" as a concept and an institution. She suggests that CanLit may

> be instrumentalized by and concerned with the Canadian state, but it also contests the stateness, and boldly points beyond it, to an elsewhereness that is not yet legible, that defamiliarizes the tropes that produce transparency and its accompanying contentment and complacency. An alternative cognitive space, this elsewhereness demands epistemic breaks that require new tools to comprehend its materiality; it calls for an understanding of temporality and space that questions the assumption that knowledge is residual, always anterior to what has come before, the product of the same epistemological gestures that have cultivated the categories of "proper" subject and "other" in the first place. This elsewhereness inscribed in CanLit intimates that Canada is an unimaginable community, that is, a community constituted in excess of the knowledge of itself, always transitioning. (x)

This evocative idea of Canada as an "un/imagined community" is the driving spirit behind the TransCanada Institute and conferences, which respond to a demand for "developing new terms of engagement with CanLit" (x) as an institution that "evokes the entirety of the geopolitical space it refers to, but [...] also siphons off large segments of this space and its peoples into oblivion at worst, and circumscribed conditions at best" (ix). The ephemeral, dynamic images of "TransCanada," "elsewhereness," and the "unimaginable community" all suggest a space that is in motion and transition, refusing the "feigned plenitude" (ix) of CanLit as an institution.

Following this current spirit of revision and transition in the study of Canadian literature, I evoke Brah's concept of diaspora space as one way of articulating the way in which diasporic communities interact with each other and with other identities within a Canadian literature in constant flux. The concept of diaspora "delineates a field of identifications where 'imagined communities' are forged within and out of a confluence of narratives from annals of collective memory and re-memory" (Brah 196). The multiple narratives of imagined communities challenge the singularity of Canada as a united and "complacent" "imagined community" (Kamboureli, "Preface" x). The Newfoundland diaspora, then, is one in a "field of identifications" whose literature challenges regionalist assumptions by breaching the borders of a place-bound identity, resists racialized visions of diaspora that limit writers to "minority literature" and the role of native informant, and problematizes the very concept of Canadian literature and the national unity such a construct implies.

...

Frequently, when I have told people what my current research is about, I have been asked, "Are you from Newfoundland?" or "What is your connection to Newfoundland?" My stock answer has been that my family is from Newfoundland, so I am a product of the Newfoundland diaspora. But it is, in reality, a question that for me does not have an easy answer. Rather, it is the asking itself that is productive, as Newfoundlanders and Canadians from a multitude of homelands negotiate a place for their literatures within the shifting space of CanLit.

NOTES

Note to Introduction
1 See Gary Burrill's oral history collection *Away* (1992) for accounts of out-migration from the Maritimes. Burrill's exclusion of Newfoundland from his study emphasizes Newfoundland's distinction from the Maritime provinces (Nova Scotia, New Brunswick, and Prince Edward Island). Many people confuse the Maritimes with Atlantic Canada, lumping in Newfoundland and Labrador as a Maritime province despite the fact that "Canada's tenth province differs substantially from its Maritime cousins" (Conrad 161). For a more involved discussion of Newfoundland's distinctive identity within the category of Atlantic Canadian Literature, see Herb Wyile's *Anne of Tim Hortons: Globalization and the Reshaping of the Atlantic-Canadian Literature* (2011).

Notes to Chapter 1
1 I will address the issue of whether or not Newfoundlanders can be considered "ethnic" in Part V.
2 Even after responsible government was granted in 1855, the imperial government maintained control over the colony's foreign affairs, and, after protests from Canada, Britain refused to ratify trade agreements that Newfoundland had negotiated with the United States. While the late nineteenth and early twentieth centuries were witness to a "surging nationalism" in Newfoundland (O'Flaherty 115), many Newfoundlanders (primarily the Protestant population) also strongly identified as British subjects, as citizens of a colony whose "face turns to Britain," as the anonymous 1869 "Anti-Confederation Song" suggests. Nor was nationalist sentiment enough to prevent a Royal Commission from recommending the suspension of responsible government in 1934, in order to give the debt-ridden colony a paternalistic "rest from politics" (Mackenzie sect. 553).

Notes to Chapter 2

1. A certain percentage of the community had to agree to move for anyone to get assistance, and many obviously felt extreme pressure to move from their neighbours, or out of fear that if they did not move now they would miss out on the opportunity for assistance. Morrissey's novel omits this policy, but the climate of fear and coercion remain in her account of the period.
2. For a detailed analysis of *Sylvanus Now*, see my article "'The Rock Beneath His Feet': Cultural Nostalgia in Donna Morrissey's *Sylvanus Now*."

Notes to Chapter 4

1. F.R. Scott wrote to A.J.M. Smith in 1934 that the Pratt poems chosen for *New Provinces* were "the less successful but more experimental and more contemporary work," which "belongs to our Anthology in spirit if not in skill" (Gnarowski xiv).
2. Interestingly, Rose credits Farley Mowat, who is not from Newfoundland but lived there for several years, with beginning the "Newfoundland Renaissance" in the 1960s, and teaching Newfoundlanders that "we were worth writing about" (xi). Michael Cook, an Irishman, is also celebrated in Rose's "Foreword" for the fact that he has "not adopted the ex-patriot Irishman's stance but has become imbedded in *this* land and its people" (xii; emphasis in original). Rose's critique, then, is not so conservative as to exclude those who, in Newfoundland parlance, are from "upalong"; rather she finds in Pratt's work a "remoteness" that Mowat and Cook have overcome. While Mowat and Cook chose to live in Newfoundland, Pratt chose to leave it. In contrast, Patrick O'Flaherty scathingly considers Mowat an "intruder" whose representations of Newfoundland were characterized by "sentimental excess" (180).
3. In Chapter 4, I discuss whether or not Newfoundlanders can be considered in "ethnic" terms; for now, I apply Radhakrishnan's use of the term "ethnic" to a Newfoundland context as a signifier of the cultural difference felt by both diasporic Newfoundlanders and other Canadians.
4. The phrase "poor bald rock" was originally Joey Smallwood's.
5. Today, according to Fowler, the myth of the old outport persists as a "powerful inspiration" ("Patrick Kavanagh" 71) for writers and stands as a symbol of Newfoundland community. To prove his point, he points to recent works like Patrick Kavanagh's *Gaff Topsails* (1996) and Bernice Morgan's *Random Passage* (1992), which look to the outport of the past as a defining emblem of Newfoundland culture.
6. The quotation is from Tom Marshall, "E.J. Pratt," *Canadian Forum* 57 (1977).

Notes to Chapter 5

1. Other Newfoundland writers have expressed similar sentiments. Patrick Kavanagh wrote his first novel, *Gaff Topsails* (1996), which is set in a small outport, in Beijing. For Kavanagh, "distance makes it easier to fiddle with the details,

to step aside from reality if it helps the story" (Vandervlist). While the novel is largely set in a fictional Newfoundland Catholic Parish in 1948, Kavanagh sets out to create an origin myth for his parishioners that predates British settlement of Newfoundland and that permeates the mid-twentieth-century community poised on the edge of Confederation. The novel's concept that Newfoundland identity is derived from a divinely ordained settlement *outside* of colonialism depends upon a romantic, mythical tone that eschews historical "fact" or the detail of realism. While I find Kavanagh's construction of Newfoundland deeply troubling for its version of history as well as its romanticization of Newfoundland culture, whether or not he is an "authentic" Newfoundlander does not seem to be the right question to ask. A more appropriate question is what is achieved (or lost) by the Newfoundland that Kavanagh imagines. See Delisle, "Nation, Indigenization, the Beothuk: A Newfoundland Myth of Origin in Patrick Kavanagh's *Gaff Topsails*."
2 The Vintage Canada edition of *The Colony of Unrequited Dreams* includes an endorsement from Proulx on the back cover: "Wayne Johnston is a brilliant and accomplished writer and his Newfoundland—boots and boats, rough politics and rough country, history and journalism—during the wild Smallwood years is vivid and sharp." While the phrase "his Newfoundland" does suggest that a variety of Newfoundlands are possible, it is interesting that she is called upon not only as a literary authority but as an authority on Newfoundland literature in particular.

Notes to Chapter 6

1 The phrase "country of no country" comes from Wayne Johnston's *Baltimore's Mansion*.
2 The Mercers may well be descended from one of the many English families that settled in Newfoundland over several centuries of colonial rule, but in order to construct Newfoundland as a civilized colony they must claim a more generalized Britishness, to accommodate the Celtic origins of much of the population.
3 This moment is dramatized in French's later play *Salt-Water Moon*.
4 Obviously, audience members at the play's original run at Toronto's Tarragon Theatre were not entirely or even mostly displaced Newfoundlanders. But the anonymity of a public audience does allow one to "imagine" a community of fellow audience members.
5 Rompkey discusses Newfoundland as a "post-colonial" entity in the sense that it is simply no longer a colony of Britain. For a more nuanced discussion of Newfoundland as post-colonial, see Paul Chafe's article on *The Colony of Unrequited Dreams*, "The Scuttlework of Empire."

Notes to Chapter 7

1 Bernice Morgan, author of the historical novels *Random Passage* and *Waiting for Time*, both claims this goal of connecting present Newfoundland identity

with Newfoundland history and connects it explicitly to out-migration: "a lot of those children, those young people who are reading [*Random Passage*] are going away, they're going to leave Newfoundland, most of them forever, and it would be nice for them to know where they came from, you know? And why people came here in the first place" (qtd. in Fuller, *Writing* 116).

2 Johnston explains to Wyile that "the people who voted for Confederation, many of them, I have no doubt (and I have spoken with them), did so very reluctantly and did so with an enormous burden of guilt on their shoulders. They believed in their own hearts that they were acting as traitors, that they were bargaining self-reliance and self-definition, for material, if not wealth, at least security. [...] My guess is that in 1948, something like seventy-five to eighty-five per cent of the population, from an emotional point of view, wanted an independent Newfoundland" ("Afterlife" 112). While Johnston's suspicions cannot be proven, what is important is that for him Confederation was, on an emotional or ideological level, much less popular than the referendum results would indicate. Smallwood's decision to bring Confederation to the table, then, is for Johnston closer to a cultural betrayal than to democratic action.

3 While *The Backhomer* is an invention of Johnston's, the magazine and the diasporic community that surrounds it do have some historical basis. Several American cities in this period had large enough populations of Newfoundland migrants to warrant clubs like the Newfoundlanders' Mutual Benefit Association and the Cabot Club. *The Backhomer* resembles *The Atlantic Guardian*, the later magazine started in 1945 by Arthur Scammell, Brian Cahill, and Ewart Young, and published out of Montreal. The title is reminiscent of the magazine *The Downhomer*, now called *Downhome Magazine*, which has been published since 1988 out of Ontario and caters to diasporic Newfoundlanders, even including a "where are they now?" section.

4 Other similar scenes occur in both *Baltimore's Mansion* and *Colony*, such as the scene of the child arriving home to discover that his family is moving, with all their possessions already loaded into a truck. Here, Wayne's childhood experience parallels Smallwood's, not Fielding's. In fact Johnston was struck when he began writing *Colony* by the many similarities between him and the real Joey Smallwood ("Afterlife" 115). Johnston has been criticized for turning Smallwood into a version of himself (Pierson, "Johnston's" 295). But as Wyile suggests in conversation with Johnston, the parallels and repetitions between the texts seem to "foreground that historical fiction like all fiction is to an extent autobiographical and to underscore Smallwood as an invention rather than a replica" (Johnston, "Afterlife" 114). By autobiographically aligning himself with both Fielding and Smallwood, Johnston emphasizes the fact that *both* narrative voices in the novel are invented—both Fielding, the entirely fictional character, and Smallwood, the historical figure.

Notes to Chapter 8

1 As Buss/Clarke informs us in the foreword, "Helen Buss," her first name and her married name, is the name she has given her "sensible side," which she uses in her academic writing. "Margaret Clarke," her middle name and her maiden name, is the name she gives her "inner child" (xii), and the pen name she has used as a creative writer. In her memoir she finds these two separated identities coming together, hence the dual authorship of the book. These two identities are in constant dialogue throughout the memoir; I refer to her as "Buss/Clarke" throughout this chapter in order to acknowledge this duality.

2 While Chariandy does not directly reference Jonathan Kertzer's 1998 *Worrying the Nation: Imagining a National Literature in English Canada*, Kertzer's definition of "worrying" as a "dogged engagement with the problematic" is illuminating. The link drawn between diaspora theory and Canadian "national" literature by this rhetorical overlap is also evocative. As Kertzer writes, the nation "promises to unify a people and/with/through their literature, but it simultaneously speaks of their irreducible plurality" (35).

WORKS CITED

Agnew, Vijay. Introduction. *Diaspora, Memory and Identity: A Search for Home.* Ed. Vijay Agnew. Toronto: U of Toronto P, 2005. 3–17. Print.

Ahmed, Sara. *The Cultural Politics of Emotion.* Edinburgh: Edinburgh UP, 2004. Print.

———. *Strange Encounters: Embodied Others in Post-Coloniality.* London: Routledge, 2000. Print.

Akenson, Donald Harman. "The Historiography of English-Speaking Canada and the Concept of Diaspora: A Sceptical Appreciation." *Canadian Historical Review* 76.3 (1995): 375–409. Print.

Alexander, David. "Newfoundland's Traditional Economy and Development to 1934." *The Acadiensis Reader: Atlantic Canada after Confederation.* Ed. P.A. Buckner and David Frank. Fredericton: Acadiensis, 1985. 11–33. Print.

———. "New Notions of Happiness: Nationalism, Regionalism, and Atlantic Canada." *Journal of Canadian Studies* 15.2 (1980): 29–42. Print.

Anderson, Benedict. *Imagined Communities: Reflections on the Origin and Spread of Nationalism.* London: Verso, 1991. Print.

———. "Nationalism, Identity, and the World-in-Motion: On the Logics of Seriality." *Cosmopolitics.* Ed. Pheng Cheah and Bruce Robbins. Minneapolis: U of Minnesota P, 1998. 117–33. Print.

———. *The Spectre of Comparisons: Nationalism, Southeast Asia, and the World.* London: Verso, 1998. Print.

Ang, Ien. *On Not Speaking Chinese: Living between Asia and the West.* London: Routledge, 2001. Print.

———. "Together-in-Difference: Beyond Diaspora, into Hybridity." *Asian Studies Review* 27.2 (2003): 141–54. *Academic Search Complete.* Web. 16 Sept. 2011.

Anonsen, Kay. "Confederation." *TickleAce* 37 (1999): 48–51. Print.

Anthias, Floya. "Evaluating 'Diaspora': Beyond Ethnicity?" *Sociology* 32.3 (1998): 557–80. Print.

"The Anti-Confederation Song." *Newfoundland Heritage,* n.d. Web. 22 Feb. 2008.

Atwood, Margaret. *Survival.* Toronto: Anansi, 1972. Print.

Bannerji, Himani. "On the Dark Side of the Nation: Politics of Multiculturalism and the State of 'Canada.'" *Literary Pluralities*. Ed. Christl Verduyn. Peterborough, ON: Broadview, 1998. 125–51. Print.

Bannister, Jerry. "Making History: Cultural Memory in Twentieth-Century Newfoundland." *Newfoundland Studies* 18.2 (2002): 175–93. Print.

Bhattacharyya, Gargi, John Gabriel, and Stephen Small. *Race and Power: Global Racism in the Twenty-First Century*. London: Routledge, 2002. Print.

Bella, Leslie. *Newfoundlanders: Home and Away*. St. John's: Greetings from Newfoundland, 2002. Print.

Bennett, Donna. "Getting beyond Boundaries: Polybridity in Contemporary Canadian Literature." *Moveable Margins*. Ed. Chelva Kanaganayakam. Toronto: TSAR, 2005. 9–25. Print.

Blackmore, G.C. "Sense of Place: Loss and the Newfoundland and Labrador Spirit." *Royal Commission on Renewing and Strengthening Our Place in Canada*, 2003. Web. 22 Feb. 2008.

Bowdring, Paul. *The Roncesvalles Pass*. St. John's: Breakwater, 1989. Print.

Boyarin, Jonathan, and Daniel Boyarin. *Powers of Diaspora: Two Essays on the Relevance of Jewish Culture*. Minneapolis: U of Minnesota P, 2002. Print.

Boym, Svetlana. *The Future of Nostalgia*. New York: Basic, 2001. Print.

Brah, Avtar. *Cartographies of Diaspora: Contesting Identities*. London: Routledge, 1996. Print.

Braziel, Jana Evans, and Anita Mannur. "Nation, Migration, Globalization: Points of Contention in Diaspora Studies." *Theorizing Diaspora: A Reader*. Ed. Jana Evans Braziel and Anita Mannur. Malden: Blackwell, 2003. 1–22. Print.

Brennan, Teresa. *The Transmission of Affect*. Ithaca, NY: Cornell UP, 2004. Print.

Buitenhuis, Peter. "E.J. Pratt." *The Canadian Imagination: Dimensions of a Literary Culture*. Ed. David Staines. Cambridge: Harvard UP, 1977. 46–68. Print.

Burrill, Gary Clayton. *Away: Maritimers in Massachusetts, Ontario and Alberta: An Oral History of Leaving Home*. Montreal: McGill-Queen's UP, 1992. Print.

Buss, Helen M. *Repossessing the World: Reading Memoirs by Contemporary Women*. Waterloo: Wilfrid Laurier UP, 2002. Print.

Buss, Helen M. / Margaret Clarke. *Memoirs from Away: A New Found Land Girlhood*. Waterloo: Wilfrid Laurier UP, 1999. Print.

Byrne, Pat. "The Confluence of Folklore and Literature in the Creation of a Newfoundland Mythology within the Canadian Context." *Canada and the Nordic Countries in Times of Reorientation: Culture and Politics*. Ed. Jorn Carlsen. Arhus: Nordic Association for Canadian Studies, 1998. 55–77. Print.

Cadigan, Sean T. "The Moral Economy of Retrenchment and Regeneration in the History of Rural Newfoundland." *Retrenchment and Regeneration in Rural Newfoundland*. Ed. Reginald Byron. Toronto: U of Toronto P, 2003. 14–42. Print.

———. *Newfoundland and Labrador: A History*. Toronto: U of Toronto P, 2009. Print.

Canada Now. CBC. 6 Jan. 2005. Television.

Chafe, Paul. "Hey Buddy, Wanna Buy a Culture?" *Nationalisms*. Ed. James Gifford and Gabrielle Zezulka-Mailloux. Edmonton: CRC Humanities Studio, 2003. 68–76. Web. 16 Aug. 2011.

———. "'The Scuttlework of Empire': A Postcolonial Reading of Wayne Johnston's *The Colony of Unrequited Dreams*." *Newfoundland Studies* 19.2 (2003): 322–46. Web. 16 Aug. 2011.

Chalykoff, Lisa. "Overcoming the Two Solitudes of Canadian Literary Regionalism." *Studies in Canadian Literature* 23.1 (1998): 160–77. Web. 16 Aug. 2011.

Chariandy, David. "Postcolonial Diasporas." *Postcolonial Text* 2.1 (2006): n. pag. Web. 29 Apr. 2007.

Cho, Lily. "Affecting Citizenship: The Materiality of Melancholia." *Narratives of Citizenship*. Ed. Aloys N.M. Fleischmann, Nancy Van Styvendale, and Cody McCarroll. Edmonton: U of Alberta P, 2011. 107–27. Print.

———. "Diasporic Citizenship: Contradictions and Possibilities for Canadian Literature." *Trans.Can.Lit: Resituating the Study of Canadian Literature*. Ed. Smaro Kamboureli and Roy Miki. Waterloo: Wilfrid Laurier UP, 2007. 93–109. Print.

———. "The Turn to Diaspora." *Topia* 17 (2007). 11–30. Print.

Chow, Rey. *Writing Diaspora: Tactics of Intervention in Contemporary Cultural Studies*. Bloomington: Indiana UP, 1993. Print.

Clifford, James. "Diasporas." *Cultural Anthropology* 9.3 (1994): 302–38. JSTOR. Web. 22 Aug. 2011.

Cohen, Robin. *Global Diasporas: An Introduction*. London: Routledge, 1997. Print.

Coleman, Daniel. *White Civility: The Literary Project of English Canada*. Toronto: U of Toronto P, 2006. Print.

Collins, Robert G. *E.J. Pratt*. Boston: Twayne, 1988. Print.

Conrad, Margaret. "Mistaken Identities? Newfoundland and Labrador in the Atlantic Region." *Newfoundland Studies* 18 (2002): 159–74. Web. 22 Aug. 2011.

Crawley, Ron. "Off to Sydney: Newfoundlanders Emigrate to Industrial Cape Breton, 1890–1914." *Acadiensis* 17.2 (1988): 27–51. Print.

Crummey, Michael. "Being There." Vancouver International Writers Festival. Granville Island, Vancouver. 22 Oct. 2005. Reading.

———. Interview by Leo Furey. *Antigonish Review* 131 (2002). Web. 29 July 2006.

———. "Journey into a Lost Nation." *Newfoundland: Journey into a Lost Nation*. Ed. Michael Crummey and Greg Locke. Toronto: McClelland & Stewart, 2004. 7–39. Print.

Culler, Jonathan. "Anderson and the Novel." *Grounds of Comparison: Around the Work of Benedict Anderson*. Ed. Pheng Cheah and Jonathan Culler. New York: Routledge, 2003. 29–52. Print.

Davis, Dona Lee. "In the Beginning: Region, Crisis, and Occupational Choice among Newfoundland's Youth." *Retrenchment and Regeneration in Rural Newfoundland*. Ed. Reginald Byron. Toronto: U of Toronto P, 2003. 177–98. Print.

Davis, Fred. *Yearning for Yesterday: A Sociology of Nostalgia*. New York: Free, 1979. Print.
Dawe, Tom. *In Hardy Country*. St. John's: Breakwater, 1993. Print.
Dearlove, Karen. "Diaspora and Community Building: Newfoundlanders and Portuguese in Cambridge, Ontario." Association for Canadian Studies Conference. Empire Landmark Hotel, Vancouver. 23 Oct. 2006. Conference Paper.
deBeyer, Michael. "Skeletons under the Lyric Skin." Rev. of *View from My Mother's House*, by Carl Leggo. *Fiddlehead* 203 (2000): 110–14. Print.
Delisle, Jennifer Bowering. "Nation, Indigenization, the Beothuk: A Newfoundland Myth of Origin in Patrick Kavanagh's *Gaff Topsails*." *Studies in Canadian Literature* 31.2 (2006): 23–45. Print.
———. "'The Rock Beneath His Feet': Cultural Nostalgia in Donna Morrissey's *Sylvanus Now*." Forthcoming in *Pathways of Creativity in Contemporary Newfoundland and Labrador*. Ed. Maria Jesus.
Djwa, Sandra. "Editors' Introduction." *E.J. Pratt: Selected Poems*. Ed. Sandra Djwa, W.J. Keith, and Zailig Pollock. Toronto: U of Toronto P, 2000. ix–xxviii. Print.
———. *E.J. Pratt: The Evolutionary Vision*. Vancouver: Copp Clark, 1974. Print.
———. "The 1920s: E.J. Pratt, Transitional Modern." *The E.J. Pratt Symposium*. Ed. Glenn Clever. Ottawa: U of Ottawa P, 1977. 55–68. Print.
Doran, Barbara, dir. *Hard Rock and Water*. Perf. Lisa Moore. Morag Productions, 2005. Film.
Dragland, Stan. "*The Colony of Unrequited Dreams*: Romancing History?" *Essays on Canadian Writing* 82 (2004): 187–213. Print.
Egan, Susanna. *Mirror Talk: Genres of Crisis in Contemporary Autobiography*. Chapel Hill: U of North Carolina P, 1999. Print.
Fee, Margery. "What Use Is Ethnicity to Aboriginal Peoples in Canada?" *Unhomely States: Theorizing English-Canadian Postcolonialism*. Ed. Cynthia Sugars. Peterborough, ON: Broadview, 2004. 267–76. Print.
Fee, Margery, and Lynette Russell. "'Whiteness' and 'Aboriginality' in Canada and Australia: Conversations and Identities." *Feminist Theory* 8.2 (2007): 187–208. *SAGE*. Web. 24 Aug. 2011.
Fiamengo, Janice. "Regionalism and Urbanism." *The Cambridge Companion to Canadian Literature*. Ed. Eva-Marie Kröller. Cambridge: Cambridge UP, 2004. 241–62. Print.
Fludernik, Monika. "Introduction: The Diasporic Imaginary." *Diaspora and Multiculturalism: Common Traditions and New Developments*. Ed. Monika Fludernik. Amsterdam: Rodopi, 2003. xi–xxxviii. Print.
Fowler, Adrian. "The Literature of Newfoundland: A Roundabout Return to Elemental Matters." *Essays on Canadian Writing* 31 (1985): 118–41. Print.
———. "Patrick Kavanagh's *Gaff Topsails* and the Myth of the Old Outport." *Essays on Canadian Writing* 82 (2004): 71–92. Print.
French, David. *Leaving Home*. Don Mills: Stoddart, 1985. Print.
———. *1949*. Vancouver: Talonbooks, 1989. Print.

———. "Of Many Coloured Glass." Interview by Peter Neary. *Canadian Forum* 53 (1974): 26–27. Print.

———. *Of the Fields, Lately.* Toronto: New, 1975. Print.

———. *Salt-Water Moon.* Vancouver: Talonbooks, 1988. Print.

———. *Soldier's Heart.* Vancouver: Talonbooks, 2002. Print.

Frye, Northrop. *The Bush Garden.* Toronto: Anansi, 1971. Print.

———. Introduction. *The Collected Poems of E.J. Pratt.* Ed. Northrop Frye. Toronto: Macmillan, 1958. xiii–xxviii. Print.

Fuller, Danielle. "Strange Terrain: Reproducing and Resisting Place-Myths in Two Contemporary Fictions of Newfoundland." *Essays on Canadian Writing* 82 (2004): 21–50. Print.

———. *Writing the Everyday: Women's Textual Communities in Atlantic Canada.* Montreal: McGill-Queen's UP, 2004. Print.

Gilroy, Paul. *Against Race: Imagining Political Culture beyond the Color Line.* Cambridge: Belknap, 2000. Print.

Gingell, Susan. "The Newfoundland Context of the Poetry of E.J. Pratt." *Essays on Canadian Writing* 31 (1985): 93–105. Print.

Gnarowski, Michael. Introduction. *New Provinces: Poems of Several Authors.* Ed. Michael Gnarowski. Toronto: U of Toronto P, 1976. vii–xxxii. Print.

Grace, Sherrill. *Canada and the Idea of North.* Montreal: McGill-Queen's UP, 2001. Print.

Grekul, Lisa. *Leaving Shadows: Literature in English by Canada's Ukrainians.* Edmonton: U of Alberta P, 2005. Print.

Gross, Konrad. "Looking to the Far East? Newfoundland in David French's Mercer Tetralogy." *Down East: Critical Essays on Contemporary Maritime Canadian Literature.* Ed. Wolfgang Hochbruck and James O. Taylor. Trier: Wissenschaftlicher, 1996. 247–64. Print.

Gunew, Sneja. *Framing Marginality: Multicultural Literary Studies.* Carlton: Melbourne UP, 1994. Print.

———. *Haunted Nations: The Colonial Dimensions of Multiculturalisms.* London: Routledge, 2004. Print.

Gwyn, Sandra. "The Newfoundland Renaissance." *Saturday Night* April 1976: 38–45. Print.

Hall, Stuart. "Cultural Identity and Diaspora." *Colonial Discourse and Post-Colonial Theory: A Reader.* Ed. Patrick Williams and Laura Chrisman. New York: Columbia UP, 1994. 392–403. Print.

———. "Ethnicity: Identities and Difference." *Radical America* 23.4 (1989): 9–20. Print.

———. "The Question of Cultural Identity." *Modernity: An Introduction to Modern Societies.* Ed. Stuart Hall, David Held, Don Hubert, and Kenneth Thompson. Malden: Blackwell, 1996. 595–634. Print.

Hiller, Harry. "Dependence and Independence: Emergent Nationalism in Newfoundland." *Ethnic and Racial Studies* 10.3 (1987): 257–75. Print.

Hiller, Harry H., and Tara M. Franz. "New Ties, Old Ties and Lost Ties: The Use of the Internet in Diaspora." *New Media and Society* 6.6 (2004): 731–52. *SAGE*. Web. 24 Aug. 2011.

Hiller, James K. *Confederation: Deciding Newfoundland's Future 1934–1949*. St. John's: Newfoundland Historical Society, 1999. Print.

Hirsch, Marianne. *Family Frames: Photography, Narrative, and Postmemory*. Cambridge: Harvard UP, 1997. Print.

Hobbs, Carol. "Trawl." *TickleAce* 37 (1999): 47. Print.

Holt, Pat. "Wayne Johnston and *The Colony of Unrequited Dreams*." 2 July 1999. *Holt Uncensored*. Web. 22 Feb. 2008.

Hutcheon, Linda. *The Canadian Postmodern*. Toronto: Oxford, 1988. Print.

———. Introduction. *Other Solitudes*. Ed. Linda Hutcheon and Marion Richmond. Toronto: Oxford UP, 1990. 1–16. Print.

Ignatiev, Noel. *How the Irish Became White*. New York: Routledge, 1995. Print.

Inglis, Gordon. "Truth and Fiction." *Newfoundland Studies* 16.1 (2000): 67–77. Web. 24 Aug. 2011.

Johnston, Wayne. "An Afterlife Endlessly Revised: Wayne Johnston." Interview by Herb Wyile. *Speaking in the Past Tense: Canadian Novelists on Writing Historical Fiction*. By Herb Wyile. Waterloo: Wilfrid Laurier UP, 2007. 105–31. Print.

———. *Baltimore's Mansion: A Memoir*. Toronto: Alfred A. Knopf, 1999. Print.

———. *The Colony of Unrequited Dreams*. Toronto: Vintage, 1999. Print.

———. "A History of Newfoundland—D.W. Prowse, *The Newfoundland Journal of Aaron Thomas, 1744*—Aaron Thomas." *Lost Classics*. Ed. Michael Ondaatje. Toronto: Alfred A. Knopf, 2000. 139–45. Print.

———. *The Old Lost Land of Newfoundland: Family, Memory, Fiction, and Myth*. Edmonton: NeWest and the Canadian Literature Centre, 2009. Print.

———. "The Time of His Life: An Interview with Wayne Johnston." Interview by Bruce Porter. *TickleAce* 27 (1994): 14–29. Print.

Jurca, Catherine. *White Diaspora: The Suburb and the Twentieth-Century American Novel*. Princeton: Princeton UP, 2001. Print.

Kalra, Virinder S., Raminder Kaur, and John Hutnyk. *Diaspora and Hybridity*. London: Sage, 2005. Print.

Kamboureli, Smaro. *On the Edge of Genre: The Contemporary Canadian Long Poem*. Toronto: U of Toronto P, 1991. Print.

———. Preface. *Trans.Can.Lit: Resituating the Study of Canadian Literature*. Ed. Smaro Kamboureli and Roy Miki. Waterloo: Wilfrid Laurier UP, 2007. vii–xv. Print.

———. *Scandalous Bodies: Diasporic Literature in English Canada*. Don Mills: Oxford UP, 2000. Print.

Kavanagh, Patrick. *Gaff Topsails*. New York: Penguin, 1996. Print.

Keefer, Janice Kulyk. "'Coming Across Bones': Historiographic Ethnofiction." *Essays on Canadian Writing* 57 (1995): 84–104. Print.

Kelly, Ursula. *Marketing Place: Cultural Politics, Regionalism and Reading*. Halifax: Fernwood, 1993. Print.

Kertzer, Jonathan. *Worrying the Nation: Imagining a National Literature in English Canada*. Toronto: U of Toronto P, 1998. Print.
King, Ruth, and Sandra Clarke. "Contesting Meaning: *Newfie* and the Politics of Ethnic Labelling." *Journal of Sociolinguistics* 6.4 (2002): 537–56. *Wiley Online Library*. Web. 24 Aug. 2011.
Kostash, Myrna. "Imagination, Representation, and Culture." *Literary Pluralities*. Ed. Christl Verduyn. Peterborough, ON: Broadview, 1998. 92–96. Print.
Leggo, Carl. *Come-By-Chance*. St. John's: Breakwater, 2006. Print.
———. *Growing Up Perpendicular on the Side of a Hill*. St. John's: Killick, 1994. Print.
———. *View from My Mother's House*. St. John's: Killick, 1999. Print.
———. "Writing Lives Is More Than Writing Lines: Postmodern Perspectives on Life Writing." *Language and Literacy* 2.2 (2000). Web. 4 Oct. 2006.
Locke, Greg. "Dispatches from Exit 0: Going Down the Road with Newfoundland's Diaspora." *greglocke.com*. Web. 20 Nov. 2007.
———. "The Fort McMurray Portraits." *Straylight*. Web. 18 Mar. 2009.
Macfarlane, David. *The Danger Tree*. Toronto: Vintage, 1991. Print.
Mackenzie, William W. *Newfoundland Royal Commission 1933*. London: His Majesty's Stationary Office, 1934. *Newfoundland Heritage*. Web. 24 Aug. 2011.
MacLeod, Alexander. "History versus Geography in Wayne Johnston's *The Colony of Unrequited Dreams*." *Canadian Literature* 189 (2006): 69–84. *Academic Search Complete*. Web. 24 Aug. 2011.
Macleod, Malcolm. Rev. of *Memoirs from Away: A New Found Land Girlhood*, by Helen M. Buss / Margaret Clarke. *Newfoundland Studies* 17.1 (2001): 98–101. Web. 24 Aug. 2011.
Mathews, Lawrence. "Report from the Country of No Country." *Essays on Canadian Writing* 82 (2004): 1–20. Print.
Matthews, Ralph, and John Phyne. "Regulating the Newfoundland Inshore Fishery: Traditional Values versus State Control in the Regulation of a Common Property Resource." *Journal of Canadian Studies* 23.1–2 (1988): 158–76. Print.
Mishra, Vijay. "The Diasporic Imaginary: Theorizing the Indian Diaspora." *Textual Practice* 10.3 (1996): 421–47. *Academic Search Complete*. Web. 24 Aug. 2011.
Moore, Lisa. "Notes from Newfoundland." *The Walrus* May 2011: 22–29. Print.
———. *Open*. Toronto: Anansi, 2002. Print.
Morgan, Bernice. Rev. of *The Colony of Unrequited Dreams*, by Wayne Johnston. *TickleAce* 36 (1999): 102–05. Print.
———. *Waiting for Time*. St. John's: Breakwater, 1994. Print.
Morgan-Cole, Trudy J. "Confessions of an Ex-Patriot." *TickleAce* 37 (1999): 52–60. Print.
Morrissey, Donna. *Sylvanus Now*. Toronto: Penguin, 2005. Print.
———. *What They Wanted*. Toronto: Viking, 2008. Print.
Mukherjee, Arun. *Postcolonialism: My Living*. Toronto: TSAR, 1998. Print.

Murphy, Rex. "Alas, Joey Smallwood Was Larger Than Fiction." Rev. of *The Colony of Unrequited Dreams*, by Wayne Johnston. *Points of View*. Toronto: McClelland & Stewart, 2003. 48–50. Print.

The National. CBC. 26 Apr. 2006. Television.

Neis, Barbara, and Rob Kean. "Why Fish Stocks Collapse: An Interdisciplinary Approach to the Problem of 'Fishing Up.'" *Retrenchment and Regeneration in Rural Newfoundland*. Ed. Reginald Byron. Toronto: U of Toronto P, 2003. 65–102. Print.

Neis, Barbara, and Susan Williams. "The New Right, Gender and the Fisheries Crisis: Local and Global Dimensions." *Weather's Edge: Women of Newfoundland and Labrador: A Compendium*. Ed. Linda Cullum, Carmelita McGrath, and Marilyn Porter. St. John's: Killick, 2006. 346–57. Print.

Newfoundland and Labrador Tourism. N.d. Web. 22 Feb 2008.

Nolan, Stephen. *Leaving Newfoundland: A History of Out-Migration*. St. John's: Flanker, 2007. Print.

O'Dea, Shane. "Culture and Country: The Role of the Arts and Heritage in the Nationalist Revival in Newfoundland." *Newfoundland Studies* 19.2 (2003): 378–86. Web. 24 Aug. 2011.

O'Flaherty, Patrick. *The Rock Observed: Studies in the Literature of Newfoundland*. Toronto: U of Toronto P, 1979. Print.

Overton, James. *Making a World of Difference: Essays on Tourism, Culture and Development in Newfoundland*. St. John's: ISER, 1996. Print.

Padolsky, Enoch. "Ethnicity and Race: Canadian Minority Writing at a Crossroads." *Literary Pluralities*. Ed. Christl Verduyn. Peterborough, ON: Broadview, 1998. 19–36. Print.

Percy, Owen D. "Melting History: Defrosting Moments in Novels by Wayne Johnston, Michael Winter, and Robert Kroetsch." *Studies in Canadian Literature* 32.1 (2007): 212–30. Web. 24 Aug. 2011.

Pierson, Stuart. "Johnston's Smallwood." *Newfoundland Studies* 14.2 (1998): 282–300. Web. 24 Aug. 2011.

———. Rev. of *The Shipping News*, by Annie Proulx. *Newfoundland Studies* 11.1 (1995): 151–53. Web. 24 Aug. 2011.

Pitt, David G. *E.J. Pratt: The Master Years, 1927–1964*. Toronto: U of Toronto P, 1987. Print.

———. *E.J. Pratt: The Truant Years, 1882–1927*. Toronto: U of Toronto P, 1984. Print.

Pollett, Ron. *Ocean at My Door*. St. John's: Flanker, 1999. Print.

Porter, Bruce. "Facing the Gulf." *TickleAce* 37 (1999): 6–7. Print.

Pratt, E.J. *Complete Poems*. Ed. Sandra Djwa and R.G. Moyles. Toronto: U of Toronto P, 1989. Print.

———. *E.J. Pratt on His Life and Poetry*. Ed. Susan Gingell. Toronto: U of Toronto P, 1983. Print.

———. *Newfoundland Verse*. Toronto: Ryerson, 1923. Print.

Proulx, Annie. *The Shipping News*. New York: Scribner, 1993. Print.

Pyper, Andrew. "Wayne's World." *Quill & Quire* 65.11 (1999): 20. *CBCA Complete*. Web. 24 Aug. 2011.
Radhakrishnan, R. "Is the Ethnic 'Authentic' in the Diaspora?" *Diasporic Mediations: Between Home and Location*. Minneapolis: U of Minnesota P, 1996. 203–14. Print.
Reeves, W.G. "Newfoundlanders in the 'Boston States': A Study in Early Twentieth Century Community and Counterpoint." *Newfoundland Studies* 6.1 (1990): 34–55. Web. 24 Aug. 2011.
Riche, Edward. *The Nine Planets*. Toronto: Viking, 2004. Print.
Richler, Noah. *This Is My Country, What's Yours?* Toronto: McClelland & Stewart, 2006. Print.
Ricoeur, Paul. *Time and Narrative*. 3 vols. Trans. Kathleen McLaughlin, David Pellauer and Kathleen Blamey. Chicago: U of Chicago P, 1984–88. Print.
Ritivoi, Andreea Deciu. *Yesterday's Self: Nostalgia and the Immigrant Identity*. Lanham: Rowman and Littlefield, 2002. Print.
Roediger, David R. *Working toward Whiteness*. Cambridge: Basic, 2005. Print.
Rompkey, Ronald. "The Idea of Newfoundland and Arts Policy since Confederation." *Newfoundland Studies* 14.2 (1998): 266–81. Web. 24 Aug. 2011.
———. "Newfoundland and Labrador: Colonial and Post-Colonial Writing." *Library and Archives Canada*. Web. 1 Apr. 2002.
Rose, Clyde. Foreword. *Baffles of Wind and Tide*. Ed. Clyde Rose. Portugal Cove, NL: Breakwater, 1974. xi–xiii. Print.
Royal Commission on Renewing and Strengthening Our Place in Canada. *Our Place in Canada*. Government of Newfoundland, 2003. Web. 24 Aug. 2011.
Rubenstein, Roberta. *Home Matters: Longing and Belonging, Nostalgia and Mourning in Women's Fiction*. New York: Palgrave, 2001. Print.
Rushdie, Salman. *Imaginary Homelands: Essays and Criticism, 1981–1991*. London: Granta, 1991. Print.
Russell, Ted. *The Holdin' Ground*. St. John's: Harry Cuff, 1990. Print.
Safran, William. "Diasporas in Modern Societies: Myths of Homeland and Return." *Diaspora* 1.1 (1991): 83–99. Print.
Salgado, Minoli. "Nonlinear Dynamics and the Diasporic Imagination." *Diaspora and Multiculturalism: Common Traditions and New Developments*. Ed. Monika Fludernik. Amsterdam: Rodopi, 2003. 183–98. Print.
Sante, Luc. "O Canada!" Rev. of *The Colony of Unrequited Dreams*, by Wayne Johnston. *New York Times Book Review* 25 July 1999: 6. Web. 24 Aug. 2011.
Scammell, A.R. *My Newfoundland: Stories, Poems, Songs*. Montreal: Harvest, 1966. Print.
Sedgwick, Eve Kosofsky. *Touching Feeling: Affect, Pedagogy, Performativity*. Durham: Duke UP, 2003. Print.
Seremetakis, C. Nadia. *The Senses Still: Perception and Memory as Material Culture in Modernity*. Chicago: U of Chicago P, 1996. Print.
Sinclair, Peter R. "Moving Back and Moving In: Migration and the Structuring of Bonavista." *Retrenchment and Regeneration in Rural Newfoundland*. Ed. Reginald Byron. Toronto: U of Toronto P, 2003. 199–225. Print.

———. "Narrowing the Gaps? Gender, Employment and Incomes on the Bonavista Peninsula, 1951–1996." *Weather's Edge: Women in Newfoundland and Labrador: A Compendium*. Ed. Linda Cullum, Carmelita McGrath, and Marilyn Porter. St. John's: Killick, 2006. 235–46. Print.

Sinclair, Peter R., and Lawrence F. Felt. "Coming Back: Return Migration to Newfoundland's Great Northern Peninsula." *Newfoundland Studies* 9.1 (1993): 1–25. Web. 23 Aug. 2011.

Smith, A.J.M. *The Book of Canadian Poetry*. Toronto: Gage, 1957. Print.

Smith, Sidonie. "Identity's Body." *Autobiography and Postmodernism*. Ed. Kathleen Ashley, Leigh Gilmore, and Gerald Peters. Amherst: U of Massachusetts P, 1994. 166–292. Print.

Statistics Canada. *2006 Census*. Web. 22 Feb. 2008.

Staveley, Helene. "Romancing Newfoundland: The Art of Fiction in David Macfarlane's *The Danger Tree*." *Newfoundland Studies* 18.1 (2002): 41–60. Web. 23 Aug. 2011.

Su, John J. *Ethics and Nostalgia in the Contemporary Novel*. Cambridge: Cambridge UP, 2005. Print.

Sullivan, Joan. "Poetry of the Everyday." Rev. of *Come-By-Chance*, by Carl Leggo. *The Telegram* [St. John's] 18 Feb. 2007: B4. *LexisNexis Academic*. Web. 23 Aug. 2011.

Sutherland, John. *The Poetry of E.J. Pratt*. Toronto: Ryerson, 1956. Print.

Taylor, Sharon. "The Wounded Gift: Meanings of Community under TAGS." *Weather's Edge: Women of Newfoundland and Labrador: A Compendium*. Ed. Linda Cullum, Carmelita McGrath, and Marilyn Porter. St. John's: Killick, 2006. 248–61. Print.

Thorne, Cory W. "Come from Away: Community, Region, and Tradition in Newfoundland Expatriate Identity." Diss. U of Pennsylvania, 2004. *Proquest Dissertations and Theses*. Web. 24 Aug. 2011.

Thornton, Patricia A. "The Problem of Out-Migration from Atlantic Canada, 1871–1921: A New Look." *Atlantic Canada after Confederation*. Ed. P.A. Buckner, Gail G. Campbell, and David Frank. Fredericton: Acadiensis, 1999. 11–42. Print. Vol. 2 of *The Acadiensis Reader*. 1998–1999.

Tölölyan, Khachig. "The Nation-State and Its Others: In Lieu of a Preface." *Diaspora* 1.1 (1991): 3–7. Print.

———. "Rethinking Diaspora(s): Stateless Power in the Transnational Moment." *Diaspora* 5.1 (1996): 3–36. Print.

Tremblay, T. Rev. of *Baltimore's Mansion*, by Wayne Johnston. *Dalhousie Review* 79.2 (1999): 269–77. Print.

Vandervlist, Harry. "*Gaff Topsails* Is Another Canadian Literary Hit Abroad." *FFWD* 2.39 (1997). Web. 31 July 2006.

Wente, Margaret. "Oh Danny Boy, Pipe Down." *Globe and Mail* [Toronto] 6 Jan. 2005: A19. *LexisNexis Academic*. Web. 23 Aug. 2011.

Whalen, Tracy. "'Camping' with Annie Proulx: *The Shipping News* and Tourist Desire." *Essays on Canadian Writing* 82 (2004): 51–70. Print.

Whitlock, Gillian. "White Diasporas: Joan (and Ana) Make History." *Australian and New Zealand Studies in Canada* 12 (1994): 90–100. Print.

Wiegman, Robyn. "Whiteness Studies and the Paradox of Particularity." *boundary 2* 26.3 (1999): 115–50. *Academic Search Complete*. Web. 23 Aug. 2011.

Wilkshire, Claire. "Family History." Rev. of *Memoirs from Away*, by Helen M. Buss / Margaret Clarke. *Canadian Literature* 168 (2001): 130–31. Print.

Williams, David. *Imagined Nations*. Montreal: McGill-Queen's UP, 2003. Print.

Wyile, Herb. *Anne of Tim Horton's: Globalization and the Reshaping of Atlantic-Canadian Literature*. Waterloo: Wilfrid Laurier UP, 2011. Print.

———. *Speculative Fictions: Contemporary Canadian Novelists and the Writing of History*. Montreal: McGill-Queen's UP, 2002. Print.

Wyile, Herb, Christian Riegel, Karen Overbye, and Don Perkins. "Introduction: Regionalism Revisited." *A Sense of Place: Re-Evaluating Regionalism in Canadian and American Writing*. Ed. Christian Riegel and Herb Wyile. Edmonton: U of Alberta P, 1997. ix–xiv. Print.

Zhang, Kenny, and Pau Woo Yuen. "National Diaspora Strategies: India, China, and Canada." National Metropolis Conference. Westin Bayshore, Vancouver. 24 Mar. 2006. Conference Paper.

INDEX

1949 (French), 102–13

affect, 3, 4, 10, 14, 32, 35–36, 39, 47–48, 50–52, 58–59, 88, 167–68; transmission of, 62
Agnew, Vijay, 146
Ahmed, Sara, 35, 37, 58–59, 160, 180
Akenson, Donald Harman, 161–62
Alexander, David, 2, 21
Amulree Royal Commission, 104, 189n2
Anderson, Benedict, 17, 98, 110–11, 129
Ang, Ien, 6, 110–11, 149–50, 154, 164, 170, 171
Anonsen, Kay, 10–11, 14, 15, 16, 17, 21, 23, 26
Anthias, Floya, 26–27
appropriation, 5, 68, 77, 96, 165, 184
assimilation, 5, 21, 80, 82, 83, 104–5, 111, 115, 117, 124, 136, 138, 142, 152, 179
Atlantic Guardian, 3, 49, 61, 192n3
Atwood, Margaret, 78, 136
authenticity, 5, 50, 65–83, 85–98

Baltimore's Mansion (Johnston), 2, 3, 115–27, 132–33, 137, 140, 142, 191n1, 192n4

Bannerji, Himani, 163
Bannister, Jerry, 22, 101
Bella, Leslie, 15, 16, 19, 26, 147, 160
Bennett, Donna, 186
Bhattacharyya, Gargi, John Gabriel, and Stephen Small, 162–63
Bowdring, Paul, 183
Boyarin, Jonathan and Daniel, 9, 15, 145
Boym, Svetlana, 40, 51, 53, 57
Brah, Avtar, 9, 17, 33, 184–85, 187
Braziel, Jana Evans, and Anita Mannur, 80
Brennan, Teresa, 62
Buitenhuis, Peter, 78–79
Burrill, Gary, 189
Buss, Helen/Margaret Clarke, 3, 5, 145–66, 169, 174, 193n1
Byrne, Pat, 50, 61

Cadigan, Sean, 20, 21, 22
Chafe, Paul, 73, 88, 91, 135, 142, 191n5
Chalykoff, Lisa, 81–82, 92, 95, 98
Chariandy, David, 145–46, 193n2
Cho, Lily, 4, 11, 12, 105, 162
Chong, Denise, 182
Chow, Rey, 184
class, 16–17, 26, 27, 32, 91, 110, 139, 155, 172–73, 184, 185

Clifford, James, 10, 14, 138, 184
cod moratorium, 2, 13, 19–21, 22, 47, 90
Cohen, Robin, 10, 11, 12
Coleman, Daniel, 106, 163
Collins, Robert, 78–79
colonialism, 11, 19, 87, 88, 93, 106, 132, 139, 161–62, 163, 165, 184, 185, 191n1, 191n2
The Colony of Unrequited Dreams (Johnston), 85–98, 101, 115, 127–42, 192n4
Come Home Year, 117
Confederation, 5, 19, 21, 23, 74, 79, 81, 82, 83, 87, 93, 98, 101–13, 115–27, 128, 131–42, 157, 172, 178–79, 181, 185, 192n2
Cook, Michael, 190n2
Crawley, Ron, 2
Crummey, Michael, 19, 96–97, 183
Culler, Jonathan, 111
cultural mourning, 47, 61
The Custodian of Paradise (Johnston), 97–98

The Danger Tree (Macfarlane), 5, 68–69, 169–80, 182
Davey, Frank, 65
Davis, Dona Lee, 13
Davis, Fred, 55, 59
Dawe, Tom, 182–83
Dearlove, Karen, 147
Department of Fisheries and Oceans (DFO), 19, 20
diaspora, Canadian, 12; and choice, 12–14; and citizenship, 105, 108, 118–19, 124, 142, 162; communities, 10, 15–17; as "condition of subjectivity," 4, 10, 162, 184; and connection to homeland, 10, 14–15; definitions, 4, 9–10, 11–12; "diasporic imaginaries," 16, 17, 60–61, 102, 110, 127–29; "diaspora space," 184–85, 187; imperial, 11; Irish, 162; Jewish, 9–10, 12, 130, 163; labour, 11, 16, 32, 42–43, 47, 48; and loss, 10–14, 32, 47, 51, 54, 57, 58, 101, 105, 117–19, 129, 182; and marginalization, 10, 24–26, 106, 158–60; and nationalism, 10, 17–24, 81
Djwa, Sandra, 65, 66, 67, 70
Doran, Barbara, 20, 90
Dragland, Stan, 9, 97, 101, 121, 127, 140

Egan, Susanna, 151
ethnicity, 5, 26, 80, 82, 111, 145–66, 167–68, 173, 179, 190n3; emergent, 170–71, 174, 179; ethnic absolutism, 146, 184; postmodern 6, 149, 166, 169–70, 174, 176
exoticization, 73, 81–82, 91–93, 147

Fee, Margery, 148, 150; and Lynette Russell, 164
Fiamengo, Janice, 93
Fish, Stanley, 148
fishery, 14–15, 19–21, 33–34, 40, 42–44, 47, 48, 90. *See also* cod moratorium
Fludernik, Monika, 5, 27, 60
Foucault, Michel, 121
Fowler, Adrian, 73–74, 190n5
French, David, 5, 102–13, 142, 182
Frye, Northrop, 65, 67, 68, 77–79, 83, 136
Fuller, Danielle, 86, 91, 94

garrison mentality, 78, 83, 136, 185
geography, 91–98, 125–27, 132–37, 142
Gilroy, Paul, 11, 12, 142, 150
Gingell, Susan, 65, 68
globalization, 17, 18, 32
Gopinath, Gayatri, 81
government, federal, 19, 20, 34, 74
Grekul, Lisa, 168–69
Gross, Konrad, 108
Gunew, Sneja, 51, 75, 93, 96, 112–13, 148

Guy, Ray, 73
Gwyn, Sandra, 3, 22, 74

Hall, Stuart, 22, 149, 150, 170–71, 174, 184
Hiller, Harry, 22; and Tara Franz, 9, 16, 147, 168
Hiller, James K., 19
Hirsch, Marianne, 176
history, 123–24; ghost history, 122, 137; historiographic metafiction, 138–39, 150, 152–53, 155–57; historiography, 138–42
home, 32–48, 50, 61, 95, 160
Hutcheon, Linda, 139, 149, 153, 157, 158; and Marion Richmond, 185–86
hybridity, 112, 150, 155, 170, 173

Ignatiev, Noel, 162–63
imaginary homeland, 87–90, 92, 94, 95, 98, 127, 137–38
imagined community, 17, 98, 101–2, 110–13, 119–26, 127, 129, 138, 186–87
Inglis, Gordon, 95

Johnston, Wayne, 2, 3, 5, 84–98, 101, 115–27, 127–42, 169, 182, 191n1, 191n2, 192n2, 192n3, 192n4
Jurca, Catherine, 161–62

Kalra, Virinder S., Raminder Kaur, and John Hutnyk, 162
Kamboureli, Smaro, 5, 6, 66, 146, 148–49, 162, 186–87
Kavanagh, Patrick, 190–91n1
Kelly, Ursula, 60
Kertzer, Jonathan, 66–67, 193n2
King, Ruth, and Sandra Clarke, 26, 103, 147
Kostash, Myra, 163
Kulyk Keefer, Janice, 156, 182

Labrador, 3
Leaving Home (French), 102, 112–13
Leggo, Carl, 4, 49–62
Lewis, David, 55
literature, Canadian, 6, 185–87
Locke, Greg, 9, 31–32, 36

Macfarlane, David, 5, 68–69, 169–80, 182
Macleod, Malcolm, 3, 92, 136
Maritimes, 189n1
Marshall, Tom, 190n6
Mathews, Lawrence, 70, 183
Matthews, Ralph, and John Phyne, 20
McCourt, Edward, 81–82
Memoirs from Away (Buss/Clarke), 3, 5, 145–66, 169, 174, 193n1
metafiction, 97
Mishra, Vijay, 16, 60, 102, 110
Moore, Lisa, 21, 27, 90, 183
Morgan, Bernice, 87–88, 183, 190n5, 191–92n1
Morgan-Cole, Trudy J., 23
Morrissey, Donna, 4, 32–48, 182, 190n2
motherhood, 36–42, 46
Mowat, Farley, 190n2
Mukherjee, Arun, 50–51
multiculturalism, 5–6, 147–49, 158, 184, 185–86
Murphy, Rex, 85

nationalism, 5, 17–24, 65, 74, 82, 83, 98, 142, 145, 178, 189n2; Canadian, 65–67, 77–78, 83, 193n2; "long distance," 111
Neary, Peter, 105
Neis, Barbara, and Rob Kean, 20; and Susan Williams, 20
"Newfie," 103, 106, 160, 171–72, 174
Newfoundland, nation of, 5, 9, 17, 19, 22–23, 71, 81, 89, 93, 101–2, 105, 109, 110, 112, 113, 115–17, 120, 121–27, 133–42, 145, 178–79, 185

Newfoundland Centralization Program. *See* resettlement
Newfoundland Renaissance, 22–23, 65, 74, 190n2
Nolan, Stephen, 9
nostalgia, 4–5, 39, 49–62

O'Dea, Shane, 9, 18, 23
O'Flaherty, 18, 50, 61, 65, 66, 70–77, 79, 81, 189n2, 190n2
Of the Fields, Lately (French), 102, 110, 113
Overton, James, 50, 91, 147

Pacey, Desmond, 65
Padolsky, Enoch, 148
Percy, Owen D., 92
Pierson, Stuart, 85–88, 95, 96
Pitt, David, 65, 75–76
Pollett, Ron, 49–50, 61
Porter, Bruce, 86, 127
postcolonialism, 12, 23, 113, 165, 186, 191n5
postmemory, 176, 179
postmodernism, 93, 95, 149–50, 152, 154, 159–60, 166. *See also* ethnicity, postmodern
Pratt, E.J., 3, 5, 65–83, 190n1, 190n2
Proulx, Annie, 95–97
Prowse, D.W., 83, 97, 138, 140

race, 96, 105–6, 146, 148, 160–65, 167, 184, 185, 187
Radhakrishnan, Rajagopalan, 69, 80, 89, 167, 190n3
Reeves, W.G., 2
regionalism, 65, 81–83, 85–86, 90–95, 98, 137–38, 186
resettlement, 34, 36, 74
return migration, 15, 117
Riche, Edward, 161
Ricoeur, Paul, 122, 127
Ritivoi, Andrea, 51, 54–55, 59
Roediger, David, 163

Rompkey, Ronald, 3, 18, 74, 113, 191n5
Rose, Clyde, 69, 81, 190n2
Royal Commission on Renewing and Strengthening Our Place in Canada, 2, 22, 24
Rubenstein, Roberta, 33, 37, 47, 51, 58, 59
Rushdie, Salman, 60, 87–89, 94
Russell, Ted, 61, 167

Safran, William, 10, 14–15
Salgado, Minoli, 57
Sante, Luc, 92, 94
Scammell, Arthur, 49–50
Scott, F.R., 190n1
second generation, 104–5, 113, 167–68, 171–73, 176–77, 180, 182
Sedgewick, Eve Kosofsky, 110
Seremetakis, C. Nadia, 58
shame, 110, 165
Shanawdithit, 164
The Shipping News (Proulx), 95–97
Sinclair, Peter R., 19–20; and Lawrence F. Felt, 13, 15
Smallwood, Joey, 74, 81, 85, 90, 117, 132, 190n4, 192n2, 192n4
Smith, A.J.M., 67
Smith, Sidonie, 159
Sollors, Werner, 148
Spivak, Gayatri, 149
Staveley, Helene, 169–70
stereotype, 5, 24, 26, 32, 50, 66, 82–83, 86, 90, 91, 93, 160, 165, 171–73
strategic essentialism, 75, 149, 166
Su, John, 51
Sutherland, John, 65, 67
Sylvanus Now (Morrissey), 32, 33–34, 47, 190n2

Taylor, Sharon, 20
The Atlantic Groundfish Strategy (TAGS), 20, 21
thematic criticism, 65, 78, 136
Thorne, Cory, 14, 16

Thornton, Patricia, 65
Tölölyan, Khachig, 11, 12, 21
tourism, 73, 91, 94, 117
Tremblay, Tony, 120
Trudeau, Justin, 91, 92, 94

unemployment, 3, 13, 15, 34, 171

Wente, Margaret, 24–25, 161
Whalen, Tracy, 96
What They Wanted (Morrissey), 4, 32–48
"white civility," 106–7, 163

whiteness 148–49, 160–66, 167
Whitlock, Gillian, 161–62
Wiegman, Robyn, 163–64
Williams, Danny, 21, 25
Williams, David, 127
Williams, Patricia, 163
Winter, Michael, 183
World War I, 69, 175–79
Wyile, Herb, 32, 89, 91, 93, 136, 189n1, 192n4; and Riegel, Overbye, and Perkins, 92

Zhang, Kenny, and Yuen Pau Woo, 12

www.ingramcontent.com/pod-product-compliance
Lightning Source LLC
Chambersburg PA
CBHW020408080526
44584CB00014B/1230